Sunset Travel Guide to
New Zealand

By the Editors of Sunset Books and Sunset Magazine

Lane Publishing Co. • Menlo Park, California

Acknowledgments

For assistance and cooperation in expediting travel arrangements and checking the manuscript, we would like to thank Lang F. Manning and John D. Davey, San Francisco office, New Zealand Government Tourist Office; and E. R. Kelsey, A. E. Shrimpton, Jim Monahan, Anthony Sturrock, and Mike Damiano, New Zealand Tourist and Publicity Department, Wellington. Bruce Clark and Ralph Anderson, National Publicity Studios, Wellington, aided us in acquiring photographs.

We also appreciate the cooperation of Jane Keator and William L. Hewes Jr. of *Pacific Travel News,* and of Helen Foerster.

During our travels, many people contributed information and suggestions, aided us in various ways, and extended personal hospitality. We particularly wish to thank the following for their assistance:

Alexandra: Peter Partridge. *Anakiwa:* Bob Ulvang. *Auckland:* Cliff Josephs, Mr. and Mrs. Ron Nolan, Mr. and Mrs. Klaus Runge, Lynn Smith. *Christchurch:* Mr. and Mrs. Joe Brown, Angus MacKenzie, T. J. Mains, Russ Parker, Brett Riley. *Dunedin:* J. C. Manning, D. D. Welsh. *Invercargill:* A. Alsweiler, Beulah Beadle, Graham D. Walker. *Kaitaia:* Maggie Boyd, Judy Evans. *Lawrence:* Ian Gray-Smith. *Masterton:* Mr. and Mrs. Phillip Evans. *Matakohe:* Mr. and Mrs. Ralph Cliff. *Napier:* Mr. and Mrs. Brian Cotter. *New Plymouth:* Bryce McPherson. *Orakei Korako:* Terry J. Spitz. *Queenstown:* Jim Gilkison, Geoff McDonald, Mr. and Mrs. Ton Snelder, Dr. and Mrs. Lindsay Stewart. *Rotorua:* W. F. Bern, W. G. Chandler, Rex Forrester, Bubbles Mihinui, John Minty. *Tauranga:* D. H. Maxwell, Noel W. Nicholls. *Te Anau:* Mr. and Mrs. Tony Barton, Keith Burrows, Mr. and Mrs. Ed Tinker. *Waimana:* Mary Allen. *Waitomo:* D. R. Stewart. *Wanganui:* Jean Frank, Gerald S. Weekes. *Wellington:* Eric Honey, Mr. and Mrs. Peter McIntyre. *Westport:* Jack Brown, Edgar Wallace. *Whangarei:* Mr. and Mrs. George Tiller, Major A. J. Voss.

Maori wood carving. Ohinemutu meeting house, Rotorua.

Edited by Cornelia Fogle

Special Consultant: Frederic M. Rea
Publisher
Pacific Travel News

Design: Steve Reinisch

Maps: William Dunn, Ells Marugg

Cover: Snow-topped peaks of the Southern Alps, Mount Tasman (left) and Mount Cook, jut above the clouds near Fox Glacier in Westland National Park. Photographed by Cornelia Fogle.

Editor, Sunset Books: David E. Clark

Fourth printing August 1982

Contents

Special Features

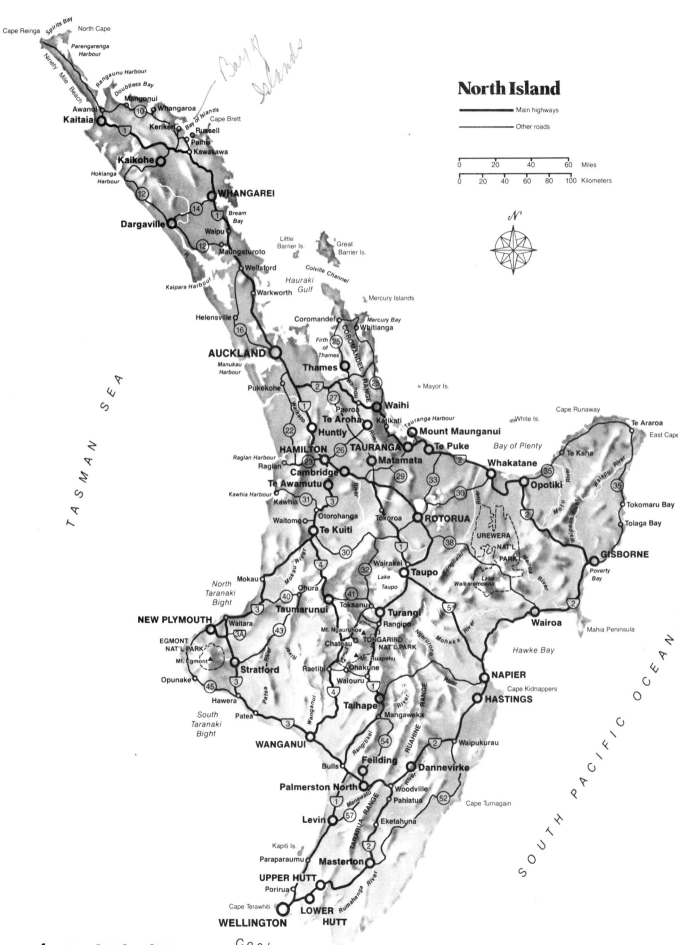

North Island

—— Main highways
— Other roads

| Miles | 0 | 20 | 40 | 60 |
| Kilometers | 0 | 20 | 40 | 60 | 80 | 100 |

Cape Reinga Spirits Bay North Cape
Parengarenga Harbour
Ninety Mile Beach
Rangaunu Harbour
Doubtless Bay
Awanui Mangonui Whangaroa
Kaitaia ⑩ Kerikeri Cape Brett
Russell
Paihia Bay of Islands
Kawakawa
Kaikohe ①
Hokianga Harbour
⑫
WHANGAREI
⑭ Bream Bay
Dargaville ①
Waipu
⑫ Maungaturoto
Kaipara Harbour Wellsford
Warkworth
Helensville ⑯
AUCKLAND
Manukau Harbour
Pukekohe ②
HAMILTON ⑳
Raglan Harbour ㉓ Cambridge
Raglan Te Awamutu
Kawhia Harbour ㉛
Kawhia ③
Waitomo Otorohanga
Te Kuiti ③⓪
Mokau ④
North Taranaki Bight ③ Ohura
Taumarunui ⑪ Tokaanu
NEW PLYMOUTH Waitara ㊸
EGMONT NAT'L PARK ③ⓐ
Mt. Egmont
Opunake ㊺ Stratford ③
Hawera
South Taranaki Bight Patea ③
WANGANUI
Bulls Feilding
Palmerston North
Levin ① ㊼
Kapiti Is.
Paraparaumu Masterton
UPPER HUTT
Porirua
Cape Terawhiti LOWER HUTT
WELLINGTON

Little Barrier Is.
Great Barrier Is.
Hauraki Gulf
Colville Channel
Mercury Islands
Coromandel Mercury Bay
Whitianga
Firth of Thames ㉕ COROMANDEL RANGE
Thames ㉕
⑳ ㉗ Waihi
Paeroa Te Aroha Katikati Tauranga Harbour
Huntly ㉖ TAURANGA Te Puke
⑳ Matamata ㉙ ㉝
Waikato River
Tokoroa ROTORUA ㉚
⓪ Wairakei ㊳ UREWERA NAT'L PARK
③② Lake Taupo Taupo Lake Waikaremoana
④① Turangi ⑤
Rangipo
Mt. Ngauruhoe TONGARIRO NAT'L PARK
Chateau Mt. Ruapehu
Raetihi Ohakune
Waiouru ①
④ Taihape
Mangaweka
RUAHINE RANGE
⑤④
Rangitikei River ② Waipukurau
Woodville Dannevirke
Pahiatua ㊼②
Eketahuna
② River

Mayor Is.
Bay of Plenty White Is. Cape Runaway
Te Araroa East Cape
Te Kaha
Whakatane ㉟ Opotiki ㉟
Waioeka River Tokomaru Bay
Tolaga Bay
GISBORNE
Poverty Bay
Wairoa ②
Mahia Peninsula
Hawke Bay
NAPIER Cape Kidnappers
HASTINGS
Cape Turnagain

TASMAN SEA
SOUTH PACIFIC OCEAN
Cook Strait Cape Palliser

South Island

Main highways
Other roads

0   20   40   60   Miles
0   20   40   60   80   100 Kilometers

N

Cook Strait

Farewell Spit

Collingwood   Golden Bay
Takaka
ABEL TASMAN NAT'L PARK   Marlborough Sounds
Tasman Bay
Motueka   Havelock
Karamea   Wangapeka Track   Nelson   Picton
Heaphy Track   Cloudy Bay
Karamea Bight   Motupiko   Blenheim
Westport   Kawatiri   Wairau River   Lake Grassmere
Inangahua Junction   Buller River   Murchison   NELSON LAKES NAT'L PARK
Punakaiki   Reefton   Clarence River
Grey River   Lewis Pass   Hanmer Springs   Kaikoura
Greymouth   Waiau   Waiau River
Kumara   Lake Brunner   Culverden
Hokitika   Taramakau River   Hurunui   River
Ross   Arthur's Pass   Otira   ARTHUR'S PASS NAT'L PARK
Arthur's Pass   Hurunui River
Franz Josef   Lake Coleridge   Waipara
Fox Glacier   Oxford
Springfield   Rangiora   Pegasus Bay
Mt. Hutt   Darfield   CHRISTCHURCH
WESTLAND NAT'L PARK   Rakaia   Lyttelton
MT. COOK NAT'L PARK   Rangitata River
Mt. Cook   Rakaia River   Akaroa
Haast   Rakaia   BANKS PENINSULA
Jackson Bay   Lake Tekapo   Ashburton   Akaroa Harbour
Haast River   Lake Pukaki   Fairlie   Geraldine
Haast Pass   Lake Ohau   Lake Tekapo
MT. ASPIRING NAT'L PARK   Lake Benmore   Timaru
Mt. Aspiring   Ahuriri River   Omarama
Milford Sound   Lindis Pass   Lake Aviemore   Waimate
Milford   Lake Hawea   Otematata   Lake Waitaki
Homer Tunnel   Lake Wanaka   Tarras   Duntroon   Waitaki River
Milford Track   Wanaka   Oamaru
Routeburn Track   Cromwell   Ranfurly
Doubtful Sound   QUEENSTOWN   Clyde   Palmerston
Lake Te Anau   Lake Wakatipu   Alexandra   River
Te Anau   Kingston   Roxburgh   DUNEDIN
Lake Manapouri   Manapouri   Mosgiel
FIORDLAND NAT'L PARK   Mossburn   Lawrence   Milton
Lake Hauroko   Lumsden   Balclutha
Tuatapere   Winton   Gore

TASMAN SEA
SOUTHERN ALPS
SOUTH PACIFIC OCEAN

Foveaux Strait
INVERCARGILL
Bluff
Oban
STEWART ISLAND

60
61
67
69
65
6
6
1
70
7
73
72
77
75
79
8
8
83
85
87
1
90
94
96
99
92

New Zealand

The Maoris called these islands "Aotearoa," the long white cloud

Haere mai! Welcome to New Zealand!

Surrounded by vast southern seas, New Zealand is one of the most isolated countries on the face of the globe. Its scenic beauty and variety are awesome—great glacial mountains upthrust above fiords, lakes, and streams; volcanoes towering above arid desert and subtropical forest.

Being isolated from the mainstream of the world is both a blessing and a problem as New Zealand and its people struggle to gain and retain the good life. Its remote location has shaped the self-sufficient temperament of its people and economy.

With Australia, New Zealand is one of only two countries in the South Pacific peopled predominantly by immigrants of European origin. Coupled with its British heritage is New Zealand's Maori culture, adding an underlying Polynesian graciousness to the country.

New Zealand is a young country with frontier zest; the first British settlers arrived less than 150 years ago. Natural barriers—rugged mountain ranges and dense bush—confined early habitation to the coast, and major cities border the sea. Except for the few large cities, land is open and sparsely populated, much of it used for farming and grazing. Meat, wool, and dairy products provide about 75 percent of the country's exports.

Enthusiasm for the agricultural life is obviously not universal. In recent years there has been a population drift as people have migrated from the country to the cities.

Yet outside the population centers you find the real New Zealand, a land of clearly defined districts, each with its distinct personality and character, molded by its landscape and its settlers.

New Zealand and its people

New Zealand lies about 10,400 km/6,500 miles southwest of San Francisco, a similar distance south of Tokyo and Singapore, and about 1,920 km/1,200 miles southeast of Sydney.

Auckland, its largest urban center, and Wellington, its capital city, are both located on North Island. The major cities on South Island are Christchurch and Dunedin, both located on the east coast.

Glaciers and volcanoes shaped the land

New Zealand's two main islands extend about 1,600 km/1,000 miles along a diagonal fault line. To the west lies the Tasman Sea, to the east, the South Pacific Ocean. Narrow Cook Strait separates the two islands. Small Stewart Island lies off the lower tip of South Island. Relatively small in area, the country encompasses an amazing variety in its land and climate.

Dominating its topography is a magnificent snow-capped mountain range—the Southern Alps—extending some 650 km/400 miles along the western side of South Island. Frequently hidden by clouds, it was probably this oft-shrouded mountain chain that earned New Zealand its Maori name of *Aotearoa*—the long white cloud. From the high peaks, glaciers gouged out long, slender mountain lakes and coastal fiords.

Much of North Island was shaped by volcanic action. Numerous volcanoes showered ash and lava over the central part of the island, burying vast forests and damming river valleys to create the Rotorua lakes. Several volcanoes are still active, particularly Mt. Ngauruhoe in Tongariro National Park and White Island in the Bay of Plenty. Thermal activity creates geysers, boiling pools, steam vents, and silica terraces from Rotorua south to Taupo.

Indenting the country's coastline are deep-water harbors, glacier-carved fiords, and "drowned" river valleys invaded by rising seas at the end of the Ice Age. Wooded headlands shelter curving bays and sandy beaches. Vast tracts of scenic wilderness have been preserved in ten national parks and two maritime parks.

In April, *autumn color brightens the hillsides north of Queenstown, and early snow dusts the summit of Coronet Peak. Travel by motorcoach or rental car offers close views of varied scenery.*

ARROWTOWN
CORONET PEAK
SKIPPERS RD.

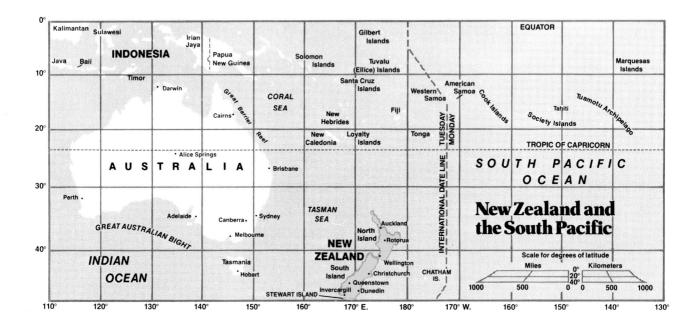

As New Zealand's land forms vary, so do its rainfall patterns and its climates. Prevailing westerlies drop most of their moisture along the western slope of the high mountains as they hit the cold, steep barrier. Depleted of moisture, the dry winds fan over the warm eastern slope.

Due to New Zealand's location in the temperate zone, temperatures are never excessively hot in summer nor uncomfortably cold in winter. Ranges are more extreme on South Island; here you'll find the wettest and driest regions of the country, as well as some of its hottest and coldest temperatures.

Seasons are reversed in the Southern Hemisphere. Summer extends from December through February; winter arrives in June.

Diverse trees and flowering plants

New Zealand's isolation from other lands and its diverse geography and climate are reflected in its unique plant life. Tree ferns and palms flourish in subtropical rain forest within sight of snow. Flowering trees brighten the bush, and tiny wildflowers carpet alpine slopes during a brief early summer display. Many of New Zealand's native plants are found nowhere else; others have Australian or South American cousins.

If you're interested in identifying and learning more about New Zealand's trees and wildflowers, you will find helpful publications in local bookstores, national park information centers, and Forest Service offices.

Forests. Northern North Island is kauri country, where this forest giant towers over lower-growing trees and shrubs. The crimson-blossoming pohutukawa tree—called "New Zealand's Christmas tree"—brightens the northeast coast and other areas in December.

Luxuriant forest covers many lowland and lower mountain areas. Tall podocarps (conifers) such as rimu, totara, and kahikatea—all valuable commercial timber—tower above lower broadleaf trees. Among the varieties you'll find in these forests are tawa, miro, hinau, puriri, kohekohe, towai, and the red-flowering rata and rewarewa trees. Other distinctive plants include the silver fern, nikau palm, and spiky-leaved cabbage tree. Ferns and mosses thrive beneath the forest canopy.

Twining through the treetops in lowland forests are the scarlet blooming rata vine and clematis with its fragrant, starry white flowers. Golden cascades of bell-shaped kowhai blossoms brighten river banks and open areas in early spring. Lacebark trees burst into hundreds of snowy blossoms along streams in autumn.

Beech forests are found in cooler mountain areas; undergrowth is usually sparse. In areas where rainfall is heavy, such as Fiordland, trees may be festooned with beardlike mosses and scarlet-blooming mistletoe.

Introduced trees. British colonists brought many European trees, planting them on their homesteads and along roads. In April these exotic (non-native) trees burst forth in glorious displays of autumn color, at its best in Canterbury and Otago.

The prime commercial tree is *Pinus radiata* (Monterey pine) which grows faster and taller here than in its native California. You may also see plantings of Oregon's Douglas fir and a few groves of California redwoods.

Dry areas. Regions too dry to support forests are frequently covered by shrubby manuka, which covers whole hillsides and valleys with its starry white flowers. Tufted tussock grasses cover much of the high inland hill country on South Island.

Wildflowers. In late spring and early summer, alpine wildflowers put on a brief flowering display.

Dotting grasslands and rocky slopes are snow grounsel, mountain gentian, mountain buttercups, mountain daisies, New Zealand edelweiss, and other plants. Most alpine wildflowers are white or yellow.

Colorful lupine varieties brighten mountain slopes and coastal areas.

Forest wildflowers include kotukutuku, the pink-flowering native fuchsia; and kakabeak, whose flamboyant red flower clusters brighten the bluffs around Lake Waikaremoana and the northeastern coast and islands. More than 70 native orchid species, some of them fragrant, grow in moist grasslands and perch on trunks and tree branches in the rain forests.

Other plants. Among other distinctive New Zealand plants you'll see the graceful, silky, ivory-colored flowerheads of toetoe and the swordlike leaf clumps of New Zealand flax. Maoris used the tall dried toetoe stems for *tukutuku* paneling and flax fiber for their clothing, ropes, and baskets.

Many native birds but few animals

The New Zealand bush teems with native birds. Best known is the flightless kiwi, a nocturnal bird that has given its name to New Zealanders, who are called Kiwis the world over.

The country's only native animals are a species of bat and the tuatara, a small dragonlike reptile that now can be seen only in zoos or on offshore islands. New Zealand has no snakes.

Flightless birds. Most characteristic is the famous kiwi, a shrill-voiced, wingless, tailless bird about .3 meter/12 inches in height with shaggy, mottled

Tuning in to Kiwi conversation

Colorful expressions and breezy slang—some borrowed from their British and Australian cousins—brighten the conversation of New Zealanders. Subtle humor, an independent tradition, and the outdoor life underlie many words and phrases you'll hear.

For many *Kiwis* (New Zealanders), social life revolves around the local pub, where they meet their *mates* (close friends, not spouses) and *shout* (treat) a round of beer. Families may spend the weekend at a *bach* or *crib* (country cabin or house), go for a *tramp* (hike) on a *track* (trail) through the *bush* (woods, forest), or perhaps *hire* (rent) a *caravan* (camping trailer) for their *holiday* (vacation).

Personal contacts. If you have a friend-of-a-friend to contact, find a *call box* (phone booth) and *ring up* (telephone) the *bloke* (fellow). If his wife invites you to their *flat* (apartment) for tea, check the time of the invitation; tea is not only a beverage, it's also the evening meal. They may invite you to join them in playing *housie*—it's just a game of bingo.

If you eavesdrop in a pub, you may hear a worker say he's *brassed off* (angry, frustrated) about his job, co-workers, or *screw* (salary). When you hear talk about a *hooker*, it's a rugby player they're discussing. If someone's called a *Pommie*, he's an Englishman; a *pakeha* is a person of European descent. You don't understand? Don't worry. It'll all *come right* (be O.K.).

On the road. If you drive a car during your travels, you'll put your luggage in the *boot* (trunk), clean your *windscreen* (windshield), stop for *petrol* (gasoline), and peer under the *bonnet* (hood) if you hear a strange noise. We hope you won't need to ring up a *breakdown truck* (tow truck), *locker* (locksmith), or *panel beater* (car body repairman).

You'll drive on *sealed* (paved) and *metalled* (graded gravel or crushed rock) roads. Warning signs you'll encounter include the following: *collision corner* (dangerous intersection), *greasy if wet* (slippery if wet), *hump* (bump), *give way* (yield), *no exit* (dead end), *change down* (shift into low gear), *no overtaking* (no passing), *road works* (construction), *special care* (caution), and *uneven surface* (rough road).

Touring tips. When traveling by coach, passengers take a break at the *wee-tea stop* (comfort stop); elsewhere, excuse yourself to *spend a penny*.

If you're motoring and get thirsty, stop for a *cuppa* (cup of tea or coffee), a *fizzy* (carbonated beverage), or—at the end of the day—even *spirits* (liquor). When you plan to picnic, buy food supplies or ask your hotel to prepare a *cut lunch* (packed lunch) for you. Then when you feel *peckish* (hungry), you can find a pleasant site beside the road or in a *domain* (park).

If you stay on a sheep station, you'll see flocks in the *paddocks* (fields). Shearers stop for a *smoko* (coffee break), then work *flat stick* (at maximum effort).

On back country trips, outdoorsmen *boil the billy* (heat water in a small can over a campfire for tea). Trampers should take along some *sticky plaster* (adhesive tape) in case of blisters and a *torch* (flashlight) if it's an overnight trip. If someone tells you to *get cracking* or *rattle your dags*, they want you to hurry up. When the weather turns cool, pull on a *jersey* (pullover sweater). Try not to *grizzle* (complain) if it starts to rain. On the beach, you can stop to *natter* (chat) with a fellow *fossicker* (beachcomber).

You'll like New Zealand. Its people are *smashing* (terrific) and the country's a *beaut*! And we're not *having you on* (pulling your leg). Cheerio!

grey-brown plumage. Its long tapering bill has nostrils at the tip; with it, the kiwi sniffs for grubs among the moss, leaves, and rotting wood on the forest floor. The hen lays an egg of remarkable size—it weighs over .45 kg/1 pound; her mate sits on the egg during its 11-week incubation period. You'll seldom see this noctural bird in the wild, but you can watch kiwis in the Auckland and Wellington zoos, and in Otorohanga, Rotorua, and Napier.

Another round-bottomed, flightless bird is the weka, a smaller relative of the kiwi.

Earliest of the flightless birds were the now-extinct moas, which grazed on open grasslands centuries ago.

Bush birds. In the bush you'll find the bellbird, whose sweet song resembles the chime of silver bells; the tui, another songster recognized by the tuft of white feathers at its black throat; friendly bush robins and fantails; the tiny rifleman; the bright-eyed tomtit; and the wood pigeon. The morepork, a small owl, is active after nightfall.

In wet, swampy places you'll often see the colorful pukeko, a long-legged swamp hen. Similar in appearance is the rare takahe, thought for many years to be extinct until rediscovered in the wild country of Fiordland.

In the South Island mountains you'll hear and see the shrill-voiced kea, a mountain parrot. Other members of the parrot family are the kaka, a bush parrot; several varieties of parakeets; and the kakapo, a very rare flightless ground parrot.

Shore birds. Along the coast you can see shore and sea birds such as penguins, petrels, shags, gannets, shearwaters, gulls, and terns. Some birds migrate part of the year. You can visit a mainland royal albatross colony at the tip of Taiaroa Head east of Dunedin. A heron colony nests at Okarito Lagoon, north of Westland National Park.

Animals. New Zealand has no native land animals. All of its wild animals—pigs, goats, deer, tahr, chamois, rabbits, weasels, ferrets, opossums—are

Dark waters of *Lake Matheson mirror the snowy peaks of Mount Tasman (left) and Mount Cook in Westland National Park.*

descendants of imported animals brought here for food, sport, fur, or as predators. Lacking natural enemies, the animals multiplied rapidly. They have severely damaged the vegetation, ruined grazing lands, and killed many native birds. Control measures have cost millions, and hunting is encouraged.

Immigrants came for a new start

New Zealand's earliest inhabitants—called "moa hunters"—were peaceful itinerant tribes who roamed the islands as early as 750 A.D. When and where they came from remains a mystery. Members of this primitive culture stalked the flightless moa birds for food.

According to Maori tradition, Polynesian voyager Kupe sailed south from the legendary Maori homeland called "Hawaiki"—thought to be in eastern Polynesia—about 950 A.D. and discovered a land he called *Aotearoa*. Eventually he returned to Hawaiki and passed on sailing instructions to the land of the long white cloud.

Ancestral canoes. Four centuries later, a number of canoes journeyed south to Aotearoa, guided by the sun and stars. It is from these ancestral canoes that most Maoris claim their descent.

The Maoris introduced tropical food plants, especially *kumara*, a variety of sweet potato. They depended on fish and birds for meat. Agricultural practices developed, and the Maori carving art flourished.

By the time Europeans arrived, most Maoris lived in the northern and central areas of North Island, where their agricultural society thrived in the warm climate. Intertribal battles were common, and several powerful chiefs dominated the territory.

Pacific exploration. Europeans had long speculated that a great unknown continent existed in the South Pacific to balance the large land masses of the northern hemisphere. In 1642 Abel Tasman was dispatched by the Dutch East India Company in search of new trade opportunities. Tasman sailed north along the west coast of South Island, anchoring in Golden Bay near the northern tip. Several of his sailors were killed in a clash with Maoris, and Tasman departed without landing.

Captain James Cook sailed to the South Pacific on a British scientific expedition. Mission completed, he turned south in search of the unknown continent. On October 7, 1769, he sighted the east coast of North Island and landed 2 days later at Poverty Bay.

Cook sailed north along the coast, passing in a storm the ship captained by French explorer Jean de Surville. During the next 6 months Cook circumnavigated both islands, charting the coastline. He and his crew recorded information on the flora and fauna and on the Maori people.

After accounts of Cook's first voyage were published, New Zealand became known to the world. Cook returned on two more voyages, making his base at Ship Cove in Queen Charlotte Sound.

Commercial exploitation. Interest grew in the Pacific and its people. In the 1790s the sealers arrived to slaughter seals by the thousands. A decade later, whalers began calling at the Bay of Islands for provisions and ship repair. It became the center of European settlement in New Zealand. In the 1830s and '40s, whaling stations sprang up on bays all along the coast south to Foveaux Strait.

While sealers and whalers plundered the seas, timber traders were razing the great kauri forests. Mill settlements mushroomed along Northland harbors and rivers.

Maoris reeled under the impact of the seamen and traders, who brought contagious diseases and firearms that disrupted and altered the pattern of Maori life.

Pressure for annexation. In 1814, missionaries began arriving in the Bay of Islands. They played a major role in attempting to protect the Maori people from exploitation by European traders and settlers. Pressure grew for British annexation due to ravaging of the country's natural resources, the threat of annexation by France, land speculation, and insistence by the impatient London-based New Zealand Company to colonize the country.

In order to exercise control over the situation, Britain reluctantly decided to negotiate with Maori chieftains for British sovereignty over New Zealand. On February 6, 1840, Captain William Hobson concluded the Treaty of Waitangi with leading Northland chiefs, and New Zealand became part of the British Empire (now Commonwealth). Maori land rights were protected, and Maoris were granted equal citizenship status with the European settlers.

Settlers arrive. Once the treaty was signed, organized settlement began. Shiploads of European colonists—most of them British—began arriving in the 1840s to establish planned settlements on both islands. Sheepherders imported large flocks to graze on the vast grasslands.

Misunderstandings arose between Maoris and land-hungry *pakeha* (European settlers) over land purchases, and fighting flared in several spots. In 1860, battles in Taranaki spread throughout the central part of North Island. The Land Wars continued intermittently for more than 20 years, and it was not until 1881 that peace was restored and the government could open the rich farming country south of Auckland to settlement.

While the Land Wars raged in the north, South Island was gripped by gold fever. After Gabriel Reed discovered gold in Central Otago in May, 1861, the stampede was on. Able-bodied men deserted the towns for the diggings, and prospectors poured in by the thousands. Dunedin became the country's richest and most influential city.

Provincial government. After the British assumed sovereignty, New Zealand was for a time administered by a governor responsible to London. The diverse backgrounds and interests of the widely scattered settlements, the lack of easy transportation and communication, and the off-center location of the capital (Auckland) made centralized administration difficult.

In 1852 provincial governments were established to control local affairs in the six main areas of settlement—Auckland, Taranaki (New Plymouth), and Wellington on North Island; Nelson, Canterbury (Christchurch), and Otago (Dunedin) on South Island. Later, four new provinces came into existence—Hawke's Bay on North Island; and Marlborough, Southland, and Westland on South Island.

Improved communications coupled with the shift of the capital to Wellington's more central site in 1865 lessened the need for local administration, and the entire provincial structure was abolished in 1876.

Industry expands. The introduction of refrigeration opened a new industry—supplying meat-hungry British markets with frozen lamb. Dairymen began exporting butter and cheese. The agricultural industry expanded as river waters were rechanneled to irrigate new areas.

At the end of the 19th century, population was about equally divided between the two islands. Since that time, North Island's growth has outpaced that of South Island due to its rich farm and grazing lands, warmer growing climate, nearness to trade routes, and increased industrialization. Today North Island has more than 70 percent of the country's population.

Government and foreign affairs

An independent member of the British Commonwealth, New Zealand is governed by an elected, single-chamber parliament modeled after that of Britain's House of Commons. Since 1865, Wellington has been the nation's capital.

Queen Elizabeth is represented in New Zealand by her appointed Governor-General, who performs the monarch's ceremonial functions in her absence. Each year he appears at the opening session of Parliament in full formal regalia to read the royal Speech-from-the-Throne that officially opens Parliament.

Unlike most Commonwealth countries, the New Zealand Parliament has no upper house. The House of Representatives is made up of 92 members (including four Maori legislators elected directly by Maori voters) elected for 3-year terms. Elections are based upon party politics and universal adult suffrage. Minimum voting age is 18.

The country has two main political parties, the National and Labour parties. The leader of the party winning a majority of seats in Parliament becomes the Prime Minister. Members of the Cabinet are selected from among the parliamentary membership of the winning party; they become the political heads of government departments and promote most of the legislation. The leader of the principal minority party becomes Leader of the Opposition.

Like Britain, New Zealand has an "unwritten constitution," and the country is ruled by convention rather than by statute. A simple majority vote in Parliament is all that is needed to execute or amend legislation.

When Parliament is in session, you can watch the proceedings from a seat in the visitors' gallery (see page 72).

Foreign affairs. Until World War II, New Zealand automatically followed Britain's lead in international affairs. Since that time, though, it has established close defense alliances with the United States and Australia and has taken a leadership role among the nations of Polynesia and the southwest Pacific. An increasing amount of New Zealand's international trade is with other Pacific nations.

Social innovations. New Zealand has gained a reputation for its innovative social legislation. As early as the 1890s, New Zealand extended the vote to women (the first nation in the world to do so), introduced arbitration procedures in industrial disputes, and established old age pensions.

Other progressive legislation includes a comprehensive health plan, use of an ombudsman to investigate citizen complaints against government departments, and compensation for victims of violent crime.

Self-reliant and friendly people

Throughout its history, New Zealand has attracted people who wanted a fresh start. With hard work and a keen sense of humor, New Zealanders have adapted to the demands of their new land.

Self-reliant and independent, the Kiwi is an amiable and friendly companion with whom you'll quickly be on a first name basis. He'll soon ask how you like New Zealand—and wait confidently for you to confirm his high opinion of his homeland.

About 90 percent of New Zealand's 3.1 million people are of British descent; Maoris make up about 8 percent of the population. Nearly three-fourths of the people live on North Island. *Pakeha* (Europeans) intermingle freely with Maoris, who have largely adopted the European life style while preserving their own traditions and culture.

Relaxed life style. Life here has a solid quality, based on virtually full employment and plenty of outdoor activities. Most people work a 5-day, 40-hour week. They treasure their weekends, and you'll find few New Zealanders engaged in commercial concerns on Saturdays and Sundays. People get their work done, but they're seldom in a hurry. You'll find some attractions close their doors for an hour during the midday lunch break.

The country's pioneering and mining heritage fostered an egalitarian society. A comprehensive system of social programs protects all New Zealanders, giving them a reasonable standard of living and safeguarding them against economic misfortune.

Zest for the outdoors. The country's ideal climate and vast expanses of open territory spawn an enthusiasm for athletics and the outdoors. In this male-oriented society, the Kiwi engages in sports with vigor and a rough-and-ready spirit. He's particularly fond of English sports—rugby, soccer, cricket, lawn bowling. No one lives far from the water.

Move to the cities. In recent decades young people have been moving to the cities in large numbers, and the transition from farm to factory is not always an easy one. It has been particularly difficult for Maoris and South Pacific immigrants accustomed only to rural communal traditions.

Traveling in New Zealand

Numerous international airlines—including the country's own Air New Zealand—serve Auckland International Airport. Trans-Tasman flights from Australia land in Wellington and Christchurch as well. Coach transportation into the city is available at all three airports.

Several steamship companies provide passenger cruise service between New Zealand and various U.S., Australian, Asian, and European ports.

Modern and efficient air, rail, and motorcoach service connects the main cities with provincial towns and resort areas. Ferries link the two islands, transporting passengers and vehicles across Cook Strait between Wellington and Picton.

Travel passes for overseas visitors

Visitors can purchase money-saving passes for travel on New Zealand's scheduled air, rail, and coach services.

Persons who travel on Air New Zealand between the United States and New Zealand can purchase an ANZ air pass, good for unlimited travel on domestic flights throughout the country. Sold outside New Zealand only, the pass may be obtained for 14 or 21 days of travel. Passengers make their own air reservations in New Zealand within two days of intended travel.

Mount Cook Line offers a coach pass, which must be purchased prior to arrival. Issued for a period of seven to 28 days, the Kiwi Coach Pass entitles the visitor to unlimited travel on scheduled services of the line's motorcoach routes as well as discounts on other Mount Cook Line services.

New Zealand Railways offers an off-season tourist pass, available from mid-April through mid-December, which allows 14 consecutive days' travel on both islands on N.Z. Railways trains, intercity motorcoaches, and interisland ferries. The pass can be extended at extra cost to a maximum of 28 days.

Air service links cities and resorts

Internal air service to the country's main cities,

resort areas, and provincial towns is provided by Air New Zealand, Mount Cook Line, and several smaller scheduled airlines. Coach and taxi transport into town is available at most airports. Charter planes operate from many local airports.

Aerial sightseeing trips by light aircraft (including float planes and ski-equipped planes) offer

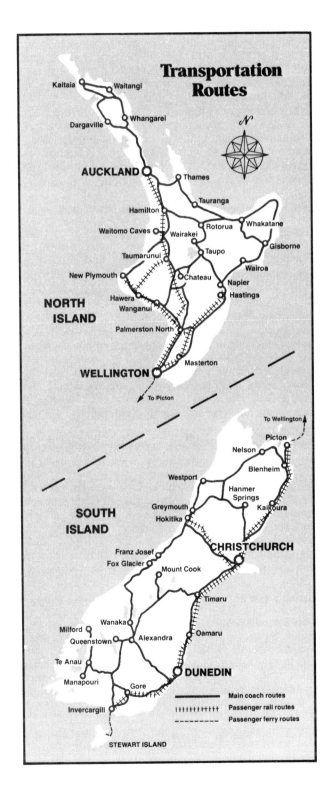

fresh perspectives (see page 97). Scenic flights are available in many towns and resorts and generally operate on demand (with a minimum number of passengers). Make arrangements after you arrive; your hotel receptionist can provide information.

Ferries steam across Cook Strait

Interisland passenger/vehicular ferries steam across Cook Strait several times daily in each direction, providing scheduled service between Wellington, at the southern end of North Island, and the town of Picton in South Island's Marlborough Sounds. Passengers, automobiles, and freight can be accommodated on the large ferries.

The crossing takes about 3 hours 20 minutes. Passage can be rough in windy or stormy weather. From Wellington you sail out between the headlands marking the entrance to Port Nicholson, cross Cook Strait, then sail up Tory Channel and Queen Charlotte Sound to Picton.

Rail service connects the main cities

Passenger rail service links the main cities on both islands. Fast, comfortable express passenger trains feature adjustable seats, smoking and nonsmoking sections, buffet cars, and refreshment service. Red-uniformed hostesses aid passengers on daytime express runs.

North Island. The main line runs from Auckland to Wellington, passing west of Tongariro National Park. Two express passenger trains provide regular service: the deluxe Silver Fern provides express daylight travel daily except Sunday, and the Northerner makes overnight runs between the two cities. The Endeavour makes a daily express run between Wellington and Napier.

South Island. Train routes branch out from Christchurch south along the coast to Dunedin and Invercargill, west to Greymouth, and north to Picton.

The Southerner provides daylight express rail service daily except Sunday between Christchurch and Invercargill. One of the country's most scenic rail routes goes from Christchurch over Arthur's Pass to Greymouth on the West Coast. Rail service also operates north from Christchurch to Picton, connecting with the interisland ferry to Wellington.

Coach service covers the country

The long-distance motorcoaches of N.Z. Railways Road Services cover the country from Kaitaia, near the northern tip of North Island, to Invercargill in the south. Regular scheduled service links most of the country's places of scenic, historic, and cultural interest.

Reservations are necessary on all routes, but no seats are assigned; if you purchase your ticket 48 hours in advance, your seat space is guaranteed. Try to be near the head of the boarding line to obtain a window seat.

Other long-distance coach companies offering scheduled service include Mount Cook Line, Hawkes Bay Motor Company, Gibsons Motors, Midland Coachlines, and Newmans Coach Lines.

Local transportation

Reliable and inexpensive public transportation is readily available in the major centers. City bus service connects the central districts with outlying suburbs; Wellington also has electric commuter train services to its northern suburbs. Bus fares vary by the number of "sections" of the route traveled.

Taxis in cities and towns operate from taxi stands or on call. The hotel desk clerk or restaurant receptionist will telephone for you. If you need an early-morning taxi, put in your request the night before.

Rates vary throughout the country but are normally charged on a per-kilometer basis. Extra charges are added for night and weekend trips and for additional luggage. You can arrange an hourly rate for sightseeing.

Traveling by car or caravan

If you enjoy leisurely touring, one of the best ways to enjoy the New Zealand countryside is by rental car. You can explore at your own pace, stay in country hotels and motels, and visit attractions of special interest to you.

You'll drive on the left side of the road in New Zealand. The speed limit is 80 kph/50 mph on the open road, 50 kph/30 mph (or posted) in built-up areas. Throughout the country, New Zealand Automobile Association signposts direct you to points of interest.

New Zealand observes the right hand rule: Unless otherwise controlled by traffic signs or lights, you give way to all traffic on your right (unless you are on a main highway). When turning, you give way to *all* traffic. Use of seat belts is compulsory. The A.A. booklet *Motoring New Zealand* contains helpful information for motorists.

Visitors from the United States, Canada, Australia, the United Kingdom, the Netherlands, Switzerland, South-West Africa, South Africa, Fiji, and West Germany may hire a car upon presentation of a current driver's license; residents of other countries should present an international driver's license. Insurance is arranged at time of car rental.

Rental cars. Major rental car companies are Mutual-Avis, Tasman-Hertz, and Dominion. All have branch offices and representatives in major towns and tourist areas throughout the country.

Companies offer a variety of plans including one way-one day rates, one way hire, unlimited kilometer rates, fly-drive trips, and plans where a rental car awaits you at the wharf or rail station.

Car with driver. Automobiles with a driver-guide are available for local sightseeing or for excursions of longer duration. Rates include a basic minimum

Music *and dance enliven an evening of Maori entertainment in Rotorua. You also can participate in a Maori* hangi *feast.*

charge plus the driver's accommodation expenses when away from his base.

Caravans and camping vans. Families and couples enjoy leisurely travel by motor caravan or smaller "campavans." Both contain sleeping and limited cooking facilities, but no toilet or shower. The caravans are roomy and comfortable but lack frills and gadgets. Some drivers find the vehicles underpowered for driving on mountain roads.

Vehicles can be rented in Auckland, Wellington, and Christchurch. Summer travelers should make rental arrangements well in advance to avoid disappointment. For information on caravan rental firms, write to the New Zealand Automobile Association, P.O. Box 1053, Wellington 1.

Motoring information. The New Zealand Automobile Association offers reciprocal membership privileges to members of other national automobile touring clubs. Bring your membership card.

At main offices of the Automobile Association you can obtain comprehensive motoring information, maps, and detailed accommodation and camping guides. District offices and representatives are located in all the main cities and towns.

Group tour or freewheeling holiday

Varied tour offerings allow you to tailor your plans to your preferred style of sightseeing. You can travel with a group by chartered motorcoach or plan your tour independently using rental car or scheduled public transportation services.

For information on current group and independent tour programs, see your travel agent. Information is also available from offices of Air New Zealand, other international carriers flying to New Zealand, Mount Cook Airlines, and the New Zealand Government Tourist Office.

Group travel by coach. Many travelers enjoy seeing New Zealand's highlights as part of a group, traveling by private motorcoach. All-inclusive trips (covering accommodations, meals, sightseeing, and transport) can be arranged in conjunction with international air travel to New Zealand for the duration of your stay or as part of a longer trip. Operators offer group tours ranging from 3 days to 3 weeks. Tours depart frequently throughout the year.

Independent holidays. If you prefer a plan that allows you to tour independently, check into the fly-drive or fly-coach plans. Most include international air fare and cover periods of 2 or 3 weeks; some can be extended.

Airlines and private tour operators offer a variety of fly-drive plans that include round-trip air fare to New Zealand and a rental car with limited or unlimited mileage. Some plans include an air pass for travel within New Zealand and a hotel pass covering accommodations at your choice of listed hotels throughout the country.

Fly-coach plans offer similar features, except that your surface travel is by scheduled motorcoach. You can select plans with or without hotel accommodations and internal air travel.

A third alternative is fly-tour plans, covering extensive local sightseeing as well as air transportation and accommodations.

Once you arrive, you'll find a variety of short fly-drive and fly-coach holidays available from Auckland and Christchurch to major tourist areas. New Zealand operators also offer camping tours and youth hostel holidays.

Enjoying your visit

In the cities and main resorts there are tourist accommodations in various price ranges. Facilities may be more limited in the countryside, but you'll find a warm welcome awaiting you.

Comfortable, modern hotels

As the number of visitors to New Zealand has increased in recent years, new hotels and motels have been built and existing facilities upgraded. You'll find modern facilities in all the main centers and tourist areas, and good accommodations are available throughout the country at moderate cost.

New Zealand hotels are not large by international standards, but they offer personal service. Rooms usually have tea and coffee-making facilities, telephone, and television. Some hotels provide daily newspapers, room refrigerators, and laundry facilities.

You can choose modern high-rise city hotels or older, smaller ones with a gracious English charm. Country hotels are generally small, with friendly, old-fashioned atmosphere.

Hotels must be licensed to serve drinks on the premises; a hotel ranks as fully licensed (liquor can be sold to the public), tourist licensed (liquor available to hotel guests but no public bar), or unlicensed (no liquor sold).

The main travel season extends from November through April. Peak demand occurs from mid-December through January and at Easter, when New Zealand families are on the road. Early reservations are recommended during peak season. Some hotels and motels apply a small surcharge for one-night stopovers. During the off-season, some offer reduced rates.

Hotel chains. Resort hotels operated by the government-owned Tourist Hotel Corporation provide excellent accommodations at most of the major scenic destinations on both islands. On North Island, THC hotels are located at Waitangi (Bay of Islands), Waitomo, Rotorua, Wairakei, and Tongariro National Park; a small motor inn is operated at Tokaanu (Lake Taupo). South Island THC hotels are located at Franz-Josef, Mount Cook, Wanaka, Te Anau, and Milford Sound.

Various private interests operate hotel and motel chains throughout the country. Some accommodations are new, others are older facilities brought up to modern standards. Among the leading hotel operators are Dominion Breweries Ltd. (DB hotels); Lion Breweries (South Pacific hotels and a chain of scattered older hotels called The Establishment, being refurbished in colonial decor); Travelodge; Vacation Hotels; Ballins Hotels; and Inns of the Pacific.

Current information. For information on hotel and motel facilities and current rates, consult your travel agent or obtain a copy of the *New Zealand Accommodation Guide*, available through the New Zealand Government Tourist Office. In New Zealand, the Automobile Association publishes the *Accommodation and Camping Guide* for its members; it contains a detailed listing of hotels, motels, and motor camps.

Motels offer good value

Many independent travelers have discovered New Zealand's fine motels, an excellent value for motorists who wish to come and go as they please. Modern, well-equipped motels can be found in all major cities and towns. Flag Inns and Best Western operate motels throughout the country.

Motel flats provide self-contained, fully furnished accommodations with kitchen facilities, refrigerator, cooking and dining utensils, and nearby laundry facilities.

Serviced motels are motorists' hotels with tea and coffee-making facilities but no kitchens. Cooked or continental breakfast is usually available; larger motels have a restaurant on the premises.

Low-cost accommodations

You don't need a big budget to enjoy a holiday in New Zealand. Public transportation costs are reasonable, and you'll find a wide range of moderately priced accommodations in smaller hotels, motels, guest houses, and cabins. If you prefer, you can stay in youth hostels or campgrounds.

Small hotels and guest houses. You'll find a variety of moderate and low-priced licensed hotels, offering clean rooms and good food without elaborate amenities.

Guest houses and private hotels have no liquor-selling licenses, and their rates vary according to their facilities. You can obtain rooms with or without private bath; most rooms contain a hand basin and an electric heater. The price may be for room only, or it may include some meals.

Youth hostels. Dormitory accommodation is available to hostel members at moderate cost. You must provide your own sleeping bag. Communal cooking facilities are provided at each hostel, and stopovers are limited to 3 nights at any one place.

For information on fees and hostels, write to the New Zealand Youth Hostel Association, P.O. Box 436, Christchurch 1.

Farm holidays

For a pleasant break in your touring, stay for a night or two with a farm family. If you like, you can help with the feeding and other chores, watch the dogs muster sheep, or just relax.

You stay in the homestead as a paying guest, having meals with the family and joining in their informal social activities. For more information, see page 85.

Maori legends and traditions reflect a unique culture

When European immigrants arrived in the early 19th century, they found a distinctive and well-established Maori culture. Tribal society was led by hereditary warrior chiefs and powerful priests.

History and traditions were memorized and passed down from father to son, mother to daughter, through legends, songs, and crafts.

Myths and legends. Colorful, imaginative, and often touching legends, handed down from generation to generation, offer insights into how the early Maori viewed his world and accounted for the origin of the universe, the elements, and man.

Tales recount a time long ago when mountains fought and walked, their tears became streams and rivers, and men and gods spoke together. In nearly every part of the country, Maori legends account for distinctive landscape features. Other stories relate tales of heroism and endurance.

Before the arrival of the missionaries, Maoris had no written language. Oratory was regarded as an important art in passing on tribal history and culture in tales that could be enjoyed by young and old alike.

Meeting house. Focal point of a Maori village is its open square (marae) and the traditional carved meeting house (whare runanga) facing it. Inside the structure, symbolic carvings depict tribal ancestors and mythical figures closely related to the tribe.

The poupou (carved wall panels) record tribal history and legends. Woven tukutuku panels in geometric patterns usually separate the wooden carvings. Posts supporting the ridgepole are also carved. Patterned kowhai-whai designs painted in black, red, and white decorate the rafters of the meeting house.

Carving. Intricately designed wood carvings were among the Maoris' primary forms of expression. Stylized figures, representing tribal ancestors and grotesque birds, fish, and animals, depicted stories of tribal history and lore. Each tribe had its distinct carving style.

Craftsmen preferred totara wood for carving. The distinctive color traditionally came from red ochre mixed with shark oil. Iridescent paua shells were used to show a figure's eyes. Distinctive motifs include curves and spiral designs, slanted eyes, and a three-fingered hand with backward turned thumb. Figures were often depicted in warlike poses, eyes bulging, and tongue outthrust in defiance.

Examples of the carver's art decorate both the exterior and interior of Maori meeting houses, as well as storehouses, gateways, and posts. In museums you'll see intricate carvings ornamenting articles once used in daily life, such as war canoes, weapons, and musical instruments.

Greenstone. Valued by the Maoris for its hardness and beauty, greenstone (nephrite jade or bowenite) was carved into prized ornaments, tools, and weapons. Maori parties made difficult overland journeys through the mountains to certain West Coast valleys in search of the comparatively rare stone. New Zealand's good luck talisman is the tiki, a greenstone neck pendant carved in the form of a fetus. Several museums have fine greenstone collections.

Weaving. Women excelled in weaving flax and reeds into geometrically patterned tukutuku panels that decorate many meeting houses, dwellings, and churches. Among other women's crafts are basket making, taniko weaving of decorative bodices and headbands, and preparation of the flax piupiu kilts worn by both men and women.

Music and dance. Traditional Maori music includes a variety of chants and poetic songs expressing joy and sadness, welcome and farewell. Familiar melodies such as Haere ra ("Now is the hour") date from the 19th century. Simple nose and mouth flutes and trumpets of shell, bone, and wood sometimes were used to accompany the singers; rhythm was supplied by stamping the feet, slapping the body with the hands, or tapping a piece of wood with a stick.

Most familiar of Maori dances is the spirited war dance (haka pukana), in which the performer engages in vigorous posture dancing as he grimaces, rolls his eyes, and thrusts out his tongue to frighten the enemy. New Zealand sports teams often perform it as an exciting preliminary to international matches. Women entertain with the gentle poi dance, twirling raupo balls on string in time with the music.

Tattooing. In traditional Maori society, tattooing was a form of adornment and status. A chief used his tattoo design (moko) as his signature.

Males were liberally embellished with distinctive patterns on face and body as well as buttocks and thighs. Women were less heavily decorated, usually only on lips and chin. Tattooing was a long and painful process. A tiny bone chisel was used to make incisions according to a pattern, and soot was rubbed into the open wounds to provide coloring.

For more information. Learning about Maori culture and crafts is an integral part of the New Zealand experience. Museums in major cities and provincial towns have fascinating exhibits of carved buildings and canoes, tools, ornaments, weapons, garments, and greenstone.

Local bookstores have varied publications on Maori customs, crafts, language, and legends.

In Rotorua you can see Maori craftsmen at work, learn about village life, attend a hangi feast, and enjoy Maori entertainment. The Waitangi meeting house represents an unusual variety of carving styles from tribes in all parts of North Island.

Maori communities are located throughout North Island, but visitors should ask permission locally before looking around a village.

Campgrounds serve families

Many New Zealanders enjoy their holidays in their own country, spending a few days at the beach, in the mountains, or at a national park; or enjoying some water-skiing, fishing, or golf.

Serving these travelers is a vast network of campgrounds, motor camps, and cabin and cottage accommodations. Many economy-minded overseas visitors have discovered these facilities also.

You'll find tent and caravan sites in campgrounds along scenic bays and beaches, near the parks, and beside lovely lakes. Most have communal kitchens, laundry facilities, and centralized shower and toilet facilities. Automobile club members can obtain campground information from the N. Z. Automobile Association.

Enjoy seafood and subtropical fruits

New Zealand lamb is world renowned and needs no introduction; you'll also find beef, pork, and poultry on restaurant menus. Venison and wild pork are available at restaurants specializing in wild game.

Seafood is superb. Rock lobster (crayfish) is available the year around but is most plentiful in spring and early summer. Tiny whitebait, netted in coastal rivers as it migrates upstream in the spring, is served in crisp, batter-fried fritters. Rock oysters are excellent, as are the tasty Bluff oysters scooped from the chilly waters of Foveaux Strait. Delectable scallops have a distinctive yet delicate flavor. The rare toheroa usually goes into rich toheroa soup; other creamy seafood soups feature the tuatua clam and the paua (abalone).

You'll see a variety of ocean fish—including snapper, flounder, and John Dory—on restaurant menus, but if you want trout, you'll have to catch it yourself.

Meals are served with a hearty salad or a selection of vegetables.

New Zealand fruits are superb in season, but you won't always find them on restaurant menus. In addition to familiar varieties, try Chinese gooseberry (kiwi fruit), tamarillo (tree tomato), and feijoa. Pavlova (meringue with sliced fruit and whipped cream) is the country's traditional dessert; it's prepared best in New Zealand homes.

Among New Zealand cheeses you'll discover local blue vein, several types of cheddar, and other varieties based on favorite international types.

Teas, lunches, snacks. Morning and afternoon tea (or coffee) breaks are widely observed, both at home and at work. Along with your hot beverage you can enjoy scones, biscuits (cookies), thin sandwiches, or a "sweet."

Fattened Wairarapa lambs, bound for the freezing works, funnel through a loading chute at Pirinoa sheep station. Additional flocks wait their turn in the grassy paddocks.

Many hotels feature smorgasbord lunches with an array of hot dishes, cold meats, salads, and desserts. If you prefer a lighter midday meal, you can purchase meat pies, savories, thin sandwiches, and other foods at milk bars, coffee lounges, and other informal food centers.

Picnicking is a pleasant alternative when you're touring. It's important to plan ahead if you're traveling in areas such as the West Coast or Fiordland where facilities are widely scattered. You can pick up crackers, cheese, fruit, and beverages for an informal repast; or, if you request it the previous night, some hotels will put up a box lunch or pack a "cut lunch" for you.

Liquor and wine. Licensed hotels may serve drinks from 11 A.M. to 10 P.M. (to 11 on Saturday nights) in bars, lounges, and licensed restaurants. Guests staying in a licensed hotel can be served at any time. Beer is the favorite drink; spirits are also available. Bars are open daily except Sundays, Christmas Day, and Good Friday.

Licensed restaurants serve liquor, beer, and wine. More informal restaurants may be unlicensed (you can call ahead and inquire); if you bring your own wine for dinner, it will be served to you for a modest corkage fee. You can buy bottled wine, beer, and liquor in bottle shops.

Restaurant wine lists offer limited imports from Australia, the United States, and Europe, and a growing list of New Zealand table wines. In general, local white wines are better than the reds. Major producers include Corbans, McWilliams, Waiherere, Montana, and Penfolds. It's customary to pay the wine steward separately for wine and drinks rather than have them added to the bill.

Entertainment and sports activities

Much of the night life revolves around the hotels, where musicians entertain and bands play for dancing. In some towns there is weekend cabaret entertainment.

Touring national and overseas artists visit the major centers, and local theater groups perform in the larger cities. Civic and university groups offer music and drama. The New Zealand Symphony Orchestra, Ballet, and Opera Company tour the major towns on both islands. Maori entertainment can be seen in Rotorua.

For information on current entertainment, check local tourist publications and daily newspapers.

The whole country is sports minded, and you'll find active New Zealanders outdoors in all seasons. For more on sports activities, see page 22.

Shopping for New Zealand crafts

You'll find a varied array of souvenirs and gift articles in New Zealand stores, shops, and craft centers. Shops are generally open weekdays from 9 to 5:30, Friday nights until 9. Most are closed on Saturday and Sunday, though shops in some tourist areas now stay open on Saturdays. In country areas, it's fun to visit the general store—the local "sell everything" retailer.

Native woods are used singly or combined in inlaid patterns in bowls, candleholders, trays, and other items. Woolly sheepskins and lambskins—by-products of the export meat industry—are converted into rugs, car seat covers, slippers, wearing apparel, and toys. Suede clothing, leatherware, and opossum fur articles are also popular. Other wool products include car robes and blankets (some in Maori designs), articles made from homespun wool, and handknitted sweaters.

Greenstone is carved into traditional *tiki* pendants and contemporary jewelry. Iridescent paua shell is used decoratively in boxes, trays, ashtrays, and jewelry.

New Zealand has a number of excellent potters, and you'll find their wares throughout the country. Other crafts include metalwork, gemstone jewelry using New Zealand stones, and weaving.

If you're captivated by the Maori culture, you'll want to look over records of Maori music and carved wood articles from native woods.

Bookstores offer a fine selection of publications on New Zealand subjects.

A limited selection of imported goods is available at duty free shops in Auckland, Wellington, and Christchurch.

Practical information

New Zealand is located close to the International Date Line and has a single time zone. New Zealand time is 12 hours ahead of Greenwich Mean Time.

Based on Standard Time, Auckland is 20 hours ahead of San Francisco, 17 hours ahead of New York. Across the date line, Auckland is 2 hours in advance of Sydney, 3 hours ahead of Tokyo, and 4½ hours ahead of Singapore. New Zealand observes Daylight Saving Time from the last Sunday in October to the first Sunday the following March, advancing its clocks 1 hour during this period.

Tourist information

New Zealand Government tourist offices can help you obtain information and answer your inquiries, both before you go and after you arrive in the country. Local public relations offices are located in larger towns throughout the country.

Before you go. U.S. offices of the New Zealand Government Tourist Office are located in San Francisco, CA 94111 (Suite 970, Alcoa Building, 1 Maritime Plaza); Los Angeles, CA 90024 (Suite 1530, Tishman Building, 10960 Wilshire Boulevard); and New York, NY 10111 (Suite 530, 630 Fifth Avenue). In Canada, write the office at Suite 1160, IBM Tower, 701 West Georgia Street, Vancouver, BC V7Y 1B6.

In Australia, consult offices of the New Zealand Government Tourist Bureau in Sydney (United

Dominions House, 115 Pitt Street, Sydney, N.S.W., 2000); Melbourne (C.M.L. Building, 330 Collins Street, Melbourne, Victoria, 3000); Brisbane (Ground Floor, Watkins Place, 288 Edward Street, Brisbane, Queensland, 4000), or Perth (16 St. George's Terrace, Perth, W.A.).

In Europe, New Zealand Government Tourist Offices are located in London (New Zealand House, Haymarket, London, SW1Y 4TQ) and Frankfurt (Fremdenverkehrsamt Von Neuseeland, 6000 Frankfurt am Main, Kaiserhofstrasse 7, West Gerany). In Japan, information is available from the New Zealand Government Tourist Office, Toho Twin Tower Building, 2F, 1-5-2 Yurakucho, Chiyoda-ku, Tokyo 100.

After you arrive. Once you land in New Zealand, you'll find offices of the Government Tourist Bureau (G.T.B.) in Auckland, Rotorua, Wellington, Christchurch, Dunedin, Queenstown, and Invercargill. Staff there can aid you in obtaining accommodations throughout the country, making travel arrangements, and providing tour information.

Local public relations offices (P.R.O.) can provide information on local attractions and special events. Free tourist periodicals in main centers offer current entertainment, dining, and shopping ideas.

Motorists who belong to an automobile club can obtain motoring information, maps, accommodation guide books, and route-planning assistance at offices of the Automobile Association.

Entry requirements

Passports are required of all visitors from overseas except Australian citizens arriving directly from Australia, and citizens of other Commonwealth countries who have been granted permanent residency in Australia or New Zealand. Passports must be valid at least 6 months beyond the date the visitor intends leaving New Zealand.

Visas are not required by U.S. citizens (except American Samoans) for visits of 30 days or less. Visitors planning a longer stay should apply to the nearest New Zealand overseas representative. Commonwealth citizens must have a temporary entry permit which is granted on arrival to those meeting requirements. Visas are required by nationals of countries with which New Zealand does not have an abolition agreement.

Persons entering New Zealand are required to be in good health and of good character, to have sufficient funds to maintain themselves during their stay, and to show proof of onward travel arrangements.

A smallpox vaccination is required for travelers arriving from an infected area. No other inoculations are necessary except for visitors arriving from South American or Asian countries.

Customs regulations

Visitors may bring in a limited amount of personal effects (such as sports equipment, fishing gear, binoculars, portable radio, tape recorder, cameras, and a reasonable amount of film), which must be declared on entry and taken out of the country when the visitor leaves New Zealand.

Each adult may bring in duty-free one 750ml bottle of wine, one 1125ml bottle of spirits, and 200 cigarettes (or up to 250 grams of tobacco or up to 50 cigars). Full details on customs limitations and restricted or prohibited imports may be obtained from the nearest New Zealand government overseas representative.

Money matters

New Zealand operates on a decimal currency system based on dollar and cent denominations. A visitor may bring an unlimited amount of foreign currency and travelers checks into New Zealand, but government restrictions do limit the importation of New Zealand currency notes or the transfer of New Zealand funds outside the country.

Banking facilities are located at international transport terminals. In New Zealand cities and towns, banks operate Monday through Friday from 10 A.M. to 4 P.M.; they are closed on Saturdays, Sundays, and holidays.

Tipping. In a word, *don't*. New Zealanders do not generally tip—nor do they expect to be tipped. It's not customary in New Zealand. Most Kiwis want to keep it that way and hope visitors will cooperate.

What little tipping there is is done rarely—and moderately—only for special service or attention. You are not expected to tip for normal service in hotels, restaurants, taxis, barbershops, or hairdressing salons—but an appreciative comment is never out of place.

It is acceptable—but not necessary—to tip hotel lounge bar stewards up to 50 cents a round of drinks, wine stewards in better restaurants, a taxi driver if he carries your luggage, and airport or railway porters up to 50 cents a bag.

Departure tax. International air passengers pay a tax of NZ$2 at the airport when leaving the country.

Keeping in touch

New Zealand's efficient internal and international communications network makes it easy to keep in touch with friends and business acquaintances.

First class mail can be sent by surface or air throughout New Zealand and to overseas destinations. Aerogrammes (for overseas air letters) may be purchased at post offices. You can ship small packets of books, maps, and other printed matter home by surface mail at favorable rates; allow 4 to 6 weeks for such surface mail to Australia and Asian countries, 6 to 8 weeks to all other destinations.

Most city hotel and motel rooms contain telephones; you'll also find public booths. Calls within direct dialing areas are free unless made from a public telephone booth. Cable and telex facilities are also available.

Daily morning and evening newspapers are produced in the main cities, and many hotels provide papers free to guests. Major provincial cities and towns also have local daily newspapers.

New Zealand has two television channels, though not all areas of the country receive both channels. There's a national noncommercial radio network, and numerous regional and local radio stations operate throughout the country.

Medical and emergency facilities

New Zealand medical and hospital facilities offer a high standard of treatment and care. Hotels and motels usually have a doctor on call for guest medical emergencies. Water is safe to drink. New Zealand has no snakes or dangerous animals. Sandflies can be a nuisance in moist lowland areas.

Visitors are covered by the national accident compensation scheme which compensates injured persons for medical and hospital expenses.

A telephone call system (phone 111) brings immediate contact with police, fire, or ambulance authorities.

Business hours and holidays

New Zealand offices and businesses are open weekdays from 9 to 5 (shops stay open until 5:30), closed on weekends and holidays. Banks are open from 10 to 4 Monday through Friday. On late shopping night (Thursday or Friday), stores are open until 9 P.M.; a few areas feature Saturday shopping.

Nationwide holidays include New Year's Day, Waitangi Day (February 6), Good Friday, Easter Monday, Anzac Day (April 25), Queen's Birthday (first Monday in June), Labour Day (fourth Monday in October), Christmas Day, Boxing Day (December 26). Most attractions close on Good Friday and Christmas Day.

Local holidays celebrating provincial anniversaries are observed on the nearest Monday to the following dates: Wellington (January 22), Auckland and Northland (January 29), Nelson (February 1), Taranaki (March 12), Otago and Southland (March 23), Hawkes Bay (October 18), Marlborough (November 1), Canterbury (November 9), and Westland (December 1).

Schools are closed from mid-December through January (the main family holiday period), for 2 weeks in May, and again in August.

Think metric

New Zealand now operates on the metric system. Throughout the country, you'll generally find distances expressed in kilometers, elevations in meters, rainfall in millimeters, weights in grams and kilograms.

For rough calculations: 1 kilometer equals 0.62

miles, 1 mile equals 1.6 kilometers. One meter is approximately 39 inches or 3.28 feet. A kilogram—1,000 grams—equals 2.2 pounds.

Temperatures are expressed in Celsius degrees. To convert Celsius degrees to Fahrenheit temperatures, multiply the Celsius number by 1.8 and add 32 for the approximate Fahrenheit equivalent.

Need a quicker rule of thumb? Try this rhyme:
"30° (C.) is hot, 20° is nice,
 10° is cool, 0° is ice."

Electricity

Electrical current in New Zealand is 230 volts, 50 cycles AC (alternating current). Most hotels provide 110-volt AC sockets for electric razors only.

Appliances that normally operate on a lower voltage require a converting transformer.

Most New Zealand power sockets accept three-pin flat plugs (top two pins angled); you'll need a special adapter plug to use most appliances manufactured outside of New Zealand.

Packing tips

New Zealand lies in the temperate zone, and its climate is seldom excessively hot in summer or uncomfortably cold in winter. Climate ranges from subtropical in the northern areas to temperate in the south. Average midsummer temperatures range from 23° C./73° F. in Auckland to 19° C./66° F. in Dunedin. In winter, average temperatures range from 14° C./57° F. in Auckland to 8° C./46° F. in Queenstown. Rainfall levels vary (heaviest on the western coast of South Island), but rainy days are distributed throughout the year.

Seasons are reversed from those in the Northern Hemisphere. Spring lasts from September to November, summer from December to February (the main holiday season), autumn from March to May, and winter from June to August.

Clothing. Informality is a way of life in New Zealand. Dress tends to be more conservative in the cities, though casual clothes are common. Bring comfortable walking shoes and a raincoat.

Men will find a medium-weight suit and sports clothes ideal the year around. In summer, you'll see men in shorts.

Women should pack dresses and casual clothes in lightweight, wash-and-wear fabrics (plus a sweater for evenings) for summer travels, warmer clothes the rest of the year. On the beach, bikinis are the rule rather than the exception.

In the evenings, men are expected to wear jackets and ties in the better restaurants, and local women tend to dress up for an evening out. In homes, informality is usually the rule.

Laundry and dry cleaning services are available on 1-day service, except over the weekend.

Other items. If you're a smoker or photographer, you'll want to bring your allotted amount of cigarettes or camera film. You'll need sunglasses if you plan to tour the Southern Alps.

Join the New Zealanders outdoors for fishing or hiking, boating or golf

Spurred on by the country's invigorating climate and inexpensive, readily available facilities, almost every New Zealander participates in one sport or another. Nearly all stores and businesses close on both Saturday and Sunday, as Kiwis (New Zealanders) scatter to enjoy their favorite outdoor events.

Families often head for the beach for a day of sunning and swimming. Or they may prefer to go bush walking, water skiing, or sailing on a sheltered bay or harbor. Many sportsmen enjoy the tranquility of a favorite fishing stream or friendly play on the local golf course.

Others seek the excitement of the racetrack or stadium, where they follow enthusiastically the fortunes of horse racing and team competition. Kiwis are renowned—not without reason—for their dedicated pursuit of "racing, rugby, and beer."

Many visitors plan their travels to include hiking on one of New Zealand's scenic tracks (trails), skiing on its challenging slopes, or fishing in its streams or offshore waters. You may enjoy watching an afternoon cricket match or a game of lawn bowls, or you can join the crowds to cheer for a favorite horse or rugby team. To learn of activities scheduled during your visit to a city, check the local newspapers and inquire at the nearest tourist information center.

Active sports

Visitors who join New Zealanders in a favorite sport see a special side of the Kiwi life style. Following are some outdoor activities you can enjoy during your visit.

Big, fighting trout await the lure

Some of the world's best fresh-water fishing awaits you in New Zealand. In fact, if you want to eat trout here, you'll *have* to catch it yourself. Trout fishing is strictly a sport, with no trout grown or caught commercially.

Even the casual fisherman can arrange a few hours' fishing with a guide before or after the day's sightseeing. Limits are generous, but in most districts, you must throw back all fish under 35.6 centimeters/14 inches. The hotel chef will cook your catch for you and your friends.

Introduced in New Zealand late in the 19th century, rainbow and brown trout thrive in the country's clear lakes and cold, fast-flowing rivers. Famed both for their size and tenacious fighting qualities, these trout can challenge the skills of the most expert angler. Yet each year hundreds of visitors who have never fished before proudly display their catch.

Steelhead (sea-run trout) and salmon migrate up a number of coastal rivers during the spawning season, and landlocked salmon are caught in some South Island lake systems.

North Island. The Rotorua and Taupo lake systems offer productive year-round fishing. Trolling is popular during the warm summer months (October through March), but in autumn the action shifts to the mouths of lake tributaries as trout congregate prior to spawning runs. Most streams are designated fly fishing only.

At Lake Rotorua, fishermen catch rainbows weighing 2 to 4 pounds. During the May-June spawning season, 9 to 10-pound rainbow trout are caught nearly every day at Lake Tarawera as they rise from the depths to gather near the stream mouths. Within a 10-mile radius of Rotorua are numerous other good fishing lakes, largest of which are Rotoiti, Okataina, and Rotoehu.

Wildlife authorities estimate that about 700 tons of trout are caught annually in Lake Taupo. Here rainbows weigh in at 3½ to 6 pounds, and brown

Sails billow in a strong breeze as yachts race on Auckland's Waitemata Harbour. The world's largest one-day regatta takes place here annually in late January.

trout average more than 5 pounds. Most of the main fishing streams, including the famed Tongariro, enter near the lake's southern end. River fishing is best here from April to September during the spawning runs. When the fishing is good, anglers in chest-high waders form a "picket fence" across the mouth of the Waitahanui River. Streams flowing into the lake from the west can be reached only by boat.

Most fishermen headquarter in the Rotorua district or at Taupo, Turangi, or Tokaanu on Lake Taupo. Accommodations, boats, tackle, and guides are available throughout the area.

South Island. Thousands of miles of uncrowded trout streams, along with the excellent lake fishing in the Southern Lakes region, attract fly fishermen to South Island.

Brown trout predominate here, but rainbows and landlocked salmon also bite in the lake systems. Rainbows and browns average 2 pounds but run to 5 pounds in some areas; 10-pounders of both species are not uncommon. Salmon spawn in some of the east coast rivers, and South Westland has large runs of sea-run brown trout in spring and late summer. Whitebait migrate up a number of coastal rivers from September through November.

Anglers planning to fish South Island streams and lakes usually stay in Queenstown, Wanaka, Gore, Te Anau, or Invercargill. In these towns you can find accommodations, rent a car, and hire a guide to help you get started.

Season, fees, guides. New Zealand has 26 different fishing districts, each governed by a local acclimatization society. The Wildlife Branch of the Internal Affairs Department controls the lake systems of Rotorua, Taupo, and the Southern Lakes.

You can fish throughout the year at Rotorua and Taupo lakes, but in most districts the angling season opens on the first Saturday in October and extends through April (in some districts through May or June). Most serious anglers try to avoid the January family vacation period.

Day licenses average NZ $1, weekly licenses $2 in each district. Overseas visitors can purchase a special 1-month trout fishing license (NZ $4 for men, $2 for women), allowing the holder to fish in any district; these licenses are available at Government Tourist Bureau offices.

Your best insurance for a successful expedition is a local professional guide; you'll find guides throughout the main fishing areas. In addition to fishing know-how, they supply all tackle, gear, boat, and surface transport to the fishing area. Most guides operate at a fixed charge per party (up to three persons), depending on services and equipment required. Rates range from NZ $100 to $150 a day or NZ $16 to $20 per hour. Most areas have "you-drive" outboards available by the hour.

Packaged excursions. Several tour operators plan 2 to 4-week fishing itineraries that include air fare to New Zealand, accommodations, and other features. You can also arrange 1-day or 3-day package trips from Auckland to the Rotorua-Taupo district. For current information, check with your travel agent, the New Zealand Government Tourist Office, or international airlines flying to New Zealand.

For more information. A comprehensive pocket guide, *Fishing New Zealand*, is available from the New Zealand Government Tourist Office. The government's Hunting and Fishing Officer in Rotorua works with travel agents in developing individual fishing-oriented itineraries.

Local information sources include the offices of the district acclimatization societies, tourist information centers, sporting goods stores, and rangers in the field.

Exciting catches for deep-sea fishermen

Fishermen come from around the world to challenge the big, fighting game fish inhabiting New Zealand's warm Pacific coastal waters.

How big is "big"? New Zealand's all-tackle records should bring a gleam to the fisherman's eye: broadbill swordfish, 673 pounds; black marlin, 976; blue marlin, 1,017; striped marlin, 465; yellowtail (kingfish), 111; thresher shark, 922; tiger shark, 947; hammerhead shark, 460; mako shark, 1,000; yellowfin tuna, 168; bluefin tuna, 519.

Deep-sea fishing is enjoyed the year around, but the best fishing comes from mid-January through April. You don't need a license.

Big game fishing centers are located along the eastern coast of North Island—from North Cape to Cape Runaway—at Whangaroa, Bay of Islands, Whangarei (Tutukaka), Whitianga (Mercury Bay), Tauranga (Mayor Island), and Whakatane (Whale and White islands).

All are less than 200 miles from Auckland. The visitor with limited time can fly to any port by amphibian airplane, spend a day fishing on a fully equipped launch, and return to Auckland by evening; longer excursions can also be arranged. Fishermen stay at hotels, motels, or fishing lodges, depending on the area.

In coastal towns licensed launches skippered by expert game fishermen may be chartered at a daily rate of NZ $100 to $225 (for the launch, not per person). Most launches have two to four chairs and are equipped with fishing equipment and tackle.

In recent years, fishermen have used lighter tackle. Charter boats normally carry 80-pound line, but some enthusiastic sportsmen take record-size catches on 50, 30, or even 20-pound line. Yellowfin tuna is the main light-tackle fish, followed by yellowtail (kingfish), skipjack, bonito, and kahawai (sea trout).

Most visiting fishermen join local deep-sea fishing clubs; membership costs NZ $5 to $10 annually and entitles members to use all club facilities, have their catches weighed and recorded, and enjoy the general club conviviality.

On weekends you can see surf fishermen on nearly any beach or rocky shoreline. Surfcasting is popular during summer, but some of the best fish-

Weekend wanderings for city visitors

New Zealanders treasure their weekends. Nearly all shops, offices, and services close or operate on a limited schedule on Saturdays and Sundays, and city streets empty as Kiwis head for home, country, or shore.

Against such potentially lackluster interludes, the savvy visitor will plan ahead. Check tourist information sources and local newspapers to learn what activities and special events are available. If you want to rent a car, reserve ahead (the earlier the better) and arrange a pick-up time. Travelers planning a weekend trip using public transportation should confirm the time schedule.

Take a boat ride. In most cities and tourist areas, you can board a harbor launch, ferry, jet boat, lake cruiser, canoe, or fishing boat for an afternoon on the water.

Head for the beach. Join local families in soaking up the sun, watching boats, and swimming in the sea.

Check the sports scene. Saturday is sports day in New Zealand. Go to the races or attend a rugby match. Check local papers to see what events are scheduled.

Explore on foot. If you've just arrived, get acquainted with the city street pattern, walk along the waterfront, or follow paths through hillside forest parks or botanic gardens.

Visit a museum. Learn about New Zealand natural history, Maori culture, and the colonial days. Ride vintage vehicles at transportation museums.

Stroll through the park. Join local families in admiring the flowers or attending a band concert.

Plan a picnic. Purchase food supplies and spread your fare on a park lawn or sandy beach.

Join the animals. Visit the zoo. See a kiwi and other birds and animals.

Visit the library. If the weather is gloomy, catch up on home news in the library's newspaper reading room or browse through the New Zealand book collection.

Attend an A & P show. Join the crowds at horse jumping events, livestock judging, homecraft displays, and sheep shearing contests. Check tourist information offices or newspapers to learn if any shows are scheduled nearby.

ing comes in the colder months of March to November. Local camps and stores near the beaches sell tackle and bait, and some rent equipment. An annual surfcasting contest on Ninety Mile Beach each January attracts hundreds of participants.

Golfers find uncrowded fairways

Sport-loving New Zealanders have embraced golf with enthusiasm; some 110,000 Kiwis enjoy the sport regularly. Hundreds of golf courses dot the country, offering views of splendid scenery along with challenging game possibilities. Every city and most towns have both public and private courses. Greens are uncrowded and fees modest, even at the finest courses.

You can arrange to use the facilities of almost any golf club in New Zealand merely by contacting the local group. Each club is self-supporting and maintains its own fairways, greens, and buildings.

Most visiting golfers bring their own clubs, but well-equipped pro shops rent pull carts (called "hand trundlers"), clubs, and other equipment items. Motorized carts are not generally used, except by persons granted special permission for medical reasons.

For information on some of the country's top courses, write the New Zealand Government Tourist Office for the illustrated brochure *Golf in New Zealand*.

Hiking and climbing amid superb scenery

New Zealand's luxuriant forests and alpine parks attract dedicated hikers (called "trampers" in New Zealand) and mountaineers, but the casual walker can enjoy many rewarding short trails and nature walks, as well.

Best known of the longer hikes is the Milford Track, described by one early hiker as "the finest walk in the world." The 53-km/33-mile tramp through Fiordland National Park begins at the head of Lake Te Anau and crosses Mackinnon Pass to end at Milford Sound.

The 40-km/25-mile Routeburn Track traverses the alpine country of Mount Aspiring and Fiordland national parks; starting near Kinloch on Lake Wakatipu, the trail crosses Harris Saddle to meet the Te Anau-Milford Road. A third facet of Fiordland National Park may be seen on the Hollyford Track, a 26-km/16-mile route down the Lower Hollyford Valley to Martins Bay.

Organized group excursions on all three tracks allow hikers to travel with minimum packs; lodging and meals are provided in huts along the route. "Freedom walkers" (independent hikers) also can hike the tracks. North Island escorted hiking trips, with tent accommodations and meals provided, depart from Taumarunui (the Wanganui Walk) and Rotorua (Te Rehuwai Safaris). For information, write the New Zealand Government Tourist Office.

Dressed in their "whites," *lawn bowlers compete on the greens in front of the handsome old Tudor Towers in Rotorua's Government Gardens. The bowling season lasts from October to Easter.*

At the northern end of South Island, the Heaphy Track starts west of Bainham, near Golden Bay. It winds through stands of native forest and tussock country to the luxuriant greenery of the West Coast north of Karamea.

In the national parks and forest reserves, shorter trails offer hikers a variety of scenic routes and nature walks. Many trails are suitable for people wearing comfortable walking shoes; other tracks demand sturdier footwear.

New Zealand's high peaks attract experienced mountaineers—the country's alpine climbers have won worldwide fame. In the Southern Alps, 17 peaks top 10,000 feet; highest of all is 3,763-meter/ 12,349-foot Mount Cook. Major climbing areas on South Island lie along the east and west slopes of the Southern Alps in the national parks. Mount Cook and Westland national parks flank the range's main divide and contain superb alpine scenery. Other high peaks are contained in Mount Aspiring, Arthur's Pass, and Fiordland national parks.

North Island's mountains are lower than those of South Island, and its major peaks are either extinct or mildly active volcanoes.

Equipment for serious hiking and mountaineering can be purchased or rented in the main towns and alpine resort hotels in New Zealand climbing areas. Guides are available at the national parks.

Information on hiking and mountaineering is available at park headquarters of each national park or from tramping and alpine clubs, which have extensive memberships. Hikers and trampers can contact the New Zealand Federation of Mountain Clubs, P.O. Box 1604, Wellington. For information on mountain climbing, write to the New Zealand Alpine Club, P.O. Box 2211, Christchurch.

Hunting is competitive

Red deer, chamois (Austrian antelope), and tahr (Himalayan mountain goat) are the main species hunted; other game includes sika and fallow deer, wapiti (elk), ferrel goat, and wild pig. Sports hunting has deteriorated due to competition from professional hunters.

All deer species are in velvet from September to mid-February; the peak time for trophy hunting is during the April-May rutting season. Since chamois and tahr do not lose their horns, they can be taken the year around (the best hunting is usually from mid-February through May). Chamois and tahr are hunted in the mountains above timberline.

New Zealand hunting country is rough and rugged. Helicopters and four-wheel-drive vehicles are often brought into service to transport hunters into remote areas or high alpine terrain.

Visiting hunters are advised to use experienced, registered guides and to allow at least a week of hunting time. Many guides operate their own areas and provide all equipment, accommodations, meals, and transportation. If necessary, they arrange for entry permits to national parks or private land. Daily rates range from about NZ $75 to $125 per hunter.

Some hunters bring their own rifles, but revolvers and pistols are illegal in New Zealand, and entry of these is prohibited. Upon your arrival, you must register your firearms with police.

Waterfowl and upland game season begins the first Saturday in May. Its duration depends on the district but is usually 3 to 4 weeks for waterfowl, 6 to 8 weeks for upland game. Licenses are required, and limits are set on waterfowl (wild ducks, Canadian geese, swans) and other game birds (pheasant, quail, chukor).

Inquiries on hunting and guide service should be directed to the Hunting and Fishing Officer, Tourist and Publicity Department, Private Bag, Rotorua.

Yachting and boating

New Zealand's sheltered harbors, gulfs, inland lakes, and rivers offer superb waters for yachting, cruising, rowing, kayaking, and canoeing. Many Kiwis enjoy these sports on weekends, both on a club and individual basis.

Visitors wishing to make contact with local yachting, rowing, or canoeing clubs should contact the local public relations officer.

In the major cities you can make independent excursions by boat. Take ferry or launch trips across Auckland's harbor or to Hauraki Gulf islands, for example, or a day return (round trip) ferry from Wellington to Picton. In Christchurch, rent a canoe or rowboat for an hour on the Avon River. Many towns and resort areas have scheduled excursions allowing you to enjoy the countryside from the water.

Skin diving and spear fishing

New Zealand's long and irregular coastline offers excellent sport for skin and scuba divers and spear fishermen. Warmer North Island waters have more abundant fish life, but underwater sport can also be enjoyed in many South Island areas. Fast-moving kingfish are the prime quarry of spear fishermen in coastal waters.

Major North Island diving areas are concentrated near the north and northeastern coasts from the Three Kings Islands off the northernmost tip south to the Bay of Islands, Hauraki Gulf, the Coromandel Peninsula, and Bay of Plenty.

Scuba diving is excellent off most islands scattered along the northeastern coast. Poor Knights Island, offshore from Tutukaka (north of Whangarei), is regarded as a marine sanctuary, and spear guns are seldom used there; huge sponges and lacy corals cluster on the vertical rock faces 100 to 200 feet below the surface. Reefs surrounding volcanic Mayor Island are particularly lush. Kawau Island in the Hauraki Gulf is headquarters for a maritime park.

There are accommodations in coastal resorts and on several islands. Divers can arrange for charter planes or vessels to ferry them from game fishing towns to offshore islands or reefs.

Good South Island diving areas are located off the northern tip of the island, along stretches of the eastern and southwestern coasts, and around Stewart Island.

The warmer months of November to April attract the most divers, but many locals dive the year around. Wet suits are necessary in winter and for prolonged diving. Winds sometimes make diving uncomfortable. Sharks are not a problem.

Diving gear can be hired or purchased in Auckland, Wellington, and other coastal towns. Some diving boats provide gear.

More than 45 diving clubs are located through New Zealand—club members are usually happy to guide visitors. Professional diving guides are also available. Some equipment firms and clubs organize excursions to the northern diving regions; the Wellington Underwater Club's excursion to Mayor Island each October is open to all divers and generally attracts more than 200 people.

All local clubs are affiliated with the New Zealand Underwater Association Inc., P.O. Box 17, Kawakawa, Northland.

Tennis—on grass or surfaced courts

Hundreds of tennis clubs guide the play of thousands of enthusiastic players. Even some farms and sheep stations have a private court for family and guests. Grass courts are used from October to April; surfaced courts are available for year-round play.

In Auckland, Wellington, Christchurch, and other cities, the visiting tennis player can arrange a friendly match with local club members. Contact regional secretaries of the New Zealand Lawn Tennis Association to make arrangements.

On the spectator side, most clubs have interclub matches during the summer, especially on weekends. Interprovincial matches and contests between visiting overseas players and locals draw large crowds to the city centers.

Lawn bowls—an organized amateur sport

One of the country's major participant sports, lawn bowls is organized by men's and women's clubs which sponsor play. Visiting bowlers are welcome to participate.

Many city parks contain immaculate lawn bowling greens, mowed and rolled with loving care. One favorite site to watch lawn bowls is Rotorua's Government Gardens.

The bowling season extends from early October until early April; Easter weekend generally marks the end of the season. Top bowlers compete in the National Association championship each January.

Spectator sports

If you're a better spectator than participant, why not spend a Saturday at the races or take in a rugby or cricket match?

Horse racing attracts large crowds

Some of the world's top thoroughbred horses are raised in New Zealand, where the breeding and racing of horses is big business. Spectators flock to racetracks throughout the country; both on-course and off-track betting is legal.

Race meetings are scheduled throughout the year on Saturdays and public holidays and during midweek as well in the larger cities. Auckland, Wellington, and Christchurch have frequent races. Other major tracks with numerous races are in Dunedin, New Plymouth, Wanganui, Palmerston North, Hamilton, Hastings, Invercargill, and Rotorua.

Racing. Most of the important gallop racing meets take place at North Island tracks, including Ellerslie and Avondale (Auckland), Te Rapa (Hamilton), Trentham (Wellington), Awapuni (Palmerston North), and Hastings (Hastings). Among main South Island tracks are Riccarton in Christchurch and Wingatui in Dunedin.

Harness racing. Major harness racing meets are held at Alexandra Park and Epsom in Auckland, Hutt Park in Wellington, Addington in Christchurch, and Forbury Park in Dunedin. Many harness race meetings take place at night under floodlights.

Admission prices to the races vary, depending on whether you buy an inside or outside enclosure. Inside is similar to reserved grandstand; outside is comparable to general admission at U.S. race courses.

Horse shows. The New Zealander's intense interest in horses is also reflected in the popularity of horse shows. Every A & P show (see page 93), similar to state or county fairs, includes jumping competitions and horse and pony judging. Horse show season runs during New Zealand's spring and summer—from about mid-October to early April.

Rugby—a way of life

In New Zealand, rugby is not merely the national sport, it is a way of life. From May through September, rugby (officially, Rugby Union football) is played in every province and hamlet throughout the country.

To be a team player on the champion All Blacks (so called because of the color of their uniforms) is the ambition of every boy from the time he first handles the oval ball. Boys begin playing rugby at the age of seven and often continue into adult life.

Rugby has much in common with American football. Each side attempts to carry a blown-up pigskin over the goal line or kick it through the goal posts with more consistency than the opposition. However, team members play without heavy padding, and action is continuous. Play does not halt until someone scores, the ball goes out of bounds, or a rule is broken. Each side has eight forwards and seven backs, and every man on the field can run, pass (laterally or backward), and kick. When tackled, the man with the ball must let go once he is pulled down.

Three types of football—Rugby Union, Rugby League, and Soccer—are played in New Zealand. All are completely amateur sports. Rugby League football is similar to Rugby Union, with some rule variations: a league team has 13 players instead of 15, as in rugby. All three football codes have large spectator followings.

Good seats for important interprovincial and international games—such as New Zealand vs. South Africa, Australia, Britain, or France—are highly prized and difficult to obtain.

Cricket—a link with the English

Amateur teams enjoy the summer sport of cricket that the English brought to New Zealand. Cricket games take place on Saturdays and holidays—sometimes Sundays as well—from November through April.

Auto racing has many fans

International motor car racing ranks high among popular spectator sports. Events begin in January, with the International Grand Prix and supporting races near Auckland. Later races take place in Tauranga, Christchurch, Feilding, and Invercargill.

Winter sports

When the weather turns chill and snow begins to pile up on the high peaks, the thoughts of many New Zealanders turn to winter sports.

Ski on hazard-free slopes

New Zealand's sleek ski slopes offer abundant powder snow, uncrowded and timber-free slopes, and fine downhill runs.

Skiing can begin as early as May and extend into November, but the main season usually lasts from mid-July through October on North Island, from early July through September on South Island.

Mount Ruapehu in Tongariro National Park is North Island's leading ski area. Top resort-developed sites on South Island are Coronet Peak (11 km/7 miles from Queenstown) and Mount Cook. The country's highest developed ski field is Mount Hutt, 104 km/64 miles from Christchurch. Equipment may be rented at all four areas. Ski package holidays are available at major resorts.

Mount Cook rates raves as a ski touring and ski mountaineering center. Ski-equipped planes and helicopters transport skiers to the high glaciers in several areas of the Southern Alps.

Smaller ski areas operate at North Island's Mount Egmont and at a number of sites on South Island. New Zealand has more than 60 ski clubs with some 11,000 members. Just about every club operates one or more huts in its particular area. National administration is handled by the New Zealand Ski Association Inc., P.O. Box 2213, Wellington.

Ice skating and curling

If ice skates are your thing, not skis, you'll find plenty of opportunities for skating, particularly in Canterbury, Otago, and Southland. Among the larger cities, Christchurch has a fine indoor rink, and Invercargill boasts a large rink that is used 10 months a year. Favorite natural skating sites include Lake Ida, west of Christchurch, and Manorburn and Idaburn dams near Alexandra.

Central Otago is the stronghold of the sport of curling; Naseby and Idaburn are major centers. Played on ice with flattened circular stones, each topped by a gooseneck handle, curling stones are slid across the ice.

Introduced here by Scottish miners and sheepherders, the sport has enjoyed a small but devoted following for more than a century. All matches are held outdoors on natural ice, and players and spectators are not averse to taking a "wee dram" between matches to help them keep warm.

Festivities dot the calendar

Festivals, carnivals, and sports events dot the New Zealand calendar. Summer (December through February) is the busiest time, but you'll find activities in all seasons. Those noted below indicate a sampling of events you can attend. Check with the New Zealand Government Tourist Office for a listing of events and current dates.

Spring

Flower festivals. Hastings and Alexandra salute their blossoming fruit orchards with September festivals, and Palmerston North hosts an October cherry blossom celebration. Local horticultural groups hold spring flower shows.

A & P shows. From October through March, Agricultural & Pastoral shows are held throughout the country (see page 93).

Racing. The New Zealand Cup Race in Christchurch highlights the early November racing calendar.

Summer

Carnival and festival season. During the Christmas-New Year holidays, many towns and resorts plan festive celebrations with sports activities, parades, flower shows, competitions, and other events.

Sports. Regattas, horse racing, and other sports activities take place throughout the country on New Year's Day. Axmen from around the country converge in Tuatapere (Southland) to compete in woodchopping events. In January, Auckland hosts the Auckland Cup Race Meeting, the New Zealand International Grand Prix, and the Anniversary Regatta. Wellington's Cup Race Meeting comes in mid-January.

Waitangi Day. An annual ceremony at Waitangi (Bay of Islands) on February 6 commemorating the Treaty of Waitangi signing in 1840.

Outdoor concerts. New Plymouth's Bowl of Brooklands is the site of a month-long Festival of the Pines. National and international artists perform music, dance, and drama in an open-air amphitheater.

Autumn

Festivals. Auckland's Easter show is New Zealand's biggest celebration. National and international artists perform in Auckland's Festival of the Arts, in the Festival of Wellington, and in Christchurch's annual Arts Festival.

Sheep shearing. The world's fastest shearers meet at Masterton's Golden Shears International Sheep Shearing Contest.

Highland Games. Bagpipes herald Hastings' Highland Games on Easter weekend. National and provincial champions meet to dance the Highland fling and compete in Scottish athletic events.

Winter

Sports. Winter race meetings take place in Auckland, Wellington, and Christchurch. Skiing begins in July on Mount Ruapehu, Coronet Peak, and other ski areas. Ice skaters and curling enthusiasts head for South Island's frozen lakes and outdoor rinks.

Orange festival. During the August school holidays, Tauranga salutes the citrus industry with an activity-packed festival and a gathering of Scottish clans.

North Island

Cities, rolling farmlands, volcanic peaks, fishing lakes, and a varied coast

More than 70 percent of New Zealand's people live on North Island, a third of them in the cities of Auckland and Wellington. Outside the metropolitan areas, you ride through rolling farmlands dotted with grazing sheep and cattle, passing through widely spaced farm towns and coastal settlements. Most of New Zealand's 250,000 Maoris live on North Island, primarily in the northern and eastern districts.

Isolated peaks and mountain ranges and a varied coastline add geographical interest. Active volcanoes and geothermal activity mark the island's center. Fruits, vegetables, and flowers thrive in the mild climate.

Maori legends and customs are still strong here. As you travel you may also become aware of the roles played by the missionaries, colonists, and farmers who developed and shaped this young country.

An island overview

Stretched out like an elongated diamond, North Island extends some 825 kilometers/515 miles from North Cape to Cape Palliser. Narrow Cook Strait separates it from neighboring South Island.

North Island's mountain backbone reaches from Wellington northeast to East Cape, a continuation of the Alpine Fault that created the Southern Alps on South Island. Volcanic activity shapes the central plateau; a series of eruptions has showered ash over the land, and lava flows dammed river valleys forming the Rotorua lakes. Deep harbors and "drowned" river valleys indent the Northland coast, the result of rising sea levels as ice melted at the end of the Ice Age.

Exploitation marked the early years

According to tradition, ancestors of the country's Maori inhabitants sailed in canoes from Polynesia, arriving in New Zealand in the 14th century.

Dutch navigator Abel Tasman skirted North Island's southwest coast in 1642, but no European set foot upon New Zealand soil until Captain James Cook and his party landed at Poverty Bay (Gisborne) in 1769.

After accounts of Cook's discoveries were published, interest blossomed. Sealers and whalers roamed the seas; by the early 1800s the Bay of Islands had become their major provisioning and repair base—and New Zealand's first European settlement.

Missionaries, who began arriving in 1814, established mission stations near the coast. Colonizing groups settled at Wellington, Wanganui, and New Plymouth. Timber speculators razed the massive kauri forests. Trading and mill settlements mushroomed on harbors and navigable rivers.

Maori tribes, which traditionally had battled among themselves, reeled under the impact of European development. In 1840 the British Government reluctantly annexed New Zealand, when representatives of the British Crown and Maori chiefs signed the Treaty of Waitangi.

Misunderstandings and ill feeling soon arose over land purchases. In 1860 fighting erupted in Taranaki between Maori warriors and Government troops and spread across the central part of North Island. The Land Wars continued for more than 20 years, and it was not until formal peace was declared in 1881 that immigrants could expand to fertile new farmlands south of Auckland.

In the early years, population centered in the Bay of Islands. As settlement increased, the capital was moved southward—from the Bay of Islands to Auckland in 1840, and to Wellington in 1865.

Inland waterways and a rugged coast

Only pockets remain of the vast forests that covered much of North Island when Captain Cook

Grazing sheep roam the rolling green hills southeast of Taumarunui in North Island's King Country. Agricultural products are the main source of New Zealand's export income.

Place names reflect a colorful heritage

New Zealand place names reflect the colorful heritage of its Maori people, the navigators and mountaineers who sailed its coastline and explored its mountains, and the settlers who colonized and developed the new land.

Early explorers named places for themselves (Cook Strait, Tasman Sea, D'Urville Island, Haast Pass); members of their party (Young Nick's Head, Banks Peninsula); their patrons (Egmont); daily events (Cape Runaway, Cape Kidnappers, Cape Turnagain, Preservation Inlet, Cape Foulwind, Cape Farewell); or geographical landmarks (Bluff, Bay of Islands).

Settlers frequently honored heroes (Wellington, Marlborough, Nelson, Hamilton); illustrious statesmen or settlers (Palmerston, Auckland, Fox, Russell, Lyttelton, Masterton); or their European origins (Norsewood, Balclutha, Dunedin, New Plymouth). Miners and sheepmen added colorful names such as Pigroot and Drybread.

Descriptive Maori names identify many settlements as well as geographical landmarks. These may reflect legendary happenings, actual events, or describe the appearance of the land. Among words often used in Maori place names are these:

Ahi (fire); *ao* (cloud); *ara* (path, road); *aroha* (love); *ata* (shadow); *atua* (god, demon); *awa* (valley, river); *haka* (dance); *hau* (wind); *hui* (assembly); *huka* (foam); *iti* (small); *iwi* (people, tribe); *kai* (food, eat); *keri* (dig); *kino* (bad); *ma* (white, clear); *ma* or *manga* (tributary, stream); *mata* (headland); *maunga* (mountain); *motu* (island); *muri* (end); *nui* (big, plenty); *o* (of, the place of); *one* (sand, beach, mud).

Other words include *pa* (fortified village, stockade); *pae* (ridge, resting place); *pai* (good); *papa* (ground covered with vegetation, earth); *po* (night); *puke* (hill); *rangi* (sky); *rau* (many); *roa* (long, high); *roto* (lake); *rua* (cave, hollow, two); *tahi* (one, single); *tai* (coast, sea, tide); *tangi* (sorrow, mourning); *tapu* (forbidden, sacred); *te* (the); *tea* (white, clear); *wai* (water); *whanga* (bay, inlet); *whare* (house, hut); *whenua* (land, country).

sailed along these shores. In the early 1800s kauri timber became the country's chief export; later, settlers carved towns out of the bush and cleared lands for farming.

Rugged capes and deep-water harbors add a dramatic touch to the island's varied coastline. Vacationers enjoy long sandy beaches bordering curving bays. The island's mild climate becomes more subtropical as you move northward.

Lake Taupo, the Rotorua lakes, and a trio of volcanoes mark the inland plateau. Numerous rivers descend from mountain watersheds to the sea. During the early years, Maori canoes and coastal sailing ships transported passengers and cargo along these water highways. Longest of the nation's rivers is the Waikato, main source of North Island's hydroelectric power.

Auckland is New Zealand's largest city, Wellington its capital. Major inland cities are Hamilton, Palmerston North, Hastings, and Rotorua. Other sizable towns—Napier, Tauranga, New Plymouth, Wanganui, Gisborne—border the coast.

Highways follow the coast

Excellent highways border the Pacific and Tasman coasts and cut through the interior of the island. Highway 1 begins at Awanui, north of Kaitaia, and follows the length of the island through Auckland, Hamilton, and Taupo to Wellington.

Highway 2 follows the eastern coast along the Bay of Plenty past Poverty Bay and Hawke Bay. Highway 3 skirts the west coast through the provinces of Taranaki and Wanganui.

Other roads and highways link the main routes and offer scenic alternatives for leisurely motoring.

Touring North Island

Outside the metropolitan areas, travelers can choose from an array of intriguing destinations and activities.

Three national parks and a maritime park preserve natural areas for recreation use. Visitors enjoy alpine activities and bush walks in Egmont National Park. You can ski, hike, or explore the varied terrain at Tongariro Park's volcanic preserve. Urewera offers a pair of lovely lakes and trails through dense forest. In Hauraki Gulf Maritime Park you sail amid scattered islands.

Fascinating thermal attractions and a look at Maori life highlight a Rotorua visit. Other travelers head for busy resorts or quiet hideaways along the coasts of Northland, the Coromandel Peninsula, Bay of Plenty, East Cape, or the west coast.

Trout fishermen aim for Lake Taupo, the Rotorua lakes, and their tributary streams. Charter launches transport big game fishermen to waters off the northeast coast.

You can walk through kauri forests, visit mission stations and colonial dwellings, learn about Maori culture and pioneer history, gaze on spouting geysers and boiling mud pools, soak up the sun on sandy beaches, fly over active volcanoes, or go fishing or skin-diving in an island-studded sea.

Auckland

Sprawling across a narrow isthmus, Auckland and its far-flung suburbs separate two magnificent harbors.

To the east, at the city's downtown doorstep, lies sparkling Waitemata Harbour guarded by Rangitoto Island; beyond spread the waters of the island-studded Hauraki Gulf and the Pacific Ocean. West of the city, the shallow turquoise waters of Manukau Harbour funnel into the Tasman Sea. Dotting the landscape are the cones of numerous extinct volcanoes. Northwest of the city rise the forested Waitakere Ranges.

New Zealand's largest city (population 800,000), Auckland contains nearly a quarter of the country's population. It is the country's business and industrial center, North Island's transportation hub, and the arrival point of most overseas visitors. Enhancing the city's cosmopolitan flavor are a large Maori community, immigrants from various European and Asian countries, and Pacific Islanders attracted by employment and educational opportunities.

New waterfront development and modern shopping and office complexes brighten Auckland's downtown. In the older suburbs, restored Victorian buildings provide nostalgic contrast. The city's most striking manmade structure is the Harbour Bridge, arcing dramatically across Waitemata Harbour and linking the city with the fast-growing North Shore.

No one lives far from the water, and Auckland's balmy year-round climate (though often hot and humid in summer) encourages water-oriented recreation. On weekends, families flock to the beaches, and hundreds of yachts cruise the sheltered harbors and gulf waters.

Before the Europeans arrived, Maoris fortified many of the volcanic cones, but warfare and successive epidemics decimated the tribes. In 1840 the capital was moved south from the Bay of Islands to Waitemata Harbour's more central location. Unlike the country's three other main cities, Auckland was not a planned settlement. Government officials, tradesmen, and laborers migrated to the new capital, but no immigrant ships arrived until 1842.

As Auckland's population grew, land-hungry settlers coveted the rich Maori lands to the south and soon embroiled Auckland in the Land Wars. In the postwar depression, Auckland lost its role of capital in 1865 to Wellington. Commerce generated by the Thames gold fields in the late 1860s aided the city's recovery.

Today's wealth comes from development of Northland and Waikato farmlands and industrial expansion on the city's outskirts.

Arriving in Auckland

Most overseas visitors arrive at Auckland International Airport, where connecting flights fan out to all parts of the country. Passengers continuing by air transfer from the new international terminal to the domestic terminal. The airport is located at Mangere, about 20 km/13 miles south of the city center. Taxis and airport buses provide transport into the city.

Cruise ships dock at Princes Wharf on Quay Street, just 2 blocks west of Queen Street, heart of the shopping district.

Auckland's railway station, east of Queen Street on Beach Road, marks the northern terminus of North Island rail service. Daylight and overnight express trains link Auckland and Wellington. Long distance buses of N.Z. Railways Road Services depart from the railway station to all parts of the island. Mount Cook Landlines coaches leave daily for Wellington from the downtown Airline Terminal on Quay Street.

Local transport. Taxis are available at all terminals and on Customs Street West just off Queen Street. Usually your hotel porter or restaurant receptionist will phone to order one for you. Avoid city driving if you can; Auckland has some 400,000 registered vehicles—one of the highest traffic-to-population ratios in the world.

Buses of the Auckland Regional Authority (ARA) and suburban companies provide public transport throughout the metropolitan area. Route information is available at the Municipal Bus Terminal on Commerce Street behind the main post office. Local buses depart from a number of downtown points.

Shuttle buses travel between the railway station and Karangahape Road via Queen Street and Greys Avenue (exact change required, varying by zone).

Ferries leave from the Ferry Terminal on Quay Street, transporting passengers to Devonport on the North Shore. Launches for several Hauraki Gulf islands also depart from the waterfront.

Tourist information. For ideas on making the most of your visit, stop at the Auckland Public Relations Office visitors bureau, 6 Queen Street; maps and guidebooks are also available. A Travellers' Information Centre at the airport aids incoming visitors and will book Auckland accommodations.

Travel arrangements, tour information, and accommodations reservations throughout New Zealand are handled at the Government Tourist Bureau, 99 Queen Street. Maps and motoring information are available to auto club members (bring your membership card) at the Automobile Association office, 33 Wyndham Street.

City hotels and motels

Auckland visitors find a full range of accommodations, both downtown and in suburban areas.

Leading downtown hotels are the Auckland Travelodge, on Quay Street overlooking the harbor; the South Pacific, corner of Queen Street and Customs Street East; the Hotel Intercontinental, at Waterloo Quadrant and Princes Street; and the Town House, on Anzac Avenue adjacent to Constitution Hill Park. A large Sheraton-Auckland hotel with convention facilities is due for completion in April 1983.

Smaller central Auckland hotels include the Royal International on Victoria Street West; the

De Brett on High Street; and Grafton Oaks Courtesy Inn, near the Domain.

Prefer a suburban location? Then consider the White Heron Regency, in Parnell overlooking Hobson Bay; Rose Park Motor Inn, opposite Parnell Rose Gardens; Vacation Hotel at One Tree Hill; or Mon Desir Hotel in Takapuna on the North Shore. Near Auckland International Airport, accommodations include the Gateway Lodge, Airport Inn, and the new Auckland Airport Travelodge.

The suburbs offer an excellent choice in motels, as well as a number of small private tourist hotels and guest houses.

Restaurants offer variety

In New Zealand's largest city you'll find restaurants offering ethnic dishes of various cultures, as well as those known for seafood, steaks, continental specialties, harbor views, or unusual settings. Reservations are recommended.

For elegant dining and dancing where the view rivals the cuisine, try Top of the Town at the Hotel Intercontinental or the Meridian Room at the South Pacific Hotel.

Among centrally located restaurants are Pelorus Jack, 27 Rutland Street (seafood); The Snooty Fox, 57B Victoria Street West (continental cuisine); and Baalbeck, 58 Wellesley Street (Lebanese cuisine). For French specialties try Bonaparte, corner Victoria and High streets; or Caballé, 14 Federal Street.

If Chinese food appeals, you can dine at the Orient, Strand Arcade; or at Diamond, 55 Customs Street East. More informal Chinese restaurants include the Dynasty, 28 Customs Street East; and the Hungry Dragon, 22 Swanson Street.

For Japanese dishes, try Yamato Restaurant, St. Kevin's Arcade, 183 Karangahape Road.

For informal atmosphere consider Tony's, 32 Lorne Street and 27 Wellesley Street (steaks and Italian dishes); The Waterfront Cafe, Ferry Building, Quay Street (seafood); and Angus Steakhouse, 35 Albert Street (steaks and grills).

Many excellent restaurants are located in suburban districts. In Ponsonby try the Deerstalker Inn, 153 Ponsonby Road (game served with traditional accompaniments); or Ponsonby's, 1 Williamson Avenue (elegant, in renovated fire station). In Parnell consider Antoine's, 333 Parnell Road (French specialties); Ascot Restaurant, 421 Parnell Road (steaks and continental dishes); La Trattoria, 295 Parnell Road (seafood specialties); or Hobson House, 223 Parnell Road (a 19th century dwelling).

Diners enjoy a pleasant harbor view at Achilles, 6 St. Heliers Bay Road, St. Heliers. In Howick's Bell House Restaurant, you dine in a restored 1851 colonial homestead.

Leading North Shore restaurants include Michael's Caprice, 2 Huron Street, Takapuna (elegant dining, seafood and continental specialties, dancing); and Fisherman's Wharf, Northcote Point, beneath Harbour Bridge (seafood, harbor view).

Shopping in Auckland

Shoppers flock to Queen Street, Auckland's main downtown thoroughfare, and to nearby side streets. Small shopping arcades and pedestrian malls add an inviting, lighthearted aspect to the commercial district. You can shop in an Edwardian atmosphere along Strand Arcade or sit on outdoor benches in Vulcan Lane to watch passersby.

Shops are generally open from 9 to 5:30 Monday through Thursday, 9 to 9 on Friday (Thursday night on Karangahape Road), closed on weekends. On Saturdays Parnell shops are open from 10 to 3, and you can shop at Mairangi Bay and Brown's Bay, both on the North Shore, from 9 to noon. Most shops in Auckland's Downtown Airline Terminal are open 7 days a week.

Near the foot of Queen Street opposite the main post office, the Downtown Shopping Complex contains several dozen specialty shops; linked to it is Haywrights, New Zealand's newest and most modern department store. Other major department stores are Farmers on Hobson Street, and Smith and Caughey Ltd. on Queen Street. The 246 Shopping Centre, in the heart of the Queen Street district, contains about 40 specialty stores. Duty-free shops are located in the Downtown Airline Terminal and several other central locations.

Crafts. Numerous city shops specialize in standard New Zealand craft and souvenir items. Rehabilitation League N.Z. (Inc.), with branch stores at several Auckland locations and in other main cities, offers a representative selection.

Handcrafted articles by New Zealand craftspeople make excellent souvenirs and gifts. They sell direct to the public at The Mill in Durham Lane (off Durham Street behind His Majesty's Theatre); the artisan-owned market is open on Fridays and Saturdays. Among suburban shops specializing in quality crafts are the Earthworks Handcraft Co-operative in Parnell Village, Parnell; and Craft Cottage, 122 Upland Road, Remuera.

Coins and stamps. Visiting collectors can purchase New Zealand coins and other items at the Coin Box, 7 Box Lane - 10 Customs Street East. Mint sets of New Zealand postage stamps are available at the chief post office on lower Queen Street.

Exploring the suburbs. One of Auckland's most intriguing shopping areas is Parnell, where old homes and stores have been transformed into boutiques and specialty shops. In Remuera, one of the city's oldest and most select suburbs, modern arcades vie with fascinating older shops to tempt passersby. Interesting shops dot Ponsonby, one of the earlier western suburbs. In the casual atmosphere of Karangahape Road, you'll find bargains, variety, and a glimpse of Polynesia.

Markets. If you enjoy browsing amid colorful market stalls, you'll want to sample several indoor markets in Auckland. The International Market, 249 Queen Street, is open weekdays, Friday nights until 9, and Saturdays from 10 to 4. The Cook Street Market, near the Town Hall, bustles with

Auckland *city skyline rises above waters of Waitemata Harbour. Colorful rooftops of Devonport frame this waterfront panorama.*

activity Fridays from 9 to 9, Saturdays from 10 to 3. Craftspeople sell their work on Saturdays from 10 to 4 at the Downtown Market, 104 Fanshawe Street. The Parnell Market, located off Windsor Road in Parnell, is open Fridays and Saturdays.

Entertainment and sporting events

A broad choice in entertainment is yours in New Zealand's largest city. For an evening out, Aucklanders and visitors can enjoy dinner followed by dancing, cabaret shows, musical acts, discotheque activity, or licensed theater restaurant. For current programs, check *Auckland Tourist Times*, *This Month in Auckland*, or daily newspapers.

Most concerts and recitals take place at the Town Hall. Touring shows, ballet, and stage plays are presented at His Majesty's Theatre; local casts perform at the Mercury Theatre and several smaller theaters. Western Springs Stadium and the Auckland Showgrounds in Epsom host special events. In addition to the City Art Gallery, Auckland has numerous downtown and suburban galleries offering changing exhibitions.

Horse racing takes place at Ellerslie Racecourse and Avondale Racecourse, trotting at Alexandra Park Raceway, Rugby Union games and cricket test matches at Eden Park, Rugby League at Car-

law Park in Parnell, soccer at Newmarket Park, and men's hockey at Hobson Park in Remuera. Basketball, wrestling, and boxing matches are held at the YMCA Stadium.

No one lives far from the coast, and the beaches and bays attract thousands of bathers and boaters from November through March. Throughout the summer yachts sail across harbor waters and amid the islands of the Hauraki Gulf. On the Monday nearest January 29, everyone heads for the Waitemata shore to watch the colorful Anniversary Day Yachting Regatta.

Other annual events include the Auckland Festival in March, and the Auckland Easter Show, largest of the country's A & P shows.

Along the waterfront

Quay Street, wide and busy, skirts the downtown waterfront. Just a few minutes' walk from the shopping district, you can watch ocean-going ships maneuver in and out of berths, and ferries chug across the harbor to Devonport on the North Shore. Recent waterfront development, including the Downtown Airline Terminal, adds a fresh modern look.

At the foot of Queen Street, the gracious old brick Ferry Terminal is a harbor landmark. Launch trips to the Hauraki Gulf islands depart

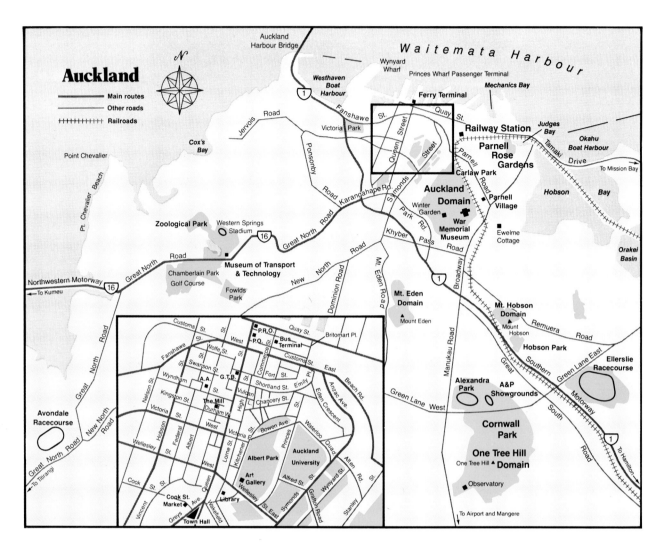

nearby; amphibian planes take off from Mechanics Bay at the east end of the downtown waterfront; passenger liners anchor at Princes Wharf.

A walk around downtown Auckland

Queen Street is Auckland's pulse—the district where everyone goes to work, eat, shop, and stroll. A leisurely walk from the waterfront to Town Hall and back through Albert Park will help you get acquainted with the city. Greenery and benches add a pleasant touch to Vulcan Lane, where black-smiths once plied their trade. If you like, pause to window-shop in some of the arcades.

Building Centre. Here you can browse amid nearly 300 free exhibits showing the newest and best in building materials and furnishings. Located on Victoria Street West at Elliott Street, the building is open weekdays and Friday evenings, as well as Saturdays from 10 to 4.

Town Hall. Topped by a clock tower, the 1911 Town Hall stands on Queen Street opposite Wakefield Street. A magnificent kauri slab, cut from a 3,000-year-old tree, dominates the foyer; kauri timber was used to panel the city council chamber. The building also houses the main town hall and a concert chamber.

City Art Gallery. A 19th century building, at the southwest corner of Albert Park (Kitchener Street and Wellesley Street East), is home for the gallery that contains the country's most complete collection of New Zealand art. Paintings, drawings, prints, and sculpture visually record the entire history of European settlement in New Zealand. A modern collection includes representative works by living New Zealand artists.

Albert Park. This pleasant retreat—a lunchtime haven for city office workers—crowns a low hill a few minutes' walk east of Queen Street. British imperial troops once occupied barracks on the site.

Students from the nearby University of Auckland relax on the lawns, and mothers bring children here to play. Beneath towering trees, a statue of Queen Victoria keeps a watchful eye on the park's fountain and flower beds. On summer Sundays you can enjoy afternoon band concerts here (and in other city parks as well).

Supreme Court. One of Auckland's first public buildings, this fine example of Gothic revival architecture was built in 1868 at the corner of Waterloo Quadrant and Anzac Avenue. Modeled after England's Warwick Castle, the turreted building is ornamented with stone gargoyles and effigies of historic figures. Public galleries in the courtrooms are usually open to visitors.

Park-topped hills offer city vistas

Numerous extinct volcanic cones jut above Auckland's flat landscape. Most were once fortified by Maori tribes, who terraced the slopes and strengthened their stockades with ditches, earth ramparts, and wooden palisades. Today sheep graze and children play on the grassy terraces. You can ride in comfort to these hilly summits for panoramic views over Auckland and its twin harbors.

Mount Eden. Auckland's highest point (196 meters/ 643 feet), Mount Eden offers the city's finest view —over buildings, parks, and water to the distant Waitakere Ranges. A direction finder identifies points of interest. You can reach the park by bus 255 from Customs Street East. Eden Garden, on Omana Road off Mountain Road, is landscaped with native and exotic trees and shrubs.

One Tree Hill and Cornwall Park. Topped by an obelisk, One Tree Hill is the city's most striking feature. This *pa*-terraced volcanic cone rises above Cornwall Park between Manukau Road and the Great South Road. Cornwall Park contains Acacia Cottage, Auckland's oldest surviving wooden building (1841). To reach the park, take bus 305 from Victoria Street East. Auckland Observatory, off Manukau Road at the entrance to One Tree Domain, schedules Tuesday evening programs.

Mount Albert. Located southwest of the downtown district, Mount Albert is reached via New North Road and Mount Albert Road. You can picnic in one of its grassy craters. Alberton House, a restored colonial homestead built in 1860, is open daily at 100 Mount Albert Road.

Other parks and gardens. The formal gardens of Ellerslie Racecourse attract visitors outside of race days. You can reach Ellerslie by bus from the Municipal Bus Terminal.

Jellicoe Park, off Manukau Road in the southern borough of Onehunga, contains a military blockhouse built in 1860. A small museum, open Thursday and Sunday afternoons, contains historic furniture and other period articles. To reach Jellicoe Park, take bus 305 from Victoria Street East.

War Memorial Museum crowns a hill

Overlooking the city and harbor from a grassy hilltop in Auckland Domain, the outstanding Auckland War Memorial Museum contains a fascinating collection of New Zealand and Pacific exhibits. To reach the museum, take bus 635 from the Municipal Bus Terminal to Domain Drive. Museum hours are 10 to 5 Monday through Saturday (to 4:15 in winter), 11 to 5 on Sunday. A free museum map guides you through the exhibits.

Dominating the museum's Maori Court is an impressive war canoe, handcarved about 1835 from a huge totara tree. You'll also see a large meeting house, storehouses on stilts, and Maori carvings. Other displays feature Maori tools and weapons, clothing (including feather cloaks), personal ornaments, and historic portraits of tattooed chiefs and maidens.

Comprehensive displays focus on New Zealand natural history—native birds, trees and plants, sea life and shells, animals, geology and paleontology. Other exhibits feature the peoples of the Pacific, decorative and applied arts, maritime and military memorabilia. Replica Queen Street shops of the 1860s line the museum's Centennial Street. Planetarium shows are presented Saturday and Sunday afternoons.

From the expansive Domain grounds surrounding the museum, you look across Waitemata Harbour to the North Shore. The Cenotaph honors

New Zealanders want to meet YOU

New Zealanders enjoy meeting overseas visitors, and they believe hospitality begins at home. Frequently they'll extend an invitation to join them informally for tea and an hour or two of conversation, or they may offer to guide you around their town.

You'll enjoy sharing the relaxed life style of these friendly, hospitable people, exchanging ideas without a language barrier and learning about daily life in a different land.

In many cities and towns, residents join voluntary hospitality programs to meet visitors. A brochure entitled "Friendly New Zealand," available from the New Zealand Government Tourist Office or local tourist information offices, lists participating towns and indicates how you make arrangements. No payment is involved except for dinner programs in Auckland, Christchurch, and Tauranga, or for overnight accommodations. Efforts are made to match occupations or special interests of host and guest.

In the Waikato, Taranaki, and Wanganui regions you can arrange to visit a farm family. If you want to stay on a farm, it's easy to arrange accommodations (see page 85).

Members of international service organizations often find local chapters in New Zealand's larger towns.

Is trout fishing your idea of a perfect vacation? You can stay with a New Zealand angler host and fish the lakes and streams of Rotorua, Taupo, and South Island. For information write to Club Pacific, 790 27th Avenue, San Francisco, CA 94121.

Shopping *is fun in historic Parnell, where refurbished Victorian structures house boutiques, shops, and restaurants.*

those who served in two World Wars. Down the slope, near the kiosk and duck pond, tropical and subtropical plants and ferns flourish indoors in the Winter Gardens.

Stroll and shop in historic Parnell

One of Auckland's oldest districts has been imaginatively restored to create a lively shopping area that retains a cohesive, small-town charm. In Parnell rejuvenated former dwellings and stores house boutiques, jewelry and craft shops, food stores, antique furniture and art galleries, bookstores, and restaurants.

From the Municipal Bus Terminal, take a 10-minute ride on bus 635, 645, or 655 up Parnell Road to the top of the hill, then stroll down to absorb the neighborhood's appeal.

Parnell Village, near the top of the hill, contains a delightful complex of small stores. Another group of boutiques and shops is located in the 1863 Stonemason's House, 29 Falcon Street (behind Parnell Road off Tilden Street).

Historic highlights. Parnell—a treat for persons who enjoy old architecture—features restored early terrace houses and small dwellings reflecting their 19th century origins.

At the top of the hill, near Parnell Road and St.

Stephen's Avenue, are Anglican church buildings associated with Bishop Selwyn, a missionary who arrived in 1842. "Selwyn churches" in the Auckland area are characterized by simple Gothic design, steep shingled roofs, exterior bracing timbers, and diamond-shaped leaded windows. St. Stephen's Chapel, built in 1857 as successor to an earlier chapel, is located off St. Stephen's Avenue at the end of Judge Street; many Auckland pioneers are buried in the churchyard. Spired and churchlike Selwyn Court was formerly the bishop's library.

Ewelme Cottage, 14 Ayr Street, was built in 1864 by the Rev. Vicesimus Lush. The kauri-wood dwelling housed his descendants for more than a century. Restored by the New Zealand Historic Places Trust, it contains many of its original Victorian furnishings and family personal effects.

Parnell Rose Gardens. Located on Gladstone Road, the gardens are at peak bloom from November to March. From the Municipal Bus Terminal, take bus 715. Mature trees, native shrubs, and hundreds of roses frame a view across Waitemata Harbour. A pleasant walk leads down to sheltered Judges Bay. Nearby is Parnell Baths, a large salt-water pool open from October to April.

Pioneer transport and a colonial village

Mechanically minded visitors enjoy the interesting collection of vintage motor cars, old steam locomotives, and pioneer aircraft at the Museum of Transport and Technology at Western Springs (open 9 to 5 daily). Other exhibits feature agriculture, printing, and photography. A Pioneer Village recreates the colonial life style; on special "live days," personnel dress in 19th century costumes.

To reach the museum on the Great North Road, take bus 045 from Customs Street East.

Watch kiwis at Auckland's zoo

Auckland's Zoological Park is one of several places in the country where you can see the kiwi, a flightless nocturnal bird that occupies a special place in the hearts of New Zealanders. In the dim light of the zoo's kiwi house, you watch these unusual birds in a bush setting. The 35-acre park contains some 300 mammals, birds, and reptiles, many exhibited in natural settings; a children's zoo; and a small aquarium.

Located in the Western Springs district, the zoo is open daily from 9:30 to 5:30. You can reach it by bus 045 from Customs Street East.

Tamaki Drive skirts Waitemata Harbour

Bordering the city's downtown waterfront, this 11-km/7-mile scenic drive follows the shore of Waitemata Harbour through the eastern suburbs to St. Heliers Bay. Along the way you pass attractive bathing beaches at Mission Bay, Kohimarama, and St. Heliers. Buses for Mission Bay and St. Heliers depart from the Municipal Bus Terminal.

Pleasure boats anchor in Okahu Bay. Savage Memorial Park honors New Zealand's first Labour prime minister. From Bastion Point, site of wartime harbor fortifications, you can watch maritime activity.

At Mission Bay the Melanesian Mission Museum contains relics from the era of bishops Selwyn and Patterson (1842-71) and native artifacts from Melanesia and the Solomon Islands. Night-lighted Trevor Moss Davis Memorial Fountain is a memorable feature of an evening drive along the harbor.

Sheltered St. Heliers Beach vies in size and popularity with Takapuna Beach on the North Shore.

Excursions from Auckland

From Auckland you can explore historic Howick, go wine tasting, or enjoy nearby beaches and the islands of the Hauraki Gulf.

Sightseeing tours and fishing trips

Half-day and full-day guided coach excursions are a boon to visitors bent on city and country sightseeing. Short tours visit points of interest in Auckland, as well as the vineyard district of Henderson and the Waitakere Scenic Reserve. Full-day tours venture farther afield—east to Howick and Maraetai Beach, and north along the Hibiscus Coast to Waiwera and Warkworth.

If your time is limited, you can visit the Bay of Islands or Rotorua on a day-return flight or a 2-day coach trip from Auckland. Numerous longer coach tours also depart from here.

Auckland flightseeing trips leave from Mechanics Bay, on the Waitemata waterfront, for aerial views of the city, harbors, and gulf islands.

If a day of fishing appeals, you can arrange an excursion departing from Auckland. Visitors can choose from a variety of day (and longer) fishing excursions; you fly to your destination, spend the day fishing, then return to Auckland the same evening.

Colonial history in Howick

Dairy farms surround the seaside town of Howick, a colonial settlement that has managed to retain some of its village atmosphere. Howick buses leave from Auckland's Municipal Bus Terminal.

Located 23 km/14 miles east of the city, Howick was established in 1847 as one of four Royal New Zealand Fencible Corps military settlements on the isthmus (others at Onehunga, Panmure, and Otahuhu) to defend the young capital of Auckland from hostile Maori tribes to the south. British soldier-settlers were given free passage to New Zealand with their families and use of a cottage and land, which became their property when their 7-year term expired.

On Selwyn Road you'll find All Saints' Anglican

Church, one of the distinctive "Selwyn churches" and the town's oldest building built in 1847. Near the beach is Shamrock Cottage; originally the Fencibles' canteen and later an inn, it has been restored and is now open as a tearoom.

Historic buildings in the Garden of Memories on Uxbridge Street include a restored Fencible cottage, the 1848 Howick Courthouse, and a small museum that is open Saturday and Sunday afternoons from 2:30 to 4:30; the garden also includes replicas of a Maori meeting house and storehouse. Stockade Hill commands a view over the countryside and harbor.

Just off the Pakuranga-Howick highway, an 1851 colonial officer's homestead has been completely restored and opened as Bell House Restaurant (reservations advised).

If you're driving, continue along the pleasant country road to Maraetai, a quiet little seaside resort; then turn inland to Clevedon and Papakura and return to Auckland on the motorway.

The beach scene

On fair weather weekends, Aucklanders head for the nearby beaches and bays that provide much of the city's ambience. Most can be reached by public transportation.

Attractive beaches rim Waitemata Harbour at Okahu Bay, Mission Bay, and St. Heliers. Others border Tamaki Strait southeast of Auckland at Beachlands, Maraetai, and Duder's Beach.

Fine beaches abound on the North Shore. Devonport's sheltered shore is backed by a grassy picnic reserve, and Takapuna is one of the district's most popular strands. Homes border the swimming beaches along the East Coast Bays, a series of coastal resorts stretching from Milford north to Long Bay. More pleasant beaches rim the Whangaparaoa Peninsula and Hibiscus Coast near Orewa.

West coast beaches sprawl at the foot of steep, bush-covered hills along the rugged Tasman coast. Ocean surfers like the waves at Piha and Muriwai Beach. Fishermen cast from the rocks, and you can hike along the beach or bluffs.

Islands of the Hauraki Gulf

For a pleasant day's outing, explore one of the islands of the Hauraki Gulf. Launches leave Auckland's waterfront on scheduled trips to several of the larger islands. Trips to Kawau Island depart from Sandspit, east of Warkworth (a connecting bus departs from Auckland's Municipal Bus Terminal). Amphibian planes take off from Mechanics Bay on regular flightseeing and charter trips.

Established in 1967, Hauraki Gulf Maritime Park encompasses most of the several dozen scattered islands off Auckland's eastern coast. Several are holiday destinations, where vacationers enjoy island walks, swimming, camping, boating, and sea fishing. Others are remote and difficult to reach, inhabited only by wildlife.

Accommodations are available on Waiheke, Pakatoa, and Great Barrier islands. The park also has several camping areas.

Blue Boat launches depart on regular fishing trips, and amphibian planes transport fishermen to offshore game fishing areas.

If you want to prolong your time cruising among the islands of the Hauraki Gulf, you can charter a fully-equipped yacht in Auckland. The New Zealand Government Tourist Office can provide information on yacht charters.

Rangitoto Island. A harbor landmark, Rangitoto's sloping cone marks many views of Auckland. The island—a favorite picnic destination—is accessible by launch. The incoming boat is met by a bus, which takes passengers on a 1½-hour tour of the island.

One of the few peaks not fortified by the Maoris, Rangitoto has little soil and no permanent source of water, yet vegetation thrives in apparently barren conditions.

Walkers can stroll from the wharf to Wilson's Park, Flax Point Bridge, and McKenzie's Bay. Wear sturdy shoes for walking on the crushed lava rock roads. It's a steep 4-km/2½-mile hike to the summit, where you have unsurpassed views of the gulf and city.

Kawau Island. A summer haven for yachters, Kawau also fascinates naturalists and those with a yen for history. Sir George Grey, an early governor of New Zealand, built his home here and transformed Kawau into a subtropical paradise of imported trees, plants, and animals. Wallabies and kookaburras still inhabit the bush. Grey's Mansion House, formerly operated as a hotel, is being restored as a museum. Old cottages and mineshafts on the island date from the 1830s and '40s, when copper and manganese were mined here.

Pakatoa Island. Accessible by launch from Auckland, Pakatoa has been developed into a holiday resort with self-contained chalets and a licensed hotel with restaurant. Honeymooners and other visitors enjoy the island's beaches and fine views.

Waiheke Island. Largest of the islands, Waiheke is dotted with small farming settlements. Many retired people have moved here. Lovely bays and beaches attract visitors, who come here for boating and fishing. Hotel and motel accommodations are available. Access is by launch, hovercraft, or amphibian plane.

Motuihe Island. Less than an hour from the city by boat, Motuihe is a popular day outing for Auckland families. Visitors find good swimming, walking trails, and picnic grounds.

Great Barrier Island. Largest of the offshore islands, Great Barrier has a rugged coastline bordered with pohutukawa trees. Cattle and sheep graze on the island. Deep-sea fishermen come here for hapuka, kingfish, and snapper. Guest houses are located at some of the bays. Access is by charter launch or amphibian plane.

Little Barrier Island. A scenic reserve and rare bird sanctuary, the island has a large forested area undisturbed by browsing animals. Permission must be obtained to land on the island.

Along the Hibiscus Coast

Bordering the Hauraki Gulf north of the Whangaparaoa Peninsula, the Hibiscus Coast is a favorite summer and weekend destination. You drive through rolling green farmlands to Orewa, a leading coastal resort and mecca for summer campers. Visitor attractions border the beach and you'll often see ocean surfers in the waters offshore.

About 48 km/30 miles north of Auckland, Waiwera is noted for its hot mineral spring pools where bathers soak away aches and cares. Visitors can picnic nearby and hike in the surrounding woods.

Just north of Waiwera is Wenderholm Reserve, a regional beach and riverside park.

The farming community of Puhoi retains some customs brought by Bohemian immigrants in 1862. Warkworth, on the Mahurangi River, is the site of a giant dishlike antenna linking New Zealand to the worldwide satellite telecommunications system. The Kawau Island ferry departs from nearby Sandspit.

Wine touring in the Henderson Valley

To get to know New Zealand wines, spend a day touring and tasting in the Henderson Valley northwest of Auckland, heart of New Zealand's wine country. Neat rows of vines sweep across the land, and huge fig trees cast welcome summer shade. Many vintners are descendants of Dalmatian settlers who originally came from Yugoslavia to work in Northland's kauri gum fields.

Near Henderson you can tour and taste at Corbans Wines, Great North Road; Penfolds Wines, 190 Lincoln Road; Delegat's Vineyard, Hepburn Road; and several smaller wineries. Western Vineyards, in the Henderson Valley, has picnic facilities. Montana Wines, Scenic Drive, Titirangi, also welcomes visitors.

Wineries are usually open Monday through Saturday for tours. For more information on wineries that encourage visitors, inquire at the Auckland Public Relations Office.

Waitakere Scenic Drive

West of Henderson, this 50-km/30-mile scenic road follows the crest of the Waitakere Ranges, between Swanson and Titirangi. Bordered by lush tree ferns, the route affords spectacular views over Auckland and the Waitemata and Manukau harbors.

A side road leads to the Cascades reserve and Kauri Park. Signposted trails lead through the native bush to a pair of waterfalls and stands of kauri trees.

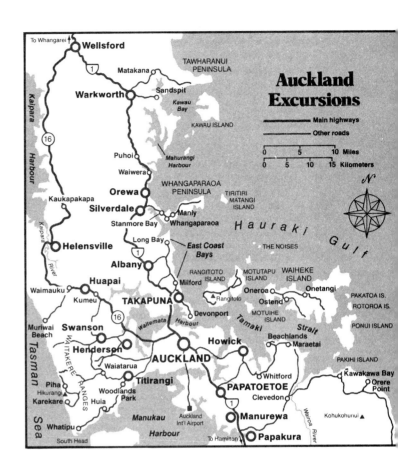

Northland

If you want to relax in scenic splendor and a balmy climate, head north! Northland's tourist mecca is the lovely Bay of Islands, cradle of New Zealand's early European settlement. But the region offers far more.

You can picnic on sheltered bays rimmed with crimson-flowering pohutukawa trees, go deep-sea fishing or cruising through scattered islands, or walk along windswept beaches or amid towering 1,000-year-old kauri trees.

More than any other region, Northland clings to its eventful history. Here you'll find links with explorers Tasman, Cook, and de Surville, as well as tales of Maori conflicts and bawdy whaling days. Anglican and Catholic missionaries set up mission stations here. Other settlements thrived on the kauri timber and gum trades. Until the 1930s, many remote farms and coastal settlements relied on sailing ships to deliver supplies and mail and to transport rural products to market.

Northland's industrial and commercial center is Whangarei, at the head of a large deep-water harbor on the east coast. Tourists head for Paihia in the Bay of Islands and Kaitaia in the Far North. Dargaville is gateway to the major kauri reserves.

Air New Zealand flies from Auckland to Whangarei and Kaitaia; Mount Cook Airlines serves the Bay of Islands airport at Kerikeri. N.Z. Railways Road Services buses operate daily from Auckland north to Whangarei, Waitangi, and Kaitaia.

From Auckland, coach excursions depart on 2 to 7-day trips to the Bay of Islands and other Northland points. Mount Cook Airlines offers a variety of holiday packages, including a 1-day excursion.

Lonely Kaipara Harbour

Northwest of Auckland, tentacles of Kaipara Harbour probe deeply into the dairylands. Highway 16 skirts its eastern shore between Helensville and Wellsford.

A century ago, ships of the kauri timber trade sailed these remote waterways, and small settlements sprang up along the shores. Today, pleasure boats cruise the intricate coastline. On the northern inlets you can picnic, swim, or camp at several beaches, including Pahi and Tinopai, both south of Paparoa. Birdwatchers head for the Pouto peninsula south of Dargaville.

Port Albert, now an isolated cluster of houses on a headland west of Wellsford, was once part of a nonconformist settlement called Albertland. A few kilometers south, tiny Minniesdale Chapel (1867) occupies a solitary setting overlooking the harbor; in the churchyard, large puriri trees shade carved wooden headstones. A two-story colonial homestead stands amid trees and gardens below.

Whangarei, Northland's port city

The thriving port city of Whangarei (population 40,000) is Northland's commercial and industrial hub. Its sheltered, deep-water harbor has attracted a number of major industries, including the country's leading oil refinery and first oil-fired power station.

Stop at the city's Information Centre on Cafler Avenue for a map and tourist literature, then drive to the summit of Mount Parahaki for views over the city, countryside, and harbor.

A 48-km/30-mile scenic drive begins at the Town Hall at Bank Street and Rust Avenue. It winds through business and residential areas and several parks, climbs Mount Parahaki, and continues east to the suburb of Onerhai.

The Hatea River flows along the city's eastern border, cutting through several fine parks including Whangarei Falls, A. H. Reed Memorial Kauri Park, and Mair Park, where the river broadens into a natural swimming pool. Bush walks and picnic sites abound.

Clapham's Clock Museum, 48 Vine Street, contains a collection of some 500 clocks of varying age, source, and design.

The tree-bordered Town Basin bustles with waterfront activity on pleasant days. You can charter a launch, hire a dinghy, or watch youngsters fish for "tiddlers" off the wharf. Water-skiers skim across the harbor, and families enjoy nearby beaches.

For an enjoyable day's outing, take the 35-km/22-mile scenic drive along the harbor's northern shore to Whangarei Heads and Ocean Beach. Along the route you pass the Parua Bay boat harbor and majestic Mount Manaia. You can picnic or swim at numerous small bays, fish from the rocks, explore a curious reef at Taurikura, or walk the lonely beach north of Bream Head.

Other good swimming and surfing beaches extend south of Whangarei along Bream Bay, from Marsden Point south to Waipu Cove.

During holiday periods, coach tours operate to the Tutukaka Coast, the Bay of Islands, and Cape Reinga. Scenic flights can also be arranged. Game fishing trips depart from Tutukaka.

The Tutukaka Coast

Northeast of Whangarei a string of beautiful bays and beaches indents the Pacific shore. Known as the Tutukaka Coast, it extends from Ngunguru some 13 km/8 miles north to Sandy Bay. Vacationers stay in the small resorts of Ngunguru, Tutukaka, and Matapouri.

Pohutukawa trees border sandy beaches, where families spread picnic lunches and children splash in the waves. Pleasure boats anchor in sheltered harbors. Along the shore, fishermen surfcast from rocky peninsulas or along the beach at Woolleys Bay. Surfers head for Sandy Bay. To reach Whale Bay's delightful cove, you follow a short trail through the woods.

At Tutukaka's marina, parties can charter deep-sea fishing launches for the day (all equipment provided) or arrange for sightseeing or skin-diving trips to the Poor Knights Islands about 12 miles offshore.

On a leisurely 80-km/50-mile loop, you can return to Whangarei through the Waro Limestone Reserve—where bare outcrops have eroded into unusual shapes and patterns—and the small farming town of Hikurangi.

Dargaville, gateway to the kauri forests

A thriving river port during the heyday of the kauri timber and gum trade, Dargaville today is a prosperous dairy center and a base for touring the kauri forests. Dargaville Museum contains articles associated with the kauri industry and local maritime displays.

You can arrange day trips by 4-wheel drive to the kauri forests and remote coastal points. Northland's longest beach stretches some 109 km/68 miles from the mouth of Kaipara Harbour north to Maunganui Bluff. Side roads from Highway 12 provide access at several points, including Bayly's Beach, a favorite summer recreation site and, in winter, a target for toheroa (clam) diggers.

Northwest of Dargaville near Maropiu, the three fresh-water lakes in Taharoa Domain attract trout fishermen and small boat owners, who come here for sailing and water-skiing.

Quiet holidays at Hokianga Harbour

Carving a ragged inlet in the northwestern coast, Hokianga Harbour and its coastal tributaries probe deeply into sparsely populated farmlands.On the southeastern shore, Omapere and Opononi are small, unpretentious beach towns. Vacationers who enjoy a quiet holiday can go boating on the harbor, fish in the sea, walk along the beach, or explore old ports and timber settlements.

A vehicular ferry provides daytime service hourly between Rawene on the south shore and the Narrows, near Kohukohu on the harbor's north coast. From Kohukohu, it's about an hour's drive to Kaitaia.

Highway 12 continues east through Kaikohe to meet Highway 1 at Ohaeawai.

The Bay of Islands

What makes the Bay of Islands special? For some visitors it's the scenery—broad vistas of sky and sea blended with wooded islands; for others it's

beaches and water sports and historic sites. Yachters and anglers regard it as one of New Zealand's finest harbors and a top game-fishing center. Residents treasure its unhurried pace, good climate, and peaceful quality of life.

Rich in legend and mystery, it is a microcosm of early New Zealand history, with ties to the Maoris, whalers, missionaries, and settlers. For decades this quiet pastoral district had few contacts with the outside world. Today it is a popular holiday resort, its tourism industry stimulated by the bay's superb deep-sea fishing.

From Auckland you can travel to the Bay of Islands by air (Mount Cook Airlines to Kerikeri) or road (rental car or N.Z. Railways Road Services coaches to Waitangi). A passenger ferry makes regular daytime trips between Paihia and Russell (in summer, evening service also); limited ferry service connects Russell and Waitangi. Daytime vehicular ferries shuttle automobiles between Opua, south of Paihia, and Okiato, southwest of Russell.

Tourist facilities and accommodations are concentrated at Paihia. Across the bay is Russell, one-time whaling port and now center of fishing activities. Other historic sites include Waitangi (across the river from Paihia), Kerikeri, and Waimate North. Farming and administrative center of the region is Kawakawa, south of the bay on High-

Verandahed *Pompallier House in Russell encloses original mud structure built to house mission printing presses in the 1840s.*

way 1. Nearby is Waiomio Caves, a series of limestone caverns where visitors see striking formations and a glowworm gallery.

The resort's leading hostelry is the THC Waitangi Hotel facing the bay at Waitangi; a fine 18-hole golf course is nearby. In Paihia you'll find the Tree Tops Hotel, along with many small motels, including the Ala-Moana, Aloha, Beachcomber, Busby Manor, and Tropicana. In Russell, travelers favor the Duke of Marlborough Hotel, facing the wharf, or Willow Bridge Motor Hotel. Accommodations are also available in Kerikeri.

New Zealand's earliest settlements

The Bay of Islands has enticed men from the earliest days of exploration. According to Maori legend, the great Polynesian explorer Kupe visited the bay in the 10th century. Captain Cook anchored here in 1769, bestowing the simple name that captures its unpretentious charm. Three years later, the French explorer Marion du Fresne established a temporary base on Moturua Island.

In the early 1800s sealers and whalers followed Cook's Pacific travels, anchoring in the harbor for ship repair and reprovisioning. An unruly settlement grew at Kororareka (now Russell), attracting assorted brigands and adventurers. Traders and colonists soon followed.

Next came the missionaries. Rev. Samuel Marsden and his party established a mission station at Rangihoua Bay in 1814; other missions followed at Kerikeri (1819), Paihia (1823), and Waimate North (1830). A Catholic mission was established at Kororareka in 1838.

By the early 1830s most of New Zealand's white population had settled along the bay, and Britain appointed a British Resident, James Busby, to deal with problems caused by haphazard settlement. In 1840 Captain William Hobson arrived to negotiate with Maori chiefs. On February 6, 1840, British and Maori representatives signed the Treaty of Waitangi, proclaiming British sovereignty over New Zealand.

Later that year the capital was moved south to Waitemata Harbour (Auckland), and the bay's era of influence was over.

The fascinating water world

Sports enthusiasts come from around the world to fish these fabled waters, first popularized by American writer-fisherman Zane Grey in the 1920s. Other visitors skin-dive in the subtropical waters or cruise the island-studded bay.

Big game fishing. The main summer season extends from November through May, capped by a big competition in early January. In winter, light tackle anglers fish for yellowtail kingfish, most prized of the small gamefish.

More than a dozen deep-sea fishing charter boats operate from Paihia and Russell. The least expensive way to go fishing is to make up a party of four

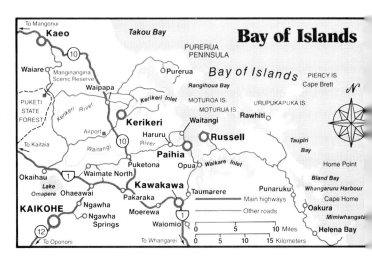

and share the charter cost. Boats usually leave about 8 A.M. and return about 5:30 P.M. Overnight charters can be arranged also.

Skin diving. Colorful subtropical fish glide through clear waters, and corals and sponges thrive in the deeper water. Cape Brett is a favorite diving spot. Arrange for transportation and equipment in Paihia.

Boat trips. Best known is the Cream Trip, named for a coastal launch route of the 1920s which collected cream and delivered mail and supplies to scattered dairy farms. A 4½-hour trip departs each morning. You sail along the coast and amid the wooded islands, stopping occasionally to deliver mail, newspapers, and freight to waiting island dwellers. A 3-hour afternoon trip covers a longer distance but does not include mail delivery.

Another favorite destination is Cape Brett, where a lighthouse marks the bay entrance. You'll circle Piercy Island, cruise into Cathedral Cave, and pass through the Hole in the Rock. Schoolfish (which attract marlin) and dolphins abound in these famed gamefish waters.

Water taxi service links the resorts with the islands and remote bays. The boat will transport your party to the site, then return at a prearranged time. Take along a picnic and your fishing tackle or skin-diving equipment. You can rent small boats, tackle, and diving equipment in Paihia.

Paihia, busy harbor resort

Strung out along the waterfront, Paihia is the accommodations and activity center for visitors. You'll find the tourist information office on Williams Road, across from the post office.

Coach tours depart from Paihia to Cape Reinga, to local historic sites, and to the kauri forests. You can arrange aerial sightseeing trips also.

Busiest spot in town is the wharf, jutting into the bay at the end of Williams Road, where excursion launches, game-fishing boats, water taxis, and the passenger ferry jockey for position. In the nearby Maritime Building you can arrange for tours and excursions, purchase tickets, charter boats, and make other travel arrangements.

Near the Waitangi River, the Church of St. Paul stands on the site of the early mission. Nearby, a carved arch marks the entrance to the Ti Beach *marae*, where Maori chiefs and warriors camped before crossing the river to discuss and sign the Treaty of Waitangi. At the meeting house, a memorial records the text of the treaty.

Gold coins, jewelry, and other articles salvaged from Northland marine disasters are displayed in the Museum of Shipwrecks. Climb aboard the restored three-masted barque *Tui*, permanently moored near the bridge, to see a film about salvage expeditions and items retrieved from the depths.

Russell—whaling port to fishing center

Russell's tranquil waterfront belies the town's wild and bawdy origins as the whaling port of Kororareka.

From the early 1800s on, sealing and whaling ships anchored here. Despite the efforts of the missionaries, Kororareka was a rough and lawless town, crowded with grog shops and Maori ship-girls who catered to the rough seafarers.

European traders and colonists soon followed, and by 1830 there was a sizable settlement. Soon after British control and administration were established, conflict developed between British troops and disgruntled Maoris who resented white authority. Four times Chief Hone Heke chopped down the British flagstaff in an effort to rid his land of the newcomers. On the final attempt in 1845, his rampaging warriors also sacked the town.

Today Russell is a peaceful retreat with an old-world charm—though it bustles in summer with vacationers and crewmen from yachts and launches anchored offshore. Big-game fishing is the leading topic of conversation, and when word spreads of a major catch, crowds gather on the wharf for the weigh-in.

A 1-hour sightseeing tour by mini-bus departs from the wharf.

Along the Strand. Buildings along the Strand—Russell's waterfront promenade—face the curve of a deep blue bay. One of them, the Duke of Marlborough Hotel, claims to hold the first liquor license ever issued in New Zealand. Farther along the street is the police station, originally the port's customs house.

At the south end of the Strand is Pompallier House, only remaining building of the Roman Catholic mission. The original two-story building

The kauri—New Zealand's magnificent forest giant

Today only a few pockets remain of the vast native kauri forests that once covered much of North Island. Now protected in reserves, these magnificent trees rival California's redwoods in age, height, and girth. Many kauri *(Agathis australis)* are more than 1,000 years old.

Kauri timber and kauri gum figure prominently in Northland's early settlement. Pioneer settlers cut the slow-growing trees at a rapid rate. The valuable timber became the country's first export—sought after for ships' masts and as a building material. Within a few decades the vast forests were depleted.

As the timber trade declined, gum diggers swarmed to Northland to "bleed" the trees and dig the resinous kauri gum—used as a base in slow-drying hard varnishes—from the beds of buried prehistoric forests.

In the forest, the massive, ashen-trunked trees grow in scattered groups, dwarfing smaller trees such as tawa, rimu, kahikatea, towai, and northern rata. They grow up to 52 meters/170 feet tall with a maximum girth of 15 meters/50 feet. As the tree grows, its lower branches drop off naturally, yielding a tall, straight-grained trunk. In mature trees, the first branches appear high off the ground.

Kauri reserves. An extensive stand of kauri is preserved in Waipoua Forest, on the west coast about 52 km/32 miles north of Dargaville. As you follow Highway 12 through the forest, towering trees loom above dense undergrowth.

Short signposted trails lead through the bush to several of the oldest and tallest trees. At forest headquarters you can see tools and other articles used by early kauri bushmen.

About 17 km/10 miles south is Trounson Kauri Park, located east of Highway 12 on the Donnelley's Crossing Road. Trails lead into the kauri grove, where you'll see young "rickers" as well as immense giants.

Two smaller reserves are near main highways northwest of the Bay of Islands. On Highway 10, turn west at Waipapa on the Pungaere Road and drive about 12 km/7 miles to the Manginangina Scenic Reserve. From Highway 1 just south of Mangamuka Bridge, turn east on the Omahuta State Forest road and drive about 14 km/9 miles. Short trails lead through the forest to the tall trees, and you can picnic nearby.

Museums. East of Paparoa on Highway 12, the fascinating Otamatea Kauri and Pioneer Museum at Matakohe focuses on the days when kauri was king. Mounted photographs depict the hard life of the bushman, and you see heavy equipment and tools used in felling and milling the trees. A typical 19th century dwelling, built of kauri, contains handcrafted kauri furniture and other period articles. Panels show the grain of various native woods, and you can study an outstanding collection of kauri gum.

You also can learn about the kauri timber and gumdigging industries at local museums in Kaitaia, Dargaville, and Russell.

Houses of Mangonui *cling to wooded slopes curving around its harbor, an inlet of Doubtless Bay. Town developed as a milling center and port for sailing ships engaged in the kauri timber trade.*

was constructed to house the mission printing presses, which are displayed inside. A century ago new outer walls were built enclosing the earthen structure, and the wooden verandahs were added. You can visit daily from 10 to 12 and 2 to 4:30.

Other attractions. New Zealand's oldest church is still in use at the corner of Church and Robertson streets. Built in 1835-36 by local settlers, Christ Church also served as courthouse and public hall. Graves in the churchyard contain the remains of whalers, early settlers, and Maoris. The battle-scarred church still bears marks of the 1845 conflict. An interdenominational service on February 6 marks the signing of the Treaty of Waitangi.

At the south end of York Street, Captain Cook Memorial Museum contains a seaworthy scale model (1/5 size) of Cook's barque H.M.S. *Endeavour* and relics of Kororareka and its inhabitants.

For a splendid panorama over Russell and the bay, take the road to the summit of Flagstaff Hill.

Waitangi, symbol of nationhood

Across the river from Paihia, Waitangi National Reserve surrounds the historic Treaty House, sym-bol of New Zealand's birth as a nation. You can walk through the restored house and stroll beneath century-old trees on the spacious, well-kept grounds.

It was here, on the lawn in front of the house, that representatives of the British government and Maori chiefs signed the Treaty of Waitangi on February 6, 1840. The Maori people voluntarily accepted British rule, New Zealand became part of the British Empire, and Maoris and Europeans were granted equal status as British subjects.

James Busby, newly appointed British Resident, built the Georgian-style house in 1833 on a knoll overlooking the bay. Wings were later added to the original three-room dwelling. Inside, visitors find a small collection of Maori artifacts, paintings and photographs, and articles associated with the area's early settlement and the treaty signing. In front of the house, a tall flagstaff marks the place of the signing.

The Waitangi *whare runanga* (meeting house) was a gift to the nation from the Maori people during the 1940 centennial celebration. It is unique in that it contains wall carvings representing many different North Island tribes. Arranged in facing pairs on the side walls, connected by painted rafters, the carvings represent notable ancestors from various tribes, each carved in that group's distinctive local style. The rafters and carved posts inside the Maori meeting house also reflect traditional craft skills.

Below the house near Hobson's landing site, an open-air pavilion shelters a 36-meter/117-foot kauri war canoe. During the centennial festivities, 80 Maori warriors paddled the canoe across the bay to Waitangi.

At Waimate North, a mission house

Inland from the Bay of Islands, about 21 km/13 miles west of Paihia at Waimate North, stands Waimate Mission House, the sole surviving building of a once-thriving mission farm. Of New Zealand's historic buildings, only the mission house (Kemp House) at Kerikeri is older.

Last of three similar houses built in the mission's early years, the colonial building is patterned after late Georgian style, built symmetrically around a central stairhall. In the 1870s, a gabled roof replaced the original hip roof and dormer windows. Period furniture and missionary items recall the early days. The house is open daily from 10 to 12:30 and 2 to 5.

Nearby you'll see the Church of St. John the Baptist, built in 1871. Its oak-shaded churchyard contains carved wooden grave markers, unique to Northland.

Kerikeri—history, citrus, and crafts

Historic Kerikeri was founded as a mission station in 1819, second of the area's settlements established by the Church Missionary Society. Two of the country's oldest buildings, both open to visitors, overlook the head of Kerikeri Inlet. At high tide, yachts and pleasure boats sail up the inlet and anchor near the wharf, as did the vessels of those early settlers.

An old-fashioned garden surrounds the verandahed Kerikeri Mission House (also called Kemp House). Completed in 1822, it is New Zealand's oldest surviving building. A succession of missionaries lived here in its early years; after 1832, members of the Kemp family occupied the house for many years.

The two-story Stone Store, built in the early 1830s, once housed Bishop Selwyn's library; now it contains a souvenir shop and a small museum of mission-related items.

The hillside across the river basin offers an attractive view of the old buildings. You also can visit Rewa's Village, a replica of a pre-European unfortified Maori village.

Upriver from the basin, travelers can picnic or camp at Peacock Gardens, where a post-European village is also on display. To reach Rainbow Falls on the Kerikeri River, take the signposted side road off Waipapa Road.

Inland, tall hedgerows hide orchards of oranges and other citrus fruits grown for both national distribution and export. Other subtropical fruits thriving in the mild climate include tamarillos, feijoas, passion fruit, and Chinese gooseberries.

In recent years Kerikeri has attracted a number of craftspeople; you can see their work in local shops.

Far North

Shaped by decades of geographical and cultural isolation, the sparsely populated Far North retains an elusive, mystical quality that attracts an increasing number of visitors. Many of the area's residents are descendants of Dalmatian gumdiggers who stayed on to wrest a living from scrubby farmlands.

Modern highways follow the northeastern coast and cut across the interior from the Bay of Islands to Kaitaia. You can reach Kaitaia by plane or bus, too.

Most visitors take the all-day coach excursion to Cape Reinga and Ninety Mile Beach. If you enjoy a taste of adventure, join one of the 4-wheel-drive trips that explore isolated beaches and bays.

In Kaitaia you can stay at the Kaitaia Hotel in the center of town, or at any of numerous motels along Highway 1 or facing the beach at Ahipara. Along the northeast coast, motorists find small hotels and motels at Whangaroa and Mangonui and along Doubtless Bay.

The coastal road

Highway 10 loops around the island's northeast coast, skirting Whangaroa and Mangonui harbors and the shore of Doubtless Bay. Narrow side roads branch off to coastal settlements and remote bays and beaches. Mangrove trees grow in many tidal estuaries in the subtropical north.

Whangaroa Harbour. North of Kaeo, a road branches off to Whangaroa, where eroded volcanic pinnacles and steep wooded slopes enclose the calm harbor. Wooden houses with gabled roofs peek out between the trees. Big game fishermen come here to fish the waters around the Cavalli Islands.

The only way to fully appreciate the inlet's scenic setting is by boat. From September through May, sightseeing cruises depart from Whangaroa, following the shoreline to the narrow-necked harbor entrance. Fishing trips and water taxi service can be arranged.

A coastal road loops east from Whangaroa to fine ocean beaches at Tauranga, Wainui, and Matauri bays with views of the Cavalli Islands offshore.

Mangonui. Houses spill down wooded slopes encircling attractive Mangonui Bay. In the early days, the harbor was the gateway to the Far North, and a whaling base and mill port for ships engaged in the kauri trade.

Today the wharf serves local fishermen and also houses the Mangonui Sea Lab and Aquarium containing marine life found in local waters. Small boats anchor at Mill Bay. For a sweeping view over Mangonui and Doubtless Bay, take the road to the Rangikapiti *pa* site overlooking the harbor.

Doubtless Bay. According to Maori legend, the great Polynesian explorer Kupe landed at Taipa centuries before the "great migration" south from Hawaiki. In 1769 Captain Cook sailed past the entrance and named the bay. De Surville anchored here and narrowly escaped being wrecked.

A series of splendid beaches along the shore attract families during holiday periods. Surfcasters and shell collectors enjoy Tokerau Beach; skin divers favor Matai Bay and Cape Karikari. Game fishermen cast outside the bay entrance.

Kaitaia, hub of the "winterless north"

Tourist and commercial center of the Far North, Kaitaia has been a Maori village, an 1830s mission station, and a boom town for kauri gumdiggers.

For today's visitors, Kaitaia is departure point for coach trips to Cape Reinga and Ninety Mile Beach and for 4-wheel-drive safaris to remote beaches. Scenic flights over Northland depart from Kaitaia Airport.

Your first stop should be the Far North Regional Museum on South Road (open Tuesday through Sunday afternoons). You can obtain regional tourist information here and learn about the history and development of the Far North.

Pride of the museum is its de Surville anchor, one of two recovered in 1974 from the bottom of Doubtless Bay. Photographs depict pioneering days in the kauri forests, gum fields, and flaxlands. You'll also see missionary relics, a collection of kauri gum, and the new colonial room.

A 15-minute drive through dairy lands takes you to Ahipara at the southern end of Ninety Mile Beach. From the hills sheltering the bay you gaze north along the magnificent sweep of sand.

If you'd enjoy an adventurous day exploring windswept beaches and secluded coves, sign up for a day's trip by 4-wheel-drive vehicle. From Kaitaia you'll head west for Wreck Bay, the gum fields, and the wave-cut Reef Point or north to the rugged Karikari Peninsula. You'll picnic on the beach, and perhaps have time for shell collecting, rock fishing, or a swim.

North to Cape Reinga

From Kaitaia a narrow road leads 116 km/72 miles north along the Aupouri Peninsula to Cape Reinga, popularly regarded as the country's northernmost point (the Surville Cliffs on North Cape actually extend slightly farther north).

Coach tours depart each morning from Kaitaia and Paihia for Cape Reinga, returning along the peninsula's Ninety Mile Beach. Depending on the time of high tide, the route may be reversed. Lunch is available at Waitiki Landing.

Buses stop at Houhora Heads for a visit to the Wagener Museum, a collector's storehouse contain-

ing exhibits that range from natural history and Maori artifacts to old-time phonographs and washing machines in working order. Houhora, once the center of gumdigging activity, still has New Zealand's most northerly tavern.

Beach grasses and the young pine trees of Aupouri Forest are reclaiming some former gum fields and sand dunes. Near the peninsula's northern tip, the road winds through Te Paki Coastal Park before emerging at the lighthouse settlement.

Cape Reinga. A trail leads out to the lonely lighthouse, perched 165 meters/542 feet above the waves. At night its light can be seen about 50 km/ 31 miles offshore. Below, two mighty bodies of water—the Pacific Ocean and Tasman Sea—collide in foamy combat. Panoramas stretch west to Cape Maria van Diemen—first sighted by Tasman in 1642 —and east across Spirits Bay toward North Cape.

Below the lighthouse, a twisted pohutukawa tree clings to the headland. According to Maori legend, the spirits of departing Maoris pass down its exposed roots into the sea on their underwater return voyage to legendary Hawaiki.

Ninety Mile Beach. On the return trip to Kaitaia, buses turn off the road and follow Te Paki Stream to the sea—quicksand in the stream bed makes this trip unsafe for other vehicles.

The magnificent white sand beach stretches along the Tasman for some 103 km/ 64 miles all the way to Ahipara. Surfcasters converge here during the New Year holidays to compete for cash prizes in a big surfcasting contest. Your bus speeds along the firm clean sand, splashing through occasional streams and scattering flocks of skittish shore birds. Off season, you'll frequently have the entire coast to yourself.

South of Auckland

Land-hungry European settlers pushed south from Auckland in the 1850s, seeking to buy—and later confiscate—rich Maori lands in the Waikato. Misunderstandings arose between Maori and *pakeha*, and for more than 20 years the Land Wars raged throughout the central part of North Island. Embittered Maoris retreated to the rugged King Country, where Europeans intruded at their peril.

In the 1860s gold miners flocked to the Coromandel Peninsula, followed by timber speculators who razed its kauri forests.

The Waikato Plains

For much of the way Highway 1 parallels the Waikato River, which gives its name to the broad area south of Auckland. From Lake Taupo the country's longest river flows some 354 km/220 miles to meet the Tasman Sea south of Manukau Harbour. Main source of North Island's hydroelectric power, the river is harnessed by a series of dams and power stations. Boaters and water-skiers enjoy the reservoir lakes behind the dams.

Stud farms cluster around Cambridge and Matamata, where thoroughbred race horses are bred and trained.

Hamilton. Hub of the Waikato Plains, Hamilton is New Zealand's largest inland city (population 155,000). It sprawls across the Waikato River in the center of rich dairy farmlands about 138 km/ 85 miles south of Auckland.

From its beginnings as a riverside military settlement, Hamilton has become a busy farming and industrial center, noted for its soil and agricultural research and experimentation.

Several pleasant parks border the river; jet boat trips operate from Ferrybank Park. You can see Maori artifacts, many of local origin, at the Waikato Art Gallery and Museum, 150 London Street.

From Hamilton you can visit the coastal port resort of Raglan, located 49 km/30 miles west on Highway 23.

Eastern Waikato. Highways 26 and 29 cut northeast across the plains toward the Kaimai Range, passing through some of the country's best pasture land and small-but-thriving country towns. Mountain streams and mineral springs feed the Waihou River, along the western base of the range.

The area's mineral springs spawned several spas and resorts. Best known is Te Aroha, a fashionable Victorian spa that retains quaint buildings in its domain. Marked trails lead through the woods, and a mountain bus transports visitors to the summit of Mount Te Aroha for wide-ranging views.

Cambridge. Both its name and its setting give Cambridge an English flavor. Stately old trees, a village green, and solid churches add charm to this riverside town southeast of Hamilton.

Trees border an attractive lake in Te Koutu Domain. On Victoria Street a museum in the Town Hall exhibits memorabilia from the Land Wars and early colonial days. Southeast of town, water sports and other recreation facilities are available at Lake Karapiro, farthest downstream of the Waikato reservoirs.

Explore underground at Waitomo Caves

In the rugged hills northwest of Te Kuiti, subterranean limestone outcroppings have been transformed into a series of spectacular caves. Three of these are open to visitors—the famous Waitomo Caves, renowned for their dramatic limestone formations and a magical glow worm grotto.

One of New Zealand's leading tourist attractions, guided cave tours are conducted daily from 9 A.M. to 4:30 P.M. on a staggered schedule, each taking about 45 minutes. Wear walking shoes and bring a sweater. Meals and accommodations are available at the THC Waitomo Hotel, a lovely old inn crowning the hill above the valley.

If you have time to explore the area, take a picnic and follow Te Anga road west from Waitomo to Mangapohue Natural Bridge, a limestone arch tunneled thousands of years ago by an underground river, and to Marokopa Falls.

Waitomo Cave. Highlight of your Waitomo tour is a silent boat ride, gliding along an underground river in a flat-bottomed punt, into a cavern spangled with the radiant blue-green lights of thousands of tiny glowworms. Covering the roof and walls of the cave, their lights shimmer in the still waters below. Elsewhere you'll see the tiny glowworms close up, their long sticky "fishing lines" hanging to snare insects attracted by the lights.

Striking limestone formations include the famous Organ and the lofty chamber called the Cathedral.

Ruakuri and Aranui caves. Less frequently visited, these caves are about 3 km/2 miles beyond the Waitomo Cave entrance.

Largest of the caves is Ruakuri, a fantastic complex of underground caverns resounding with the reverberating roar of a hidden waterfall. An underground river mysteriously appears and disappears in the cave.

Smallest and loveliest of the three caves is enchanting Aranui, noted for its delicate fluted limestone formations and unusual colorings.

The rugged King Country

It was not until formal peace was made in 1881, ending the Land Wars, that the government could extend its North Island rail line south to open up new farmlands. Highways 3 and 4 link the farming centers of Otorohanga, Te Kuiti, and Taumarunui with major markets. On the Tasman coast, remote Kawhia attracts away-from-it-all vacationers.

Otorohanga. Located on Highway 3 north of the Waitomo turnoff, Otorohanga is one of several places where you can see a kiwi. A small zoo here includes a nocturnal kiwi house open to visitors daily from 10 A.M. to 4 P.M.

Kawhia Harbour. Remote Kawhia, 60 km/37 miles west of Otorohanga on Highway 31, offers the timeless fascination of a remote settlement—one of the finest natural harbors on the coast—bypassed by main road and rail routes. Traders and missionaries arrived here in the 1830s. White settlers were ousted during the Land Wars, and the port never regained its early vigor.

Launches depart from Kawhia's wharf on harbor sightseeing trips. On Te Puia Beach, hot springs well up through the sands, and you can scoop out your own hot pool at low tide.

Te Kuiti. South of the Waitomo turnoff, Te Kuiti is a farming, mining, and timber town with a rich Maori history. Of special interest is the carved meeting house built in 1878 (ask permission before visiting).

South of Te Kuiti, Highway 3 bends southwest, cutting through the scenic Awakino Gorge to the coast.

Taumarunui. In the heart of the King Country midway between Hamilton and Wanganui, this farming and sawmill center marks the confluence of the Ongarue and upper Wanganui rivers. For generations, Maori canoes plied these inland rivers; today you might see a canoe party paddling down the scenic Wanganui.

From mid-December through March, hiking groups depart from Taumarunui on the Wanganui Walk, a 5-day escorted tramp operated by Venturetreks Ltd. of Auckland. Hikers follow the Mangapurua Valley to the Wanganui River, sleeping in tents and eating meals cooked over open fires. Jet boats return hikers upriver to Taumarunui.

From Taumarunui highways lead east to Lake Taupo and south to Tongariro National Park. Scenic but slow Highway 43 winds through forested hills and the Tangarakau Gorge to Stratford.

The Coromandel Peninsula

Southeast of Auckland, the rugged Coromandel Peninsula thrusts clawlike into the sea, separating the Hauraki Gulf from the Bay of Plenty. Along its coast the sea crashes against rocky cliffs and gently laps sandy crescents. Its forested mountain backbone contains remnants of gold mining and kauri milling days.

Coastal roads border the shoreline, and several mountain roads wind across the Coromandel Range, linking the west and east coasts.

The peninsula's population has fluctuated wildly with its changing fortunes. Prospectors flocked here in the late 1860s in search of gold. Timber traders and gumdiggers razed its forests and plundered its lands. Today swimmers, skin divers, fishermen, and yachtsmen enjoy these waters. Gemstone collectors find fine specimens on west coast beaches, in rivers and creeks, and near abandoned mining shafts.

Quaint old Victorian buildings recall the Coromandel's period of prosperity and indicate its slow development in recent decades. Largest of the towns is Thames, the peninsula's western gateway; you can obtain tourist information here. Other centers are Coromandel, nestled between mountains and sea on its northwest harbor; and the east coast resorts of Whitianga and Whangamata, headquarters for deep-sea fishing excursions and water sports.

The west coast. Located about 120 km/75 miles southeast of Auckland, Thames is a convenient base for exploring the peninsula. A mineral museum in the Thames School of Mines is open afternoons except Sunday. The Kauaeranga Valley road leads to pleasant riverside picnic sites and bush walks in Coromandel Forest Park.

From Thames it's a pleasant 56 km/35 mile coastal drive to Coromandel. Charming Victorian buildings snuggle beside the harbor, rekindling memories of the 1867 gold rush that brought quick prosperity to the area. You can continue north to Long Bay, a popular picnicking and camping area;

to Kennedy's Bay, a yachter's haven; and to secluded bays and beaches near the tip of the sparsely-populated Colville peninsula.

Slow but scenic Highway 25 winds 48 km/30 miles from Coromandel high above Coromandel and Whangapoua harbours and Mercury Bay to Whitianga. Narrow and winding Highway 309 is the direct route across the mountains.

East coast resorts. Summer vacationers come here for swimming and water-skiing, deep sea fishing and surfcasting, gemstone hunting, and bush walking.

The peaceful harbor town of Whitianga takes on a carnival atmosphere in summer as vacationers flock here for big game fishing on Mercury Bay and water sports along the coast. You can arrange fishing and sightseeing excursions. A passenger ferry makes the 4-minute trip across the Narrows to Ferry Landing, where you can walk to several interesting destinations.

Busy Whangamata attracts surf-swimmers and water-skiers. Offshore is Mayor Island, one of the coast's major deep-sea fishing bases.

Rotorua

Rotorua offers two unusual attractions for visitors: an intriguing variety of thermal activity, and an opportunity to learn about the Maori culture. Anglers come here for some of the country's best trout fishing.

The resort town (population 45,000) curves along the southwest shore of Lake Rotorua, largest of a cluster of tree-rimmed lakes at the northern end of North Island's volcanic plateau. To the southeast looms Mount Tarawera, violently split open by a volcanic eruption in 1886. For a view over the lake basin and plateau, drive to the top of Mount Ngongotaha northwest of town.

An important part of Rotorua's history and culture revolves around the Maoris, members of the Arawa tribe, who settled here. Ancestors of the present residents landed on the Bay of Plenty coast about 1340. Migrating inland, they established scattered villages on defensible hills, peninsulas, and islands. Violent battles between warring tribes were a common occurrence.

After the Land Wars ended, the area's thermal attractions—including the famous Pink and White Terraces bordering Lake Rotomahana—began to draw an increasing number of visitors. And after Mount Tarawera's 1886 eruption, Rotorua developed and flourished as a turn-of-the-century spa, highly regarded for the curative powers of its mineral waters.

A busy tourist center, Rotorua is the hub for numerous excursions to nearby lakes and thermal attractions. A local fishing guide can introduce you to some of the area's renowned fishing; your hotel chef will cook your catch for dinner.

Billowing steam, *spouting geysers, and boiling mud await Whakarewarewa visitors in Rotorua.*

To learn more about the Maori culture, you can visit settlements at Whakarewarewa and Ohinemutu, observe craftsmen at work, sample Maori foods at a *hangi* feast, and enjoy programs of traditional songs and dances.

Getting settled in Rotorua

Visitors arrive in Rotorua by air or road. Flights of Air New Zealand, Mount Cook Airlines, and Air North Ltd. land at Rotorua Airport northeast of town, with direct service to Auckland, Wellington, Christchurch, and Queenstown.

Coaches of N.Z. Railways Road Services connect Rotorua with Auckland, Wellington, and other North Island points; they also transport visitors on numerous local sightseeing excursions and link Rotorua passengers with the railway at Hamilton. Local and long-distance buses depart from the Travel Centre on Amohau Street.

Hotels and motels. North Island's main tourist resort offers a full range of accommodations. You'll find the larger tourist hotels and motels located in town (Vacation Hotel, Rotorua Travelodge, and the cozy old Prince's Gate Hotel); near Whakarewarewa Thermal Reserve 3 km/2 miles south of town (THC International, Geyserland Motor Hotel, Shaw Savill Caravel, Puhi Nui Motel); and along Fenton Street—Highway 5—connecting the two areas (DB Rotorua Hotel, Four Canoes Inn). Rotorua has dozens of small motels, many of them located along the highway.

If you're a dedicated fisherman or prefer a secluded location, consider the Okataina Tourist Lodge on the shore of Lake Okataina, 30 km/19 miles northeast of town.

Tourist information. For suggestions on making the most of your Rotorua visit, stop at the city's Public Relations Office on Haupapa Street. And for assistance with travel arrangements and accommodations throughout the country, contact the Government Tourist Bureau at the corner of Fenton and Haupapa streets. Inquire at the G.T.B. office or the Travel Centre on Amohau Street for information on local sightseeing tours.

Enjoy Maori-style food and entertainment

Rotorua's the place to sample a Maori *hangi,* a Polynesian feast traditionally steam-cooked in an underground pit. *Kai* (food) may include pork, lamb, chicken, seafood, marinated fish, venison, kumera (Maori sweet potato), salads, Maori bread, and fresh fruit.

After dinner, Maori entertainers serenade guests with traditional songs and perform Maori dances featuring twirling *pois* (balls on string) and the fierce *haka* (a posturing war dance).

The THC International Hotel presents a traditional hangi every Sunday night at 6:30 throughout the year (additional Maori feasts in summer). If you arrive early, you may see the food being lifted from the earth oven, where it has been

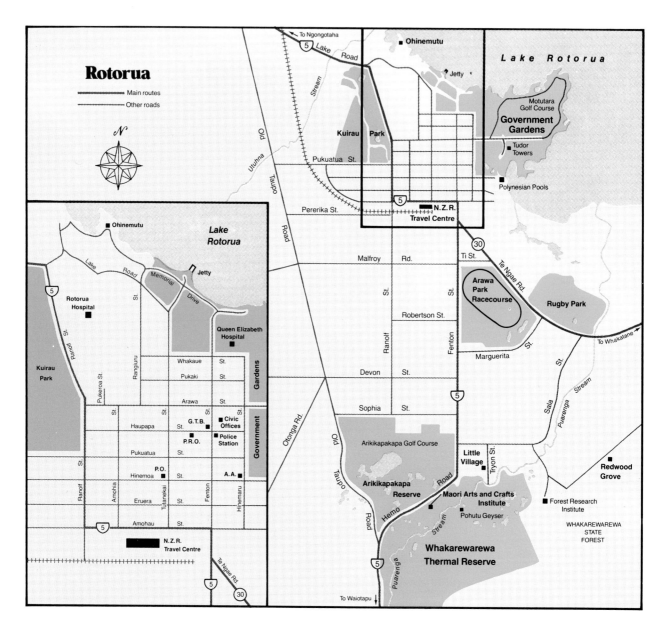

cooked by natural steam. Other hangi feasts and entertainment are presented at the Geyserland Motor Hotel, Four Canoes Inn, and Travelodge Hotel.

You can enjoy Maori food and entertainers nightly at Top of the Towers cabaret in Government Gardens. Cabaret acts and dancing follow the Maori program.

Other restaurants. You'll find comfortable dining rooms in the major hotels. Among the city's restaurants are The Bushman's Hut, 163 Tutanekai Street (traditional New Zealand game and seafood specialties); the Five Doors on the lakefront (a la carte menu, dancing); and Ruedi's Restaurant, 41 Arawa Street (French cuisine).

Maori concerts. Regular programs of Maori songs and dances that chronicle events in tribal history and village life are presented at the Rotorua Maori Cultural Theatre on Eruera Street, and at the Tamatekapua Meeting House at Ohinemutu.

Sports and outdoor activities

Rotorua's sports facilities are concentrated in Government Gardens east of the business district. Watching lawn bowlers or croquet players is a pleasant pastime, though you can participate in more active pursuits if you prefer. Many travelers enjoy a relaxing dip in a hot mineral pool at the end of a busy day.

Sports enthusiasts can obtain fishing and hunting information at the Government Tourist Bureau on Fenton Street. If you want to go trout fishing, you can arrange for a guide who will pick you up at your hotel and take you out in a launch (all equipment provided) for a few hours on one of the local lakes. Chartered floatplanes transport anglers to secluded fishing sites. Deep-sea fishing trips on the Bay of Plenty depart from Tauranga and Whakatane, about an hour's drive northeast of Rotorua.

Golfers can choose from several local courses. You'll find something different in course hazards at Arikikapakapa Golf Course, where thermal vents dot the links with escaping steam.

Horse racing events take place at Arawa Park.

Relax in thermally heated pools

Bring along your bathing suit and relax in one of Rotorua's thermally heated pools.

Developed as a spa town, Rotorua for decades attracted visitors who came to "take the waters" to treat rheumatism and other ailments. Today's bathers enjoy these mineral-rich waters primarily for the feeling of well-being they bestow. Some spa facilities are available; you can arrange for a sauna or an *aix* massage with coconut oil rubdown —guaranteed to make a new man or woman of you!

Many hotels and motels have pools for their guests, and there are large swimming pools in the Blue Baths in Government Gardens.

At the Polynesian Pools, located at the east end of Hinemoa Street, you can relax in the deep warmth of heated mineral waters or plunge into a thermal swimming pool. Children have their own pool in a separate wing. For those who prefer to soak *au naturel*, small private pools are available. Pool hours are 9 A.M. to 10 P.M. daily.

You can rent bathing suits and towels at both the Polynesian Pools and Blue Baths.

A walk through Government Gardens

From the city center, walk east to Government Gardens, a spacious peninsula park extending east from Hinemaru Street. A distinctive Maori carving greets visitors at the main Prince's Gate entrance on Arawa Street. Thermal attractions are interspersed amid the park's sports fields and flower beds.

From October to Easter you can watch lawn bowlers, dressed in their proper "whites," competing in matches on the greens in front of the dignified old Tudor Towers building. Elsewhere residents and visitors enjoy croquet, tennis, golf, roller skating, or a plunge in a thermal pool. Indoor sports activities take place in the nearby sports and conference center.

Tudor Towers. One of New Zealand's most photographed buildings, the elegant Tudor Towers was built in 1906-07 as the bathhouse for those who came for curative mineral and mud baths. Transferred to the town in 1963, the building has been restored and now houses Rotorua's museum and art gallery, a licensed restaurant, and the area's only cabaret.

In the building's southern wing, the museum is open from 10 to 4 daily. Geological displays offer information on the volcanic plateau, thermal activity, and the great Tarawera eruption of 1886. Maori cultural exhibits contain family and tribal treasures contributed by local Maoris. On the mezzanine, a colonial cottage has been furnished with period items. In the northern wing, the City Art Gallery is open 10 to 4 daily.

Whakarewarewa Thermal Reserve

One of Rotorua's top attractions is Whakarewarewa Thermal Reserve (popularly called Whaka), located south of town along Highway 5. Here you'll learn about the Maori people and their crafts and get a close view of thermal activity. Maori guides conduct groups through the reserve, or you can stroll the paths at your own pace. The reserve is open daily from 8:30 to 4:30.

Outside the main entrance, the Maori Arts and Crafts Institute trains promising young Maori carvers in the skills of their elders. Women fashion skirts out of flax, make baskets, and demonstrate the *taniko* weaving of bodices and headbands. Visitors are welcome weekdays from 8:30 to 4:30.

Carved wooden figures of fabled Maori lovers Tutanekai and Hinemoa embrace above a gate in

Harnessing geothermal energy at Wairakei

Dramatic clouds of billowing steam mingle with silvery pipes and towers to greet the traveler at Wairakei, in the center of North Island's thermal belt. Dozens of deep bores tap superheated underground water, releasing steam under pressure which is converted to electricity.

One of the world's foremost geothermal power projects, Wairakei has attracted considerable international scientific attention. It began generating electricity in 1959.

Visitors learn about the development at the power project's information office alongside Highway 1, about 10 km/6 miles north of Taupo. You can also join a guided tour at one of the power stations.

Several thousand feet below the surface, hot volcanic rocks heat underground water reservoirs to above-boiling temperatures. To tap the geothermal steam, engineers drill deep bores intersecting this layer. The steel-encased bores channel escaping steam to the surface, where hot water is extracted. "Dry" steam funnels through insulated mains to electricity generating stations along the Waikato River. "U"-shaped loops in the pipes allow for expansion and contraction.

Inside the power stations, vast quantities of cold water pumped from the river condense the steam; water is then returned to the river. The stations operate 24 hours a day at full output.

the palisaded walls of the model *pa*. Inside the reserve, walkways lead down to a kiwi house and viewpoints of Pohutu Geyser and the thermal valley.

You'll see pools of bubbling mud edged in greenery, spouting geysers, silica terraces, and steam escaping from ground vents. Mighty Pohutu Geyser plays spasmodically—for a few minutes or for hours at a time—erupting to 60 feet, with occasional spurts rising to twice that height.

At the lower end of the valley you walk past Whakarewarewa village, where Maori residents use the hot pools for cooking, bathing, laundering, and heating.

A lakeside Maori village

The village of Ohinemutu borders Lake Rotorua northwest of town. For generations its residents have used the escaping steam and thermally heated water in daily activities.

Maori carvings and *tukutuku* panels decorate the interior of the Tudor-style St. Faith's Anglican Church, built in 1910. In the side chapel, a magnificent window depicts Christ, wearing a chief's cloak of kiwi feathers, apparently walking on the waters of the lake. In front of the church, a regal bust of Queen Victoria contrasts with its ornate shelter and pedestal, carved and painted Maori-style. In the churchyard, tombs are above ground because of thermal conditions.

Facing the church is a meeting house enhanced by traditional carvings. Some of the interior decoration dates from the early 1800s and depicts ancestors who arrived in the Arawa canoe. Evening programs of Maori songs and dances are often presented here.

Other places to visit

Local families enjoy Kuirau Park for its children's attractions. Located at Ranolf and Pukuatua streets, Kuirau Park features the "Toot 'n Whistle" miniature steam railway (runs weekends except July, daily during school holidays), a children's playground, aquarium, sports fields, and an aquatic center. Walkways link the park's small lake with gardens, boiling mud pools, and a large thermal fountain.

You can browse and shop in an old-time atmosphere at Little Village, a refreshment and crafts center on Tryon Street, Whakarewarewa, across from the tall THC International Hotel. Artisans demonstrate their skills in colonial-style shops at the rear.

If you'd enjoy a quiet walk in the woods, head for Whakarewarewa State Forest southeast of town. Tracks of varying lengths wind through the forest. A popular trail loops through a grove of towering redwood trees south of Sala Street. Maps at park entrances indicate the routes, and posts marked by colored bands guide you along the trails.

The large forest park extends from the Whaka thermal reserve and the Taupo highway east to the Blue and Green lakes.

Lifts *transport skiers up Mount Ruapehu in Tongariro National Park (see page 58). Season usually lasts from mid-June through October.*

Excursions from Rotorua

As a tourist, you're part of one of Rotorua's main industries, and you'll find plenty of excursions to nearby attractions.

If thermal activity intrigues you, take a look at spouting geysers, steaming cliffs, boiling pools, and colorful silica terraces.

You can cruise secluded lakes rimmed by native forest, walk down a thermal valley, explore a buried village, feed trout by hand, climb the side of a volcano by 4-wheel-drive vehicle, or take a flightseeing trip over the lakes and thermal valleys.

Bus trips. Half-day and full-day sightseeing excursions depart from the Travel Centre on Amohau Street. Most trips are scheduled daily from December through April, on alternate days the rest of the year.

One full-day excursion covers the Waimangu Valley, boat trips on lake Rotomahana and Tarawera, and a visit to Te Wairoa buried village. Another loops south to visit Huka Falls, Wairakei, Lake Taupo, and Orakei Korako. There's also a day excursion to Waitomo Caves.

Up Mount Tarawera. Four-wheel-drive vehicles transport passengers on a mountain safari up the slope of Mount Tarawera. From the summit you peer into the volcano's deep, color-streaked craters and enjoy an awesome panorama over Rotorua's green forests and sparkling lakes.

Flightseeing. One of the best ways to view the lakes and thermal attractions is by air. Floatplanes depart from Rotorua's lakefront jetty; other flights leave from the Rotorua Airport on the lake's east shore. You can fly over Rotorua and the lake district, the gaping craters of Mount Tarawera, and steaming geothermal areas. Longer flights also circle smoking volcanoes at White Island or Tongariro National Park.

Cruising on the lakes

Good roads provide access to most of the larger lakes, and you'll enjoy them even more if you cruise their clear, tree-rimmed waters.

The lakes figure prominently in local history as links in the Maori canoe route to Lake Rotorua. In 1823 Hongi Hika and his warriors paddled across the lakes, portaging the heavy wooden canoes when necessary, on their way to attack the fortified Arawa settlement on Mokoia Island.

Launch excursions depart daily on Rotorua and Rotoiti lakes; extra trips are scheduled during peak periods. Rental boats are available at the main lakes.

Lake Rotorua. Largest of the lakes is Rotorua, nearly circular, with wooded Mokoia Island near its center. The island is the site of the Maoris' greatest love story, the romance of the maid Hinemoa and young chief Tutanekai.

You board the sightseeing launch at the jetty at the north end of Tutanekai Street. After circling the island, the launch docks and you have time for a short walk on the island, and perhaps a quick swim in Hinemoa's Pool and a wish by the Arawa wishing rock. If you prefer, take the morning cruise, picnic on the island, and return on the afternoon trip. Summer evening excursions include a barbecue dinner on the island.

Lake Rotoiti. Renowned for its trout fishing, this tree-bordered lake is a favorite of many visitors. Tourist facilities are concentrated at the west end of the lake. The launch trip departs from Okere Falls township daily at 10 and 2:30. You'll cruise past Moose Lodge, a lakeside retreat where Queen Elizabeth II relaxed during her 1953-54 visit.

Around Lake Rotorua

On a circuit of Lake Rotorua you can visit trout springs, watch trained sheep perform, view the countryside from atop Mount Ngongotaha, walk among redwood trees, and visit a waterfall renowned in Maori legends.

Trout springs. Clear, pure, cold water wells up from underground springs northwest of Rotorua. At each of four areas, visitors follow fern-lined paths along clear trout streams and toss food to the fish. The springs are cool, woodsy retreats to visit on hot days.

You can stop at Paradise Valley Springs, west of Rotorua on the Valley Road; Rainbow Springs or Fairy Springs, both bordering Highway 5 west of the lake; or Taniwha Springs, near Awahou on the lake's northwestern shore.

Fish are free to swim between the lake and the various streams. Fairy Springs is the oldest and least developed of the attractions. The other three trout springs feature underwater viewing windows and animal parks or native bird enclosures. Rainbow Springs has a nocturnal kiwi house.

Sheep on parade. Nineteen trained champion rams, each representing a different New Zealand breed, take the stage during a 1-hour pastoral show at the Agrodome, set in lush pastureland northwest of Rotorua at Riverdale Park, Ngongotaha. Originally developed for Expo 70 in Japan, the program tells the story of wool, one of the country's most important industries.

As each breed is announced and described, the ram trots onto a tiered platform. A sheep shearing demonstration finishes the inside show; you then move outside to watch sheepdogs maneuver sheep around a fenced paddock. Shows are presented daily at 10:30 and 2:30, with extra performances during busy visitor periods.

Mount Ngongotaha. Looming above the countryside northwest of Rotorua, this peak offers a sweeping view over the town and lakes toward the Bay of Plenty.

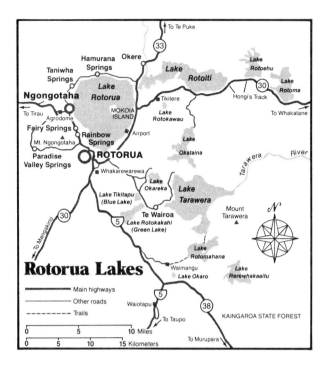

Rotorua Lakes

Main highways
Other roads
Trails

0   5   10 Miles
0   5   10   15 Kilometers

Hamurana Springs. You can walk through a grove of lofty redwood trees at Hamurana Springs, on the north shore of the lake. More than 1,000 trees planted in the 1920s have already grown taller than 30 meters/100 feet. You also can rent a boat and paddle along the willow-bordered stream, watch trout in an upstream pool, feed tame deer in the deer park, or golf on the nine-hole course.

Okere Falls. The clear green outflow of lakes Rotorua and Rotoiti surges and foams through a narrow rift, then plunges into a broad pool of the Kaituna River. Rocky steps lead down the steep wooded slope to the foot of the falls and to caves where Maori women reputedly hid in time of war.

East to fishing lakes

Northeast of Rotorua, the Whakatane road (Highway 30) skirts the southern shore of three bush-rimmed fishing lakes—Rotoiti, Rotoehu, and Rotoma. A side road south of Rotoiti leads to unspoiled Lake Okataina. Southeast of Rotorua, thermal pools bubble furiously at Tikitere, site of the country's only thermal waterfall.

Tikitere (Hell's Gate). The district's most active thermal area, Tikitere is an inferno of sulphurous steam, boiling water, and bubbling mud. White pumice and golden sulphur combine to shape bizarre formations. Take the short bush walk through native trees and ferns to Kakahi Falls, where thermal waters (averaging about 38° C./100° F.) cascade into an inviting pool.

Lake Okataina. A bush-bordered avenue south of Lake Rotoiti leads to this lovely lake. Totara trees and punga ferns shade the road, and red-flowering *kotukutuku* (native fuchsia) brightens your way

in late spring and early summer. Dense forest covers the steep slopes enclosing the lake.

Okataina attracts people who enjoy peace and quiet—along with some of the area's best trout fishing. Inquire at the lodge regarding guides, fishing equipment, and rental boats.

Other visitors can picnic on the sandy beach; follow the shoreline path to Maori Point, site of an old *pa,* or climb to Lookout Rock.

Hongi's Track. Linking lakes Rotoiti and Rotoehu, this short route curves through magnificent forest. It commemorates Hongi Hika's expedition along this route in 1823 (see page 55). Travelers traditionally pause at the 400-year-old matai tree—called Hinehopu's Wishing Tree—to make a wish and leave an offering of greenery for protection against evil spirits on the rest of the journey.

Waimangu Valley–Lake Tarawera loop

South of Rotorua you can stroll through the steaming Waimangu Valley, cruise on lakes Rotomahana and Tarawera, and visit the buried village of Te Wairoa. Wear your walking shoes and bring a lunch if you're taking the full-day excursion.

Early on the morning of June 10, 1886, Mount Tarawera erupted in tremendous volcanic fury, awakening Aucklanders nearly 280 km/175 miles away. Splitting open from end to end, the volcano spewed forth a cubic mile of molten rock, boiling mud, and volcanic ash, covering the countryside for miles around. Three villages were buried, and more than 150 people died. The eruption destroyed Lake Rotomahana's famous Pink and White Terraces, fan-shaped silica staircases world-renowned for their beauty and shimmering colors. When the smoke cleared, Mount Tarawera was left with a gaping chasm and craters up to 700 feet deep.

Waimangu Valley. You see examples of the area's thermal activity on a guided 4-km/2½-mile walk down the valley to Lake Rotomahana. Steam rises from the surface of the Waimangu Cauldron, a large thermal lake fed by subterranean boiling springs. Off the main path is Ruamoko's Throat, a turquoise lake of fluctuating level rimmed by colorful cliffs. Your path down the valley follows a scalding stream. Near the lake, thermal waters fan over Warbrick Terrace, its silica deposits patterned with colorful algae.

Visitors not making the loop excursion must retrace their route up the valley.

Lakes Rotomahana and Tarawera. If you take the full-day excursion, you'll board a launch and cruise slowly past Lake Rotomahana's stratified cliffs, laced with steaming fumaroles. Visitors in the 19th century came here to see the renowned Pink and White Terraces; Mount Tarawera's eruption changed that.

You disembark on the lake's north shore and hike across a narrow saddle separating it from larger Lake Tarawera. Another launch waits at the Tarawera dock for a leisurely trip across the lake, where a bus waits to transport passengers on the final leg of the trip.

Te Wairoa buried village. Before the 1886 eruption, Te Wairoa was the departure point for excursions to the terraces. Buried by 5 to 6 feet of volcanic mud, the village has been partially excavated. A self-guided walk links a museum and several structures. You can follow Te Wairoa Stream, Green Lake's outlet into Lake Tarawera, as it tumbles over Te Wairoa Falls.

Gemlike lakes. On the way back to Rotorua you'll stop for a view of a pair of jewel-like lakes—Green Lake (Rotokakahi) and Blue Lake (Tikitapu). Off the main route is secluded Lake Okareka, a relaxing spot for a picnic, a swim, or a bit of fishing.

South to Waiotapu

Located 30 km/19 miles south of Rotorua near the Taupo road (Highway 5), Waiotapu is noted for the colorful silica surrounding its thermal attractions.

Lady Knox Geyser erupts daily at 10:15 A.M. Other attractions include the Artist's Palette silica terraces, tinged in delicate colors; lovely Bridal Veil Falls; and the shimmering Champagne Pool, which bubbles when sand is tossed into it.

The Volcanic Plateau

Dominating the center of North Island are a vast volcanic plateau marked by Lake Taupo, the country's largest lake, and a trio of active volcanoes in the heart of New Zealand's first national park.

Those who love the outdoors come here for superb lake and stream fishing, for water sports on Lake Taupo, and for hiking, climbing, and skiing in Tongariro National Park. Thermal energy is transformed into electricity at Wairakei's steaming geothermal bore field and at power stations along the Tongariro and Waikato rivers.

Buses of N.Z. Railways Road Services, Mount Cook Line, and Hawkes Bay Motors connect the major tourist centers on the plateau. Air New Zealand flights land at Taupo airport. Trains on the Auckland-Wellington run stop at National Park and Ohakune, both west of the park.

Tourist information centers are located at Taupo and Turangi and in Tongariro National Park.

Fishing lodges and a mountain chateau

Most overseas visitors stay near Taupo or in Tongariro National Park, though fishermen range far afield. Taupo accommodations are geared toward families. Larger lakefront motels include Manuels and the Oasis motels.

North of Taupo at Wairakei is the comfortable THC Wairakei Hotel, a favorite of golfers for its excellent 18-hole course. Upstream from Huka Falls is Huka Lodge, a historic fishing retreat on the Waikato River.

Anglers find small fishermen's motels scattered along Lake Taupo's eastern shore. In Turangi, accommodations include the DB Turangi Motor Hotel, Bridge Fishing Lodge, and several motels.

You'll find one of the country's most renowned hotels at Tongariro National Park, the newly renovated THC Chateau. Visitors can also stay at the Ruapehu Skotel (skier's hotel) in the park or in Tokaanu, National Park, or Ohakune.

The upper Waikato River

Near Taupo, travelers satiated with thermal wonders enjoy a scenic change of pace as the powerful yet placid Waikato River cascades over Huka Falls and Aratiatia Rapids. The district's most interesting thermal attraction—Orakei Korako—borders the river farther downstream.

Huka Village. A North Island pioneer village typical of the late 19th century has been recreated north of Taupo beside the Huka Falls Road. Pioneer buildings, moved here and restored, depict life during the era of the 1860s Land Wars and the days of the Armed Constabulary in the Taupo area. Artisans demonstrate crafts of a bygone era. The village is open daily from 10 A.M to 5 P.M.

Huka Falls. About 5 km/3 miles above Taupo, the Waikato suddenly narrows, its waters abruptly funneled into a narrow chasm. Surging and foaming through the rocky gorge, the roaring waters catapult over a ledge into a wide, calm pool below. Though not a high waterfall, Huka is impressive in its savage power.

The Huka Falls loop road follows the river between Taupo and Wairakei. Near the top of the falls, a footbridge spans the river leading to several overlooks. A riverside trail parallels the Waikato between Huka Falls and Aratiatia Dam.

Aratiatia Rapids. Long regarded as one of the loveliest stretches of the Waikato Valley, Aratiatia reflects a compromise between the gorge's scenic attraction and the nation's power needs. To reach Aratiatia, turn east off Highway 5 north of Wairakei.

At the head of the valley, a control dam holds back the Waikato, whose waters are rechanneled to a power station. Each afternoon from 2:30 to 4 the pent-up river is released to thunder down the deep rocky ravine. From viewpoints on the right bank, you watch the frothing waters crash down the narrow gorge.

Orakei Korako. Extensive silica deposits and a legendary cave draw visitors to Orakei Korako, located 27 km/17 miles north of Wairakei. To reach the area, you board a jet boat and skim across the river at the upper end of Lake Ohakuri.

Largest of New Zealand's silica terraces, the broad cascade called the Great Golden Fleece extends along an ancient fault scarp. Above it is the Artist's Palette, a large level basin riddled by dozens of small geysers and hot springs. Algae create color variations in the crusty silica deposits.

Tall tree ferns frame the entrance to Ruatapu

(Aladdin's) Cave, filtering sunlight to a small mirrorlike pool far below. For generations the cave was used only by Maori women who came here to bathe and beautify themselves. It's traditional to dip your left hand in the warm pool and make a secret wish.

Relaxing at Taupo

Approaching Taupo from the north, Highway 1 crests a hill and Lake Taupo's sparkling panorama spreads before you. Fed by dozens of streams, the lake occupies a gigantic volcanic crater. Its only outlet is the Waikato River, which leaves the lake alongside the town of Taupo. In the distance rise the huddled peaks of Tongariro National Park.

Maoris lived in the area before Europeans arrived, but the settlement dates from 1869, when an Armed Constabulary garrison was built here. Later, thermal activity attracted visitors. The town's development spurted in the 1950s during construction of the Wairakei geothermal project.

At the Information Centre on Tongariro Street you can obtain maps and brochures, arrange local accommodations, and inquire about fishing and hunting trips, boat rentals, and flightseeing and coach excursions. Fishing licenses and gear are available in local sports shops.

Along the river. Pleasure boats and fishing launches anchor near the head of the river, upstream from the gates that control the lake's water level and regulate the flow of water downstream. You can rent small boats at the marina. Boat excursions leave from the wharf.

Just below the bridge you can see the earthworks of the A.C. Redoubt, built to house the militia and protect their ammunition supply. Nearby is the old courthouse, originally a soldiers' hall.

Spa Road leads downriver toward Cherry Island, a wooded island in the river developed as a family attraction. From a viewpoint above the Waikato you look down on steaming pools and geysers at Hell's Gate.

Thermal pools. If you missed a swim in a thermal pool in Rotorua, you'll get another chance in Taupo. A favorite place to soak away stiffness is De Brett Thermal Hotel in the Onekeneke Valley, about 1½ km/1 mile up Highway 5 (the Napier road).

Outdoor heated fresh-water pools and private mineral pools await bathers at the A.C. Thermal Baths. If you'd rather swim in the lake, Waipahihi Hot Springs bubble from the lake bed along the northeast shore (access off Lake Terrace).

Waipahihi Botanical Reserve. South of the Napier turnoff, this wooded reserve overlooks the lake east of Highway 1, at the end of Shepherd Road. Loop trails lead walkers through groves of young native trees, ferns, and flowering native shrubs to an alpine garden and seasonal displays of rhododendrons, azaleas, and camellias.

The lake's south shore

At the south end of Lake Taupo, fly fishermen cast near the mouths of the Waitahanui and other tributary streams. Other anglers prefer the famed trout pools of the fast-flowing, snow-fed Tongariro River. The town of Turangi mushroomed during construction of the nearby Tongariro hydroelectric power project and expansion of the district's farming and forest industries. Information on local recreation, the power project, and area history and geology can be obtained at the Power Project Information Office alongside Highway 41 at Turangi.

Tokaanu has a small thermal reserve with hot pools, boiling mud, geysers, and a small bathhouse. St. Paul's Anglican Church, decorated in Maori style with *tukutuku* panels and painted rafters, is a memorial to early missionaries.

A side road leaves Highway 41 and curves along the lake to Waihi, a picturesque Maori village backed by a steep wooded cliff.

Highway 41 continues north to Kuratau, then turns west toward Taumarunui.

Hydro project. Dominating the lake's southern shore are the hydro works of the Tongariro Power Development Scheme. This massive engineering project diverts the headwaters of several major rivers (including the Tongariro, Wanganui, and Rangitikei) from one watershed into another. Long tunnels (beneath the slopes of active volcanoes) and open canals rechannel the water through Lake Rotoaira and the Tokaanu power station into Lake Taupo and the Waikato River. Another power station is planned near Rangipo.

Pihanga Saddle Road. South of Turangi, a scenic mountain road curves across the shoulder of Mount Pihanga. It climbs to a viewpoint overlooking the lake, winds through luxuriant forest, and skirts Lake Rotoaira on its route southwest to meet Highway 47.

About 10 km/6 miles from Tokaanu, a signposted trail leads south from the road to Lake Rotopounamu, a small green lake nestled in a bush-rimmed crater. A naturalist's delight, the 25-minute walk goes through thick forest abundant with ferns.

Volcanoes shape Tongariro Park

South of Lake Taupo, three volcanic peaks loom above the surrounding plateau in a terrain unique in New Zealand. One of the country's prime recreation areas, Tongariro National Park is an unspoiled wilderness shaped by eruption, glaciation, and erosion.

For generations Maoris regarded these high mountains with awe, weaving legends about them. In 1887 Chief Te Heuheu Tukino presented the peaks to the government as a reserve, and 7 years later they became the nucleus of New Zealand's first national park.

The park takes its name from the northernmost and lowest of the peaks, 1,968-meter/6,458-foot Tongariro, whose truncated crest is a maze of craters—some mildly active. A docile plume of

Mount Egmont's snowy cone, *partially shrouded by clouds, hovers above Taranaki's dairy pastures. Hikers, climbers, and skiers enjoy the peak's wooded trails and alpine slopes (see page 61).*

smoke drifts from Ngauruhoe's symmetrical cone; every few years the 2,291-meter/7,515-foot volcano erupts spectacularly, belching lava and ash over its slopes. Highest of the three is 2,797-meter/9,175-foot Ruapehu, North Island's highest peak and main ski area. Snow-capped the year around, it has a simmering acid crater lake and small glaciers on its high slopes. Seismologists keep a continuing monitor on volcanic activity.

Among the park's most fascinating aspects are its varied terrain, vegetation, and bird life. Wet lowland forests, lush with ferns and orchids, on Ruapehu's southwest slope contrast dramatically with tussock grasslands, wildflower-sprinkled alpine rock gardens, and stark volcanic formations at higher elevations. More than 500 native plant species and many bird varieties have been identified in the park.

Year-round park pleasures

Center of park activity is the Chateau at Whakapapa Village. Skiers flock here in winter; summer activities include golf, tennis, and lawn bowling.

Nearby at park headquarters you learn about the park's geology and volcanic activity, history, plants, and birds. You can also obtain trail information and maps and check the weather forecast. In summer, rangers conduct guided walks and evening nature programs. They also arrange for climbing guides, hunting permits, and use of mountain huts. A ranger station is located on the Ohakune Mountain Road.

Skiing on Mount Ruapehu. From Whakapapa Village the Bruce road (Highway 48) continues about 7 km/4½ miles up to the main ski area. You can rent skis and boots at the Chateau and take lessons at the ski school. The season usually lasts from late June through October.

From Top o' the Bruce, chairlifts, Poma lifts, and T-bars give access to Ruapehu's downhill runs and ski-touring trails. Helicopters transport skiers to the upper slopes.

The new Turoa Skifield on Ruapehu's southwest slope, reached by the Ohakune Road, is expected to relieve pressure on the main ski area.

Walks and tramps. Several short walks begin near Whakapapa Village. The easy 20-minute Ridge Track winds through the bush to a scenic viewpoint. Not far away is the Alpine Garden, a pleasant stroll through high-altitude plants. The 1-hour Whakapapanui Track follows a tumbling stream through dense mountain beech forest below the Chateau. Tawhai Falls is a 10-minute walk off Highway 48.

Half-day hikes cut through varied terrain— beech and fern forests, golden tussock, boggy areas, alpine meadows. Try the trail to Silica Springs, the bush walk to lovely Taranaki Falls, or the climb to Tama Lakes in a pair of ancient craters. From Highway 47 it's a steep uphill tramp to Ketetahi Hot Springs, but a soak in the warm waters below the springs rejuvenates tired climbers.

Longer hikes lead to the Tongariro Craters and to Mount Ruapehu's hot acid lake surrounded by ice and snow. A round-the-mountain tramp curves from the Chateau to the Ohakune Mountain Road.

Several fine walks begin along the Ohakune Road; consider the Mangawhero Forest Walk through a pocket of lush subtropical rainforest, or the bush walk to Waitonga Falls, the park's highest waterfall.

Drives. The varied topography can be appreciated best on a round-the-mountain drive. The snow and ice of the high peaks contrast with the northern tussock country, near-desert on the southwest, dense fern forest on the western slope.

Most scenic of the park routes is the Ohakune Mountain Road, climbing from Ohakune straight up Ruapehu's southwestern flank. Ask at park headquarters for a descriptive leaflet. As you ascend, you traverse a cross-section of the park's varying climate and vegetation zones—from lowland rimu forest through silver and mountain beech into high tussock shrublands to alpine gravel fields at road's end. You can picnic beside the Mangawhero River as it falls over the edge of old lava flows.

Across the Rangipo Desert

One of North Island's most unusual drives crosses the desolate, windswept Rangipo Desert just east of the park. From Turangi 63 km/39 miles south to Waiouru, Highway 1 is known as the Desert Road. Generations of Maori travelers hurried across the forbidding plains, not daring to stop or look at the sacred mountains for fear of antagonizing the gods, who might punish them with storms of snow and ice.

Dry, cold winds sweep down from snowy Mount Ruapehu, and only sparse and stunted plants survive in the harsh climate. Sculptured by wind and frost, road cuttings expose the region's layered volcanic deposits.

South of Waiouru, Highway 1 passes through the railway town of Taihape and follows the Rangitikei River southwest through white-walled gorges. Several splendid bush reserves are located near Hunterville, in the heart of the district's farmlands. Highway 1 meets the west coast road (Highway 3) at Bulls, another Rangitikei farming center.

Along the west coast

From the King Country, Highway 3 veers southwest across Mount Messenger and follows the wooded Awakino River gorge to the coast. A trio of small fishing settlements—Awakino, Mokau, and Tongaporutu—mark the mouths of coastal rivers.

New Plymouth is the hub of the rich Taranaki farmlands, a city of splendid parks and gardens, and the gateway to mountain recreation in Egmont National Park.

The coastal highway continues southeast to Wanganui, at the mouth of the Wanganui River, and through the Rangitikei and Manawatu farming districts to Wellington.

N.Z. Railways Road Services and Gibsons Coachlines provide regular motorcoach service from the

---

Explore rural New Zealand leisurely by car

One of the best ways to see New Zealand is to rent a car and head for the country, exploring out-of-the way places at your leisure. Outside the metropolitan areas traffic is usually light. In rural districts you may meet a herd of sheep or cattle being prodded along the road to pasture.

A variety of fly-drive touring programs are available for independent travelers. Or you can arrange a day or weekend excursion when city activities slow down.

Roads are sealed (bitumen surfaced) or metalled (graded gravel, usually all-weather). Country roads have improved considerably in recent years, but city drivers may find some unfamiliar conditions.

Use care and common sense on narrow roads, keeping left and driving at country speeds. Resist the impulse to brake suddenly on metalled roads; it's easy to skid on the loose gravel. Corrugations form in sandy road surfaces despite regular grading, so drive slowly and learn to spot ridges in advance. On one-way bridges, traffic in one direction has the right-of-way; oncoming traffic yields.

In rural areas you'll often meet stock on the roads, particularly in early morning and late afternoon. Usually the farmer will direct his dogs to make a path through the group for you. Move slowly but steadily; don't toot your horn or rev your engine unnecessarily. If the herd is moving toward you, it is simplest just to stop and let them move past. When you're driving after dark, don't overdrive your lights; occasionally animals wander onto the roads.

west coast towns to Auckland, Wellington, and intermediate points.

Taranaki's rich farmlands

Renowned for its lush pastures, Taranaki is frequently called the "garden of New Zealand." Solitary Mount Egmont dominates the province, its snowy cone looming above the surrounding green fields and dairy farms.

A historic Maori battleground, Taranaki was invaded many times by fierce Waikato tribes from the north. In 1860 Waitara was the scene of the first major battles in the Land Wars. Hostilities spread through the central part of North Island, continuing until 1881.

The meeting house at historic Manukorihi Pa in Waitara contains outstanding examples of characteristic Taranaki carvings and *tukutuku* work.

In the early 1960s natural gas was discovered at Kapuni, south of Mount Egmont, and offshore drilling rigs tapped the vast Maui natural gas field off the Taranaki coast in 1969.

New Plymouth, city of parks and gardens

Located about midway between Auckland and Wellington, New Plymouth is Taranaki's only large city. An important agricultural center, it has also become the mainland point for development of the offshore natural gas deposits. The Port Taranaki complex serves coastal and overseas shipping.

The New Zealand Company settlement was laid out in 1841, its first settlers drawn from the British counties of Devon and Cornwall. The town's main commercial area extends along Devon Street (Highway 3). Numerous parks and reserves dot the town.

Stop at the Public Relations Office, 81 Liardet Street, for information on city and district attractions, scenic drives, and other excursions.

Largest of the city's numerous hotels and motels is Devon Motor Lodge; other accommodations include Westown Motor Hotel and DB Bell Block Hotel.

Pukekura Park. A 10-minute walk up Liardet Street from the downtown district is Pukekura Park, one of the country's outstanding city parks. Footpaths wind around two manmade lakes and through the wooded reserve. From the tea kiosk, park visitors enjoy a fine view of Mount Egmont.

Azaleas and rhododendrons flower here from September through November. Rare ferns are displayed in the Fernery, and begonias, orchids, and fuchsias bloom in the Begonia House. During summer and holiday periods, you can rent rowboats on the upper lake.

Brooklands. Adjoining Pukekura Park is Brooklands, a park occupying the wooded site of a pioneer homestead. It contains New Zealand's only outdoor theater, a children's zoo, and some of Taranaki's oldest trees.

Native pines form a backdrop to the Bowl of Brooklands, a natural amphitheater that accommodates up to 19,000 people. During the annual Festival of the Pines in January and February, families sit on the grass to enjoy music, dance, and drama under the stars. Programs usually conclude with a spectacular fireworks display.

Other city attractions. Taranaki Museum at the corner of Brougham and King streets contains an outstanding collection of primitive Maori stone implements and stone-tooled wood carvings salvaged from swamps near Waitara. The museum is open afternoons except Saturday. Nearby is the 1853 Richmond Cottage, furnished with period furniture.

The Govett-Brewster Art Gallery on Queen Street is open daily except Monday.

For a view over the city and port, follow the scenic drive west to Moturoa Lookout above the port and power project. Inland, Mount Egmont's snowy peak looms above Taranaki dairylands.

Lake Mangamahoe. Located 10 km/6 miles south of New Plymouth off Highway 3, Lake Mangamahoe is famed for its greenery-framed, mirrored view of Mount Egmont. For the best reflections, come in early morning and drive to the far end of the lake.

Pukeiti Rhododendron Trust. Some 800 varieties of rhododendrons—plus many alpine, bog, and woodland plants—bloom in this large, internationally known private garden about 24 km/15 miles southwest of New Plymouth. Reached by Upper Carrington Road, the reserve is open the year around, but peak blooming season begins in September. Grassy paths and bush tracks wind through the valley.

Egmont National Park

Loneliest and loveliest of North Island's peaks, Mount Egmont was sighted and named by Captain Cook in 1770. Called Taranaki by the Maoris, the snowcapped mountain figured prominently in their legends.

To reach the park, drive south from New Plymouth on Highway 3 to Stratford and turn west. The park preserves Egmont's mountaintop and its densely wooded slopes. Climbers and hikers come here in summer, skiers enjoy its slopes in winter. Information on the park is available at the Public Relations Office in New Plymouth or at the Dawson Falls information center.

Mountain guest houses offer simple but cozy family-style accommodations for visitors who desire a brief break from urban activities. Dawson Falls Tourist Lodge perches on the south slope near the start of several bush walks. Stratford Mountain House occupies a site on the east slope near the main ski fields.

Often shrouded by clouds, Egmont's tranquil appearance masks a dormant volcano that last erupted in the early 17th century. Great variations in altitude (from sea level to 2,518 meters/8,260 feet) and rainfall (60 to 300 inches annually), coupled with the mountain's isolation from other high peaks have given it an unusually varied flora, including a number of plants unique to Egmont.

In good weather, the day climb to the summit is not difficult, but weather conditions can change rapidly. You can join a guided excursion. On clear days, hikers gaze inland to the peaks of Tongariro National Park and over undulating dairylands to the sea.

Motorists can make a "round the mountain" day's drive to enjoy contrasting views of mountain, forest, sea, and farmland.

Friendly Wanganui

From Taranaki, Highway 3 cuts southeast through a belt of coastal farmlands to Wanganui, nestled in a broad curve along the west bank of the Wanganui River. Victoria Avenue is the city's main thoroughfare. Attractive parks, a well-planned central district, an outstanding regional museum, and hospitable residents make Wanganui an inviting town for visitors. Boat trips depart up the river.

Among the city's leading hotels and motels are Vacation Hotel (Wanganui) and Bryvern Motor Inn, both along Victoria Avenue north of the business district; and Grand International Hotel, in the center of town.

For information about city attractions, boat trips, walking tours, and other activities, stop in at the visitors' information center (Hospitality Wanganui Inc.) beside the City Council Chambers, St. Hill and Guyton streets.

Wanganui's hospitality program for overseas visitors (see page 37) is one of the best in the country. Inquire at the visitors' center if you'd like to have a resident show you around the city. "Home hosting" can include dinner or an overnight stay. You also can arrange to visit a nearby sheep or dairy farm.

Civic Centre. Wanganui's cultural center is attractive Queen's Park, a block east of Victoria Avenue at the top of Maria Place. It occupies the site of an early stockade. Here you'll find the museum, art gallery, memorial hall, and public library.

A block west of the main street bordering St. Hill Street is Cooks Gardens, the city's sports center.

Wanganui Regional Museum. A Maori-style entry invites visitors to view the museum's outstanding Maori collection, encased around a long war

Open-air museum in Tauranga (see page 64) features early buildings transplanted from various Bay of Plenty towns. Museum also contains replica Maori pa, sawmill and gold mining settlements.

canoe once paddled by Maori tribesmen on the Wanganui River. Especially notable are the greenstone exhibit, ancient tools and carvings, a smoked head, and Maori godsticks. You can also see attractively displayed natural history exhibits and a replica settler's cottage.

Located at Watt Street and Maria Place at the entrance to the park, the museum is open 9:30 to 4:30 weekdays, 1 to 5 weekends and holidays.

Sarjeant Art Gallery. Visitors enjoy changing exhibitions and displays from the gallery's permanent collection of 19th and early 20th century British and New Zealand paintings. The gallery's domed building is located in Queen's Park above the Veterans' Steps.

Virginia Lake. Wanganui's floral showplace and favorite picnic spot is serene and lovely Virginia Lake, surrounded by attractive residential areas north of the city on St. John's Hill. Highway 3 skirts the lake's south end.

You can walk around the large lake or through the woods, feed the waterfowl, or enjoy flower displays in the Winter Gardens. At night, colored lights illuminate the lake fountain.

St. Paul's Memorial Church. Completed in 1937, the Anglican church at Putiki is an outstanding example of Maori craftsmanship. Magnificent carvings, *tukutuku* panels, and painted rafters decorate the entire interior. To reach the church, located southeast of the river near the Putiki *pa*, cross the Wanganui River on the Cobham Bridge (Highway 3). Turn left at the first street (Wikitoria Road) and left again on Anaua Street.

Durie Hill Lookout. For a splendid view of the city, river, coast, and distant peaks, cross the river on the City Bridge, at the end of Victoria Avenue, and go to the top of Durie Hill. Motorists drive up Portal Street to reach the summit.

From Anzac Parade at the bridge, pedestrians walk through a tunnel to the hill elevator, a commuter service for hilltop residents. For the best views, climb the spiral stair to the top of the elevator building, or ascend the nearby Durie Hill Memorial Tower, a city landmark.

Kowhai Park. An imaginative children's playground and picnic areas attract families to this riverside park along Anzac Parade by the Dublin Street Bridge.

Other activities. Wanganui supports a full-time professional theater, the Four Seasons, housed in a remodeled residence southeast of the river in Putiki.

You can swim in the sea at Castlecliff beach west of town or go bush walking at Bushy Park homestead and bush reserve at Kai-Iwi, northwest of Wanganui.

Up the Wanganui River

Excursions operate up the river from Wanganui, departing from the east bank off Anzac Parade, up-river from the Dublin Street Bridge. From Christmas to Easter, trips range from a 1¼-hour trip on the broad tidal river to an all-day excursion into the unspoiled bush-bordered gorge upstream from Pipiriki.

Maori canoes and flat-bottomed river steamers once plied this long, historic river which rises high on Mount Tongariro's northwest slope. The Wanganui's most scenic stretch is from Pipiriki upstream to Taumarunui, accessible only by canoe, jet boat, and trail. The river winds through perpendicular fern-draped valleys, tumbling over some 240 rapids as it passes caves and plunging waterfalls.

The Wanganui River Road closely follows the water north to Pipiriki, then turns east to meet Highway 4 at Raetihi, southeast of Tongariro National Park. Several of the riverside settlements began as mission stations. In season, 1-hour jet boat trips operate upriver from Pipiriki.

The Bay of Plenty

Gentle waves lap the golden sand beaches curving around the Bay of Plenty. The coastal towns of Tauranga, Mount Maunganui, and Whakatane are magnets for summer visitors who come here to relax on the beach, frolic in the surf, and go deep-sea fishing.

Citrus and subtropical fruits thrive in the balmy climate. Timber from Kaingaroa State Forest is processed into paper and wood products in the mill town of Kawarau at the foot of Mount Edgecumbe.

Accommodations are concentrated in Tauranga and Mount Maunganui, but you can also stay in Whakatane, Ohope Beach, and Opotiki at the eastern end of the bay. Leading hotels include the Willow Park Motor Hotel and Greerton Hotel in Tauranga; DB Mount Maunganui in Mount Maunganui; and Commercial Hotel in Whakatane. Numerous motels are located along beachfront roads and town thoroughfares.

Tourist information offices are located in Tauranga, Whakatane, and Opotiki.

N.Z. Railways Road Services and Midland Coachlines schedule daily bus service from Tauranga to Rotorua and Auckland. Scheduled Air New Zealand flights and aerial sightseeing excursions depart from the Tauranga airport on the Maunganui peninsula.

Tauranga—mission station to busy port

Sprawling along the shore of its harbor, Tauranga is a busy commercial center—serving local farmers and the regional forest products industry—as well as a busy summer resort. Across the water on the harbor's eastern shore is Mount Maunganui, a holiday town named for the peak rising above it.

Daytime ferry service operates between Tauranga's Coronation Pier, at the east end of Wharf Street, and Mount Maunganui's Salisbury Wharf.

You can arrange sightseeing and fishing excursions in both towns. The Tauranga tourist information office is located on The Strand, near Coronation Pier.

Missionaries established a mission station on the Te Papa peninsula in 1835, but the settlement did not begin to thrive until the 1860s when military troops arrived. On a short walk you can visit the mission house and walk around "The Camp", site of the military settlement on a cliff overlooking the harbor. An excellent new open-air museum is located south of town.

Visitors and residents picnic and swim in Memorial Park, a waterfront beach bordering Devonport Road. City sports facilities are located in Tauranga Domain, west of Cameron Road.

"The Elms." One of the country's oldest homes, the handsome old Te Papa mission house on Mission Street (now known as "The Elms") was built in 1847 by Rev. Alfred N. Brown. It has been occupied continuously by his descendants. The mission station was a peaceful oasis during the troubled days of 1864-65, when Maoris and Government troops battled at Gate Pa and Te Ranga.

The elegant house faces a large garden shaded by spreading trees, including a pair of Norfolk pines that marked the mission station gateway and guided early sailors into port. On the tour you'll visit a small one-room library, built by Brown to house his large collection of books and a piano imported from England. The replica chapel contains the old 1835 mission bell.

"The Camp." Robbins Park links two wooded knolls, sites of the old mission burying ground and military cemetery and the well-preserved earthworks of Monmouth Redoubt. Trees ring the old cemetery off Mirrielees Road, where lichen-encrusted tombstones and a monument recall the early years.

At the south end of Robbins Park, well-preserved earthworks outline the redoubt, which housed soldiers and sheltered European women and children during the warfare.

Tauranga District Museum. History comes alive at this new open-air museum on 17th Avenue West. Original and replica buildings typical of those used in early Bay of Plenty settlements have been erected here.

Museum areas include a small town (with shops, school, church, dwellings, jail, livery stable, and blacksmith); a farm, Maori *pa*; gold mining town; sawmill settlement; and specialized exhibits.

A century-old steam locomotive circles the grounds, and visitors can ride in vintage vehicles or horse-drawn wagons. On "live days" staff members dress in period costume.

Mount Maunganui's peak and beach

Across the harbor from Tauranga, Mount Maunganui's wooded peak rises 232 meters/761 feet above the bay. Allow about 1½ hours if you want to hike to the summit for a magnificent view along the coast.

A long, slim sandy peninsula connects "The Mount" to the mainland. The resort of Mount Maunganui clusters at the base of the peak; you can swim in a hot saltwater pool here.

Nearby off Marine Parade is Marineland, where marine animals cavort and perform several times daily.

A coastal road parallels the town's famous golden beach, which curves gently along the bay southeast to Papamoa Beach and beyond.

Day trips from Tauranga

Narrow-necked Tauranga Harbour, sheltered from the sea by Matakana Island, indents the coast northeast to Katikati. Pleasant tidal beaches border the harbor at Omokoroa and Pahoia. Several hot mineral springs have been developed along this coast.

On the wooded southern slope of the Coromandel Range, Waihi blossomed during the local gold rush; many of its buildings—and exhibits in the local museum—reflect that era. One of New Zealand's largest gold strikes was made here at the Martha Mine.

Highway 2 cuts inland toward Paeroa through the Karangahake Gorge, where mining settlements boomed—and subsequently vanished—in the late 19th century.

East of Tauranga Highway 2 veers inland to Te Puke, center of a thriving fruit-growing and dairying district. At the small coastal village of Maketu, a cairn near the mouth of the Kaituna River marks the traditional landing site of the Arawa canoe.

Two bay islands

From Tauranga and Mount Maunganui you can arrange excursions to Mayor Island, a big game fishing center, and to White Island, an active volcano.

Deep-sea fishing. Mayor Island lies about 35 km/22 miles off the coast in waters teeming with game fish. Peak season extends from late December to early May; fishermen compete in an annual contest. Charter fishing boats operate from Tauranga and Mount Maunganui.

Skin divers come here to view colorful marine life. The pohutukawa-bordered island has twin volcanic craters, each with its small lake. Hikers enjoy walks through the bush, where bird life abounds.

An active volcano. White Island rises about 50 km/30 miles offshore at the north end of Taupo-Rotorua volcanic zone, part of a volcanic chain that extends far into the Pacific.

Riddled with thermal activity, the volcanic island has boiling pools, steam and gas vents, and holes filled with sulphuric acid. Periodically the volcano erupts, spewing lava and ash over the island. Scenic flights operate from Tauranga, Whakatane, Rotorua, and Taupo.

Whakatane and the eastern bay

Located 100 km/62 miles southeast of Tauranga, the timber and farm town of Whakatane traces its beginnings back to the landing of the Mataatua canoe, one of the ancestral canoes that brought Maoris to New Zealand in the 14th century. The town has its own waterfall—behind the Commercial Hotel on Mataatua Street.

Inquire at the Public Relations Office on Commerce Street about big game fishing trips, a jet boat excursion, and scenic flights.

Ohope Beach. East of Whakatane, this attractive seaside settlement has a long ocean beach backed by pohutukawa trees. A slim peninsula shelters Ohiwa Harbour, where fishermen seek flounder and shellfish and water-skiers skim across the water. Skin divers cross the headland at the west end of the beach to Otarawairere Bay.

Jet boat river trip. Rangitaiki River jet boat trips depart above Lake Matahina dam, south of Whakatane, skimming upstream through the Waiohau Gorge to Aniwhenua Falls. The river links the Galatea Plains with the eastern Bay of Plenty.

On the exhilarating 1½-hour excursion, you'll pass farmland and forest, and skip over whitewater rapids. Willows overhang the river's lower stretches. Farther upstream, ferns drape the banks, and tributary waterfalls plunge into the river.

Opotiki. Once a large Maori settlement, Opotiki is a coastal farm town known for its martyr's church and as the starting point for the trip around East Cape. Hukutaia Domain southwest of town offers pleasant bush walks in unspoiled forest.

Around the East Cape

Cut off by wooded mountains from the rest of North Island, sparsely-populated East Cape clings to the leisurely pace of an earlier era. Crimson-flowering pohutukawa trees border the cape's curving bays and deserted, log-strewn beaches. Plan to break your drive with a picnic.

From Opotiki the coastal road (Highway 35) closely borders the Bay of Plenty northeast to Cape Runaway, then loops around past New Zealand's most easterly point and continues south, briefly touching the shore at Tokomaru and Tolaga bays before reaching Gisborne. The direct route, Highway 2, cuts across the base of the cape.

Captain Cook sailed along this shore in 1769, anchoring at Tolaga Bay to take on water and wood. In the 1830s whalers operated along this coast. The cape traditionally has had a sizable Maori population; excellent examples of Maori carving and art decoration are located in churches and meeting houses in Te Kaha, Hicks Bay, Tikitiki, and Ruatoria.

You'll pass Te Kaha, set in an attractive cove, and Hicks Bay, a popular campground. Te Araroa is New Zealand's most easterly village. Hot mineral springs are located at Te Puia. Attractive Tolaga Bay offers good swimming and fishing.

The east coast road

Highway 2 follows the eastern coast from Poverty Bay, site of Captain Cook's first landing in 1769, to Napier and Hastings in the fruit, vineyard, and vegetable-growing area of Hawkes Bay. It continues south through Wairarapa sheep farms to Wellington.

Two mountain highways cut inland to central tourist areas. From Wairoa, Highway 38 heads northwest through Urewera National Park and Kaingaroa State Forest to Rotorua. Highway 5 follows a historic Maori track and stagecoach route northwest from Napier to Lake Taupo.

Regular coach service links the larger east coast towns with Auckland, Rotorua, and Wellington. The Endeavour express train operates daily between Napier and Wellington.

Captain Cook's landing site

Bordering the shore of Poverty Bay, prosperous Gisborne belies the name bestowed by Captain Cook. His party came ashore at Kaiti Beach, near the mouth of the Turanganui River, on October 9, 1769, the first Europeans to land on New Zealand soil. A monument on Kaiti Beach Road marks Cook's landing site.

From a lookout atop Kaiti Hill you have a splendid view over the city, harbor, and surrounding river valleys. Across the bay are the white cliffs of Young Nick's Head, named for Nicholas Young, the 12-year-old surgeon's apprentice on the *Endeavour* who first sighted land. Nearby is Cook Memorial Observatory.

Information on local attractions may be obtained at the Public Relations Office, 209 Grey Street. The town's museum and art gallery are located in Kelvin Park. The Botanical Gardens border the Taruheru River.

In summer families enjoy Waikanae Beach, near the center of town at the end of Grey Street. Good swimming beaches extend north of Gisborne from Wainui to Whangara.

Gisborne accommodations include the Sandown Park Motor Hotel, DB Gisborne Hotel, Teal Motor Lodge, and Blue Pacific Beachfront Motel.

Urewera National Park

Dense virgin forests cover the rugged Urewera ranges southeast of Rotorua. Highway 38 follows an old Maori route, winding through mountains and valleys to remote Urewera National Park and its sparkling gem, Lake Waikaremoana. The mountain route meets the east coast highway at Wairoa, southwest of Gisborne.

You can enjoy the park's bush and lake scenery from the highway, but if possible, allow time for a short stroll through the bush. Many trails begin near park headquarters at Aniwaniwa, where visitors obtain trail and other park information, fishing licenses, and shooting permits. Trail huts are maintained for hikers and hunters. In summer, rangers conduct field trips and nature programs.

Walks vary from a few minutes' stroll to nearby waterfalls to a 5-day tramp around the lake. Near park headquarters, short easy tracks lead to lovely Bridal Veil and Aniwaniwa falls and to Papakorito Falls. A half-day excursion goes through beech forest and ferny glades to Lake Waikareiti.

Many trout fishermen cast near Mokau Landing, a river inlet on Waikaremoana's north shore. Picnickers enjoy Rosie Bay south of park headquarters. Water sports enthusiasts come here for swimming, boating, and water-skiing. Hunters range the dense bush for deer and wild pig. Naturalists enjoy the park's varied flora and abundant bird life.

Napier, busy seaside resort

One of North Island's prettiest towns, Napier aims to create the activity-filled atmosphere of a British coastal resort. Along its shingle beach runs a long esplanade bordered with tall Norfolk pines and a varied array of recreation facilities.

White houses spread down the slope of Bluff Hill above the blue waters of Hawke Bay. Most of Napier's buildings were rebuilt after a 1931 earthquake and fire ruined the town.

Stop at the Napier Development Association office on Marine Parade at Tennyson Street for information about current activities and a street map outlining the city's scenic drive. Hastings and Emerson are Napier's main shopping streets.

Centrally located accommodations include Napier Travelodge, Tennyson Motor Inn, and the older Masonic Establishment Hotel. Modern motels cluster along Kennedy Road in the suburb of Pirimai and along Highway 2 north of town.

Marine Parade. Most of Napier's attractions face this pine-bordered oceanfront avenue. Thousands of tiny sparkling lights festoon the trees during the New Year holidays.

At the south end of the Parade is the handsome new Hawkes Bay Aquarium, containing an 86,000-gallon saltwater oceanarium; a wave-action tank and tidal pool; New Zealand fish in a freshwater stream; and display tanks containing local marine life and imported freshwater tropical fish. On the top floor you can see native tuatara lizards.

Trained marine animals—dolphins, leopard seals, penguins, and sea lions—perform daily at Marineland of New Zealand.

You can see New Zealand's famous native bird at the Kiwi House at 11:15 A.M. daily except Monday during holiday periods, twice weekly the rest of the year.

Other seaside attractions include the Sunken Gardens, built on rubble from the 1931 earthquake; a boating lake; outdoor roller skating rink; putt-putt golf; outdoor saltwater pool (open summer only); floral clock; and children's play areas. The Pania statue is located near the night-lighted fountain.

On alternate summer Saturdays, craftsmen set up open-air stalls near the band shell.

Bluff Hill. For viewpoints over Hawke Bay, follow the city's scenic drive to a pair of overlooks atop Bluff Hill. At the top of Lighthouse Road you look down on the harbor, where cranes load cargo onto freighters bound for overseas ports.

A streetside platform beside Clyde Road offers a rooftop view over the town and tree-lined waterfront south to Cape Kidnappers.

Lilliput Village and Railway. Around the corner from the tourist office on Marine Parade, miniature trains circle a model village populated by tiny animated figures engaged in daily chores and play.

Other attractions. The Hawkes Bay Museum and Art Gallery on Herschell Street features exhibits on the 1931 earthquake, Maori displays dating from the moa hunter era, historic articles of the region, and changing art exhibitions.

Napier's Botanical Gardens spill down the slopes of Hospital Hill. Trees give way to formal gardens, an aviary, and an outdoor amphitheater where open-air concerts are staged.

Small boats anchor in the Iron Pot, an Ahuriri district inlet named by early whalers. Acres of lowlands, upthrust here during the earthquake, have been reclaimed. The scenic drive continues along the waterfront past the new port.

Flower lovers enjoy rose gardens in Kennedy Park. Up to 70,000 orchid plants bloom under glass from August to mid-December at South Pacific Orchids, a commercial growing and exporting nursery southwest of town on Oak Road.

You can see sheep skins converted to fluffy rugs during weekday morning tours at the Classic Decor Ltd. tannery on Thames Street.

Safari trip to a gannet colony

Getting there is half the fun when you take the Gannet Safari trip southeast from Napier to visit the mainland bird colony at the tip of Cape Kidnappers. Usually birds breed on isolated islands.

The large seabirds, white with a golden crown and black-tipped feathers, congregate here in late July. Chicks hatch in late November and December. The best period to visit is early November to late February, when migration begins.

The 4-wheel-drive Safari Wagon leaves Napier on weekends from Labour Weekend in October to Christmas, then twice daily to mid-March. Beyond Clifton, your route follows a rocky riverbed, crosses a sheep station, and climbs steep hills on the roadless cape. You also can reach the colony by a beach route at low tide.

Sampling Hawkes Bay wines

Vineyards thrive in the sunny Mediterranean climate of Hawkes Bay, second largest of the country's wine-producing areas. Several wineries welcome visitors Monday through Saturday for informal sampling; two offer afternoon tours.

Sheltered *by a pair of Norfolk pines, tiny Jesus Christ Anglican Church overlooks the reef at Raukokore, on the East Cape Road between Te Kaha and Waihau Bay. A picket fence surrounds the burial ground.*

After a mission station was established here in 1851, the French missionaries planted vineyards and soon began producing wine for church and table use. About 1,400 acres of vineyards now cover the sunny slopes and plains around Napier, Hastings, and Havelock North.

The country's oldest established operation is the Mission Vineyard at Greenmeadows, where you can sample wines and tour the cellars at 3 P.M. Other Napier vineyards that invite visitors are Glenvale Wines, north of town in Bay View; and Brookfields Wines, south on Brookfields Road in Meeanee. In Hastings you can combine tasting and touring at Seppelt Vidal Ltd. (Villa Maria), 906 Avenue Road East; a 1-hour tour begins at 3:15 P.M. You can also visit Lombardi Wines Ltd., on Te Mata Road north of Havelock North.

The Winecraft shop in the Marewa Shopping Centre, on Kennedy Road in Napier, invites shoppers to sample New Zealand wines while browsing through articles made by numerous potters of the Hawkes Bay area.

Fruit orchards surround Hastings

Orchards and market gardens surround Hastings, a city of parks and gardens on the Heretaunga Plains. Often called the Fruit Bowl of New Zealand, it is renowned for its productive orchards—apples, peaches, pears, plums, nectarines, and other fruits —which bloom handsomely in September and October.

Food processing factories can and freeze most of the locally-grown vegetables, though farmers sell produce direct to the public at roadside stalls.

Hastings' tourist information office faces Russell Street North a half block from the post office. Ask for a scenic drive folder routing motorists to the area's highlights.

Hawkes Bay accommodations include the Angus Inn, Mayfair Hotel, and Elmore Lodge Motel, all in Hastings; and the DB Te Mata Hotel in Havelock North.

Parks. Hastings' best known landmark is Fantasyland, a community playground in Windsor Park east of the business district. Built around a fanciful castle, the imaginative play equipment depicts children's storybook characters. Visitors can ride a train around the playground or hire a boat to paddle on the lake. Families camp near a tree-shaded stream in the adjacent campground.

You can stroll through Cornwall Park's formal gardens and see birds in its aviary, or picnic beneath rare trees in Frimley Park. Drive through a mile-long tunnel of oak trees on Oak Avenue, northwest of the city off Omahu Road.

Havelock North. Southeast of Hastings, this choice residential area spreads along hilly slopes.

For the finest view of the Hawkes Bay district, follow Te Mata Peak Road 6 km/4 miles up to the mountain's summit. Your view extends over the region's orchards, gardens, vineyards, rivers, towns, and coast. Trails wind through the woods.

Getting acquainted with New Zealand wines

One of the nicest ways to learn about New Zealand's wines is to go wine touring, sampling a winemaker's specialties right at the winery. Spontaneity is part of the fun at small family-owned wineries, where the winemaker himself may show you through the cellars. Take along a picnic lunch, and enjoy it with a bottle of wine from one of the places you visit.

Missionaries planted vineyards bordering the Bay of Islands before 1820, and mission vintners began producing sacramental wines in the Hawkes Bay district in the mid-19th century. Later, European immigrants made wines for their own consumption. But, the New Zealand wine industry's rapid growth and increasing sophistication has come within the past 30 years.

The heart of the table wine industry lies north of Auckland in the Henderson Valley and nearby Kumeu, where you'll find most of the major producers and some of the most attractive vineyards. The other main winemaking area is Hawkes Bay. Table wines are also produced near Thames and Gisborne on North Island, and in the Wairau Valley near Blenheim on South Island.

Local tourist offices can provide maps and direct you to wineries that welcome visitors. You can visit operations ranging from small family-owned wineries to automated commercial ventures. Vineyards are busiest from February through April, when the grapes are picked and pressed. Wineries are usually open to visitors Monday through Saturday.

Through the Wairarapa farmlands

South of Hawke Bay, Highway 2 veers inland, cutting southwest through rolling pasturelands and small farm towns toward Wellington. In the 1870s Scandinavian settlers carved Norsewood, Dannevirke, and Eketahuna out of the vast totara forest then covering the region.

At Woodville, Highway 3 heads west through the magnificent Manawatu Gorge to Palmerston North and the fertile valleys bordering the Tasman coast. Pahiatua marks the northern end of the rugged Tararua Range.

Rare native birds breed in captivity at Mount Bruce Native Bird Reserve. Visitors can see the takahe, kakapo, kiwi, pukeko, and other birds on weekends (except during the October to mid-December breeding season) and during the summer holidays.

Heart of the Wairarapa farming district is Masterton, about 100 km/62 miles north of Wellington. The highway continues south through rolling dairy and sheep-fattening farms and market gardens to Carterton, Greytown, and Featherston. Roads lead west from the highway to the edge to Tararua Forest Park.

Wellington

Wooded hills curve like a green amphitheater around Wellington's sparkling harbor, giving New Zealand's capital city its character and charm. From atop Mount Victoria and other lofty viewpoints, your gaze sweeps over a magnificent vista of ever-changing moods.

Located at the southwestern tip of North Island, Wellington is the country's second largest city, its metropolitan population exceeding 350,000. Forested peninsulas and port wharves jut into the harbor. In the heart of the city, commercial and government buildings rise along a narrow shelf rimming the waterfront. The winding thoroughfares of Lambton and Thorndon quays mark the city's original shoreline. Nostalgic Victorian buildings mingle pleasantly with more modern structures. Above the business district, dwellings cling precariously to the steep slopes.

Wellington was the first settlement organized by the London-based New Zealand Company. Early shiploads of settlers sailed into the sheltered waters of Port Nicholson in 1840. In 1865, the seat of government was transferred from Auckland to Wellington, setting the permanent character of the young town.

Many of Wellington's residents staff the government offices or work in the "home office" headquarters of the country's major banks and commercial organizations. Foreign embassies and the diplomatic corps add a cosmopolitan element. The city's easy pace makes sightseeing a leisurely affair.

Wellington's marine climate is generally free from extremes of heat and cold. Bracing winds funnel through Cook Strait, clearing the air and adding zest to daily life. A nearby geologic fault subjects the city to occasional earth tremors.

Arriving in Wellington

Wellington Airport, about 8 km/5 miles southeast of the city at Rongotai, handles Air New Zealand service to main towns on North and South Islands plus trans-Tasman traffic from Australian cities.

Interisland ferries link Wellington with Picton on South Island. Departing several times daily from the Aotea Quay terminal, they carry rail cars and automobiles as well as passengers and cargo. Cruise liners moor at the Overseas Passenger Terminal during Wellington stopovers.

Wellington Railway Station on Waterloo Quay is the southern terminus for North Island rail service. A block away on Stout Street, the buses of N.Z. Railways Road Services arrive from Auckland (via Rotorua, Wairakei, and Taupo), Wanganui, and New Plymouth. Newmans Coach Lines and Mount Cook Landlines also serve the capital.

Local transport. You'll find taxi ranks at the terminals and on Lambton Quay, between Grey and Hunter streets.

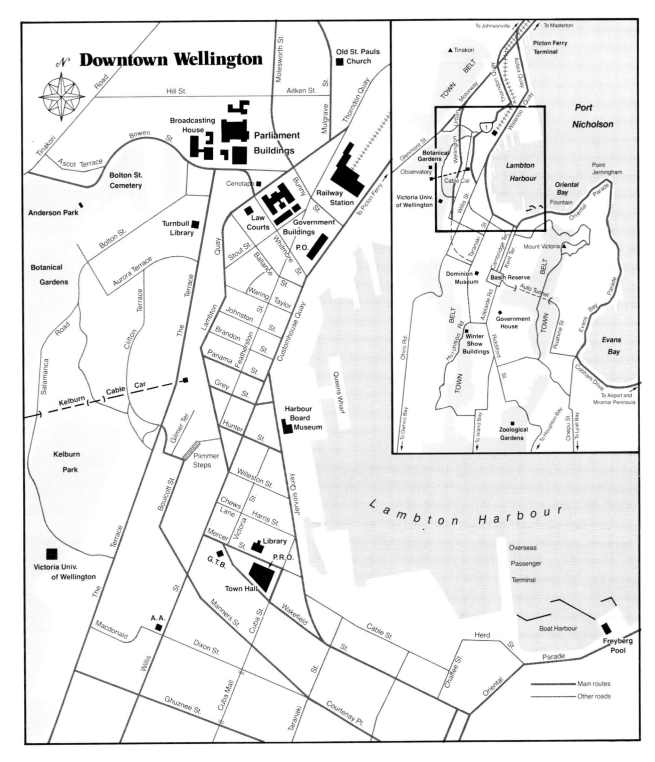

Downtown Wellington

Trolley and diesel buses of the Wellington City Transport Department fan out to the city's residential areas. Most bus lines begin at the railway station or on Courtenay Place and run along Lambton Quay at some point. Cash fares are paid by sections, depending on distance traveled. A city sightseeing excursion departs daily at 2 P.M. from Mercer Street, opposite the Town Hall.

Electrified suburban trains depart from the railway station for Hutt Valley towns and west coast settlements as far north as Paekakariki.

Tourist information. For ideas on how to enjoy Wellington, stop in at the Public Relations Office in the Town Hall, Mercer and Cuba streets. You might ask for leaflets on walking tours and scenic drives, for many inviting trails wind through the wooded hills of the Town Belt, and the city has three scenic routes—in the north, west, and southeast districts of the city.

Travel accommodations and arrangements throughout the country are handled at the Government Tourist Bureau, a block away from the P.R.O. at 26-31 Mercer Street. Automobile club members can obtain motoring information and maps at the Automobile Association office at Willis and Dixon streets.

Hotels and motels in the capital

Largest of Wellington's downtown hotels is the James Cook Hotel, towering above the business district from its hillside site on The Terrace.

Other modern, centrally located hotels include the comfortable Abel Tasman at Willis and Dixon streets; and the Town House Motor Inn, Wellington Travelodge, and new Parkroyal, all on Oriental Parade near the Overseas Passenger Terminal. Older hotels, all within walking distance of Lambton Quay, include the St. George, De Brett, and Waterloo.

Visitors who prefer to stay outside the central district enjoy the Sharella Motor Inn, about a mile from the city center near the entrance to the Botanic Gardens; and the Shaw Savill Lodge, about a mile from the airport.

Dine elegantly or informally

Wellington's restaurants offer a choice of elegant or informal surroundings. Reservations are recommended, especially on weekends.

French specialties are featured at Pierre's, 342 Tinakori Road; Orsini's, 201 Cuba Street; Toad Hall, 115 Dixon Street; and The Coachman, 46 Courtenay Place. Other centrally located restaurants include Plimmer House, 99 Boulcott Street (1873 dwelling, European cuisine); Le Normandie, 116 Cuba Street (game specialties); and Bacchus, 8 Courtenay Place (international dishes).

If you enjoy an informal atmosphere, consider The Woolshed, Plimmer Steps off Boulcott Street (rural decor, steaks and grills); Wellington Settlement Trading Co., 155 Willis Street (casual); the 1860 Victualing Co., Lambton Quay (colonial decor); Packing Case, 191 Featherston Street (New Zealand specialties); and Flanagan's, Kent Terrace near the Overseas Passenger Terminal (oysters).

Shopping in Wellington

Heart of Wellington's shopping district is Lambton Quay, curving through the center of town. Shops, boutiques, and department stores flank a mile-long thoroughfare extending south along Willis and

For a splendid view *of Wellington, its harbor, and the port's encircling hills, ride the Kelburn cable car from Lambton Quay to the Kelburn summit. Sleek new enclosed cars recently replaced the open cars.*

Manners streets to Courtenay Place. Another lively shopping district is the Cuba Mall.

Downtown stores are generally open weekdays from 9 to 5:30, Fridays until 9.

The city's main department stores are Direct Importing Company Ltd. (D.I.C.) and Kirkcaldie & Stains, both on Lambton Quay; and James Smith Ltd., at Cuba and Manners streets. Plimmer's Emporium on Plimmer's Steps contains an interesting complex of small shops.

Tourists find a representative selection of New Zealand souvenirs at Rehabilitation League shops at 29 Willis Street and at the Overseas Terminal. A duty-free shop is located at 56 Willis Street with a branch at the airport.

Stamp collectors can obtain New Zealand postage stamps at the Post Office Philatelic Bureau, 66A Courtenay Place, and coin collectors purchase souvenir coins on the ground floor of The Treasury, State Fire Building, on Lambton Quay and Stout Street.

You'll find local handcrafted goods at the Victoria Market, 188 Willis Street, open Fridays from 9 A.M. to 8 P.M., Saturdays from 10 to 3.

Entertainment and sports activities

Most after-dark entertainment in Wellington centers on the city's hotels and taverns. You can go dancing or enjoy musical acts varying from folk singers to jazz to Bavarian beer hall bands. Check the monthly *In Wellington* booklet, the *Capital Visitor*, or daily newspapers to find out what's available.

New Zealand and overseas artists perform at the Town Hall, and in January and February the N. Z. Symphony Orchestra plays promenade concerts. Plays are presented by the Downstage Theatre repertory group and by Wellington Repertory Theatre. In summer, musical groups perform in the Botanic Gardens sound shell.

Horse racing fans head north of the city for Trentham Race Track in the Hutt Valley; trotting events take place at Hutt Park in Petone. Rugby Union games are held at Athletic Park, Rugby League at Rugby League Park, soccer and cricket matches at Basin Reserve. Championship tennis matches are held at Central Park, and you can watch bowls and croquet at Kelburn Park. Golfers find several fine courses in and near the city; the seaside links at Paraparaumu, a 45-minute drive north of the city, rank among the country's top courses.

Oriental Bay's boat harbor is the center of yachting activities; in summer you often see yachting and rowing races on the harbor. Swimmers can choose salt or fresh water, beach or pool, surf or calm harbor waters. No matter what the weather, swimmers enjoy Freyberg Pool off Oriental Parade. Near the city's heart, the beach fronting Oriental Bay becomes crowded on summer days. Surf swimmers take bus number 1 to Island Bay or bus number 3 to Lyall Bay, Seatoun, and other Miramar Peninsula destinations.

Gaze down from Mount Victoria

To savor the sight of Wellington, make your way to the top of Mount Victoria. Below you, the city and its hills encircle the sparkling harbor.

Along the base of the northern hills, the Hutt road links the Hutt Valley with Wellington's commercial heart. Rising behind the eastern bays is the Rimutaka Range. To the south you look across the harbor and Cook Strait toward South Island. Near the viewpoint, a memorial honors American polar explorer Rear Admiral Richard Byrd.

Other favorite Wellington viewpoints are from atop the Kelburn heights and from the Massey Memorial on Marine Drive.

Getting acquainted with Wellington

Despite its steep hills, you can explore much of Wellington on foot. Stairways and footpaths climb the slopes. Buses and a hillside cable car take you to viewpoints and suburban destinations.

Along the waterfront. As you walk along Wellington's waterfront, you'll often see ships docking at downtown wharves and Cook Strait ferries steaming across the harbor. From the Wellington Boat Harbour, look up at the pastel wooden houses climbing the hills above Oriental Bay.

At Queens Wharf on Jervois Quay, stop at the Maritime Museum in the fine old Wellington Harbour Board building. Here you'll see models and relics of ships that have sailed these waters, and paintings, photographs, charts, and other articles of port history. The museum is open weekdays from 10 to 4, Saturdays from 2 to 5.

One of the last of the wood-hulled coastal freighters has been refitted as a cruise vessel. On weekends and holidays the *Te Aroha* departs from Inter Island Wharf on summer harbor cruises.

The commercial center. Shops and businesses line Lambton Quay, curving along the line of the city's original waterfront. Reclamation has added land for commercial expansion along the shore.

Higher up on the hills, office and apartment towers indicate a building boom along The Terrace. Many of the city's older wood dwellings have fallen victim to the new motorway that cuts a broad swath along the northern foothills.

Several routes link Lambton Quay and the upper level commercial and residential areas along The Terrace. You can walk up the Plimmer Steps, a pedestrian stairway flanked by shops and restaurants, ascending near the south end of Lambton Quay (near Hunter Street) to Boulcott Street. Near the James Cook Hotel, an elevator descends to Lambton Quay.

Kelburn cable car. The quickest and cheapest route to a panoramic view of Wellington harbor is aboard bright red cable cars which climb from Lambton Quay to the Kelburn heights. Sleek new enclosed cars recently replaced the historic vehicles which have transported government workers, businessmen, shoppers, and students since 1902.

You'll find the lower terminal on Kelburn Avenue (Cable Car Lane), off Lambton Quay opposite Grey Street. In 3½ minutes the electrically operated cars ascend 122 meters/400 feet above city traffic to the upper terminal at Kelburn. A companion car descends as yours climbs.

For a look at the campus of Victoria University of Wellington, get off the cable car at Salamanca Road and walk down past the school. From the upper terminal, you can walk down through the Botanical Gardens to return to Lambton Quay.

A stroll through Government Centre

The part of Wellington that belongs to all New Zealanders is the country's political center, located on a knoll near the north end of Lambton Quay, above its intersection with Bowen and Molesworth streets. Visitors can join guided tours of the Parliament Buildings and Broadcasting House. If Parliament is in session (usually from May through October), you can observe the proceedings from a seat in the visitors' gallery.

Parliament Buildings. The dignified Parliament House, built in 1922, contrasts with the distinctive domed "Beehive" of the new executive wing— opened by Queen Elizabeth in 1977—and the lighter Gothic architecture of the 1897 General Assembly Library. New Zealand materials, especially Takaka marble and native woods, have been used liberally in their construction.

The buildings are not open to casual sightseers, but you can arrange to join a guided tour. For tour information and booking, telephone 738-288 ext. 538.

Parliamentary procedures, modeled after those of Britain's Parliament, are explained during the tour.

Other buildings. Behind the Parliament Buildings at Museum and Bowen streets is Broadcasting House, Wellington's center of the Broadcasting Corporation of New Zealand. For a studio tour, inquire at the reception desk. Tours depart at 10:15 and 2 on weekdays, at 2 on Saturdays, Sundays, and holidays.

Facing Lambton Quay opposite the Cenotaph are the Government Buildings, a marvelous example of Wellington's early architecture. The 152-room wooden building, built in 1876 on reclaimed land, translates traditional 19th century stone architecture into timbered Italianate style.

Open on weekdays, the buildings of the Law Courts on Ballance Street contain three levels of New Zealand's law hierarchy—Magistrate's Court, Supreme Court, and the Court of Appeals.

Reminders of an earlier era

In older parts of the city, Victorian dwellings and other historic buildings add nostalgic contrast to more modern structures. Gabled houses climb the hills, their brass doorknockers and tall bay windows adding touches of 19th century elegance.

Old St. Paul's Church. Just a short walk from the Parliament Buildings, Wellington's historic old Anglican church is a Mulgrave Street landmark. Built in 1866, it adapted traditional Victorian Gothic architecture to colonial conditions. It is renowned for its timber construction, simplified style, and human scale. Inside, stained glass windows and brass plates provide a valuable century-long record of its parishioners.

Supplanted by a new cathedral in 1966, the church has been preserved and restored as a tranquil setting for musical and dramatic events. You can visit Monday through Saturday from 11 to 5:30, Sundays from 2:30 to 5:30.

Early houses. Among former dwellings still in use are Plimmer House, an 1870s gem on Boulcott Street, now a fashionable restaurant; and the stately, turreted Williams residence at 53 Hobson Street, incorporated into Queen Margaret College.

Ascot Terrace, off Tinakori Road near the top of Bowen Street, is a delightful pocket preserving the charm of a bygone era. Other fine old buildings are located along Tinakori Road and its side streets.

Enjoying the Botanical Gardens

From the upper cable car terminal, it's a pleasant downhill walk through the Botanical Gardens, a 62-acre reserve extending down to Glenmore Street.

Tropical flowering plants and ferns are on view daily from 10 to 4 in the Begonia House. In season, Wellingtonians enjoy the formal Lady Norwood Rose Gardens and the early October display of blooming tulips. Band concerts are presented in the sound shell on Sundays and summer evenings. Just outside the Rose Gardens on Glenmore Street, you can board a number 12 bus back downtown.

To learn more about the southern skies, attend a Tuesday evening public lecture at Carter Observatory on Upland Road, near the top of the gardens.

New Zealand's national museum

Overlooking Wellington Harbour, the Dominion Museum features exhibits on the natural history and culture of the peoples of New Zealand and the nearby Pacific islands. To reach the museum on Buckle Street, take bus number 1 or 3 from the railway station to Basin Reserve and walk 2 blocks west. Museum hours are 10 to 4:45 daily.

The museum's fascinating Maori collection concentrates on articles from Taranaki and the central districts. Highlight of the colonial history section is an early Wellington dwelling furnished in 1840s style. Relics obtained during Captain Cook's voyages are also on display.

In the National Art Gallery are works of 19th and 20th century New Zealand artists and special exhibitions.

The imposing tower in front of the museum contains a carillon and the Hall of Memories, the national war memorial.

Other places to visit

Depending on your interests, you may wish to visit some of the following places:

Alexander Turnbull Library. Visitors as well as scholars come here to see the original signed parchment sheets of the Treaty of Waitangi, as well as changing displays from the library's fascinating collections. The Turnbull Library is renowned for its valuable works dealing with Pacific exploration and New Zealand history. Located at 44 The Terrace, it is open weekdays and Saturday mornings.

Katherine Mansfield Memorial. A shaded garden on Fitzherbert Street, off Hobson Street just east of the motorway, honors the famous New Zealand-born writer of short stories (real name: Kathleen Beauchamp). Many of her best-known stories have a Wellington setting.

Newtown Park Zoo. Located about 4 km/2½ miles south of the city center, Wellington's zoo is open daily from 8:30 to 4:30. To reach the zoo, take bus number 11 from the city railway station.

You can visit the kiwi house daily from 10 to 4. Leopards and tigers are fed in midafternoon. On Saturday and holiday afternoons, ride a miniature train around the edge of the zoo's waterfowl pond.

Native plant garden. New Zealand's largest and most complete collection of native flora has been assembled at the Otari Museum of Native Plants in the northwest suburb of Wilton. To reach the garden, located off Wilton Road, take bus number 14 from the city. Paths lead through formal areas and into a sheltered, wooded valley where visitors can picnic.

Harbor views along the Marine Drive

From the city center, a 39-km/24-mile drive follows the harbor shore to suburban beaches. The route skirts Oriental and Evans bays on the inner harbor, then loops around the Miramar Peninsula past a series of attractive bays. Along the way you'll pass moored pleasure boats, pleasant swimming beaches, and boating and surfing clubs.

City dwellers enjoy the popular beach fronting Oriental Bay, where they come to lunch, swim, and soak up the sun. On the northern tip of the Miramar Peninsula, the Massey Memorial offers a fine harbor viewpoint and picnic facilities. Along the peninsula's eastern shore, the beach road curves past a series of inviting beaches at Scorching, Karaka, and Worser bays. Outer harbor beaches at Lyall and Island bays attract hardy swimmers. Island Bay is the home of a small fishing fleet.

Excursions from Wellington

Regular sightseeing coach tours operate from Wellington to nearby destinations, and you can arrange scenic flights over the district.

If the day is pleasant and the seas are calm, you might enjoy the day-return ferry excursion across Cook Strait to Picton.

The Hutt Valley and beyond

Hemmed in between hills, Lower Hutt and Upper Hutt sprawl over alluvial plains along the Hutt River. The forests and market gardens that once covered this rich valley have given way to housing areas and manufacturing industries. Lower Hutt is a center of scientific and industrial research. Upper Hutt is the site of Trentham Racecourse.

North of Upper Hutt, the Akatarawa road branches northwest off Highway 2, winding through the wooded Akatarawa range to meet the coastal road at Waikanae. Motorists can make an all-day circuit from Wellington, returning to the capital along the coast.

Wellington trampers and hunters enjoy the rugged hills of Tararua Forest Park, an hour's drive north of the capital. Access routes to the vast reserve are signposted off the main highways. Many trails wind through the bush and along streams. Information on forest recreation is available from N.Z. Forest Service officials in Wellington and Masterton.

Eastbourne and the Eastern Bays

A pleasant excursion follows the harbor northeast through Petone to prime residential suburbs bordering the Eastern Bays. By bus, it's a 40-minute ride from the Wellington railway station to Eastbourne.

The road passes a series of sheltered beaches bordering Lowry, York, Mahina, and Days bays before reaching Eastbourne. Houses spill down the steep wooded slopes, and some hill dwellers have private cable cars to transport them between street and home. From Kowhai Street, a signposted trail winds over a hilly ridge (good harbor views) and down to the peaceful wooded valley of Butterfly Creek.

Golden Coast beaches

Coastal towns dot the Tasman shore from Plimmerton north to Otaki. From Wellington, Highway 1 parallels the western coast along the Tararua foothills, with side roads branching to the sea. Suburban trains link Wellington with the larger beach towns. Saturday shopping draws weekend visitors. Many Wellingtonians have built beach cottages or retirement homes along this coast.

A popular destination is Queen Elizabeth Park at Paekakariki. You'll find Wellington's Tramway Museum near the park's McKay's Crossing entrance; on weekends and holidays, cars that once clanged along Lambton Quay now clatter along the park's track.

If you're driving, take the Horokiri hill road from Paekakariki south to Pauatahanui for superb coastal views.

South Island

The Southern Alps tower above rain forest, sea, and glacial lakes

On the sparsely populated South Island, lofty mountains flanked by icy glaciers set the scenic tone. Subtropical rain forests, coastal fiords of awesome beauty, vast grazing lands, deep alpine lakes bordered by thick forest, windswept headlands, and sunny beaches add to the visual drama. The island proudly carries the imprint of the hardworking 19th century colonists, sheepmen, and prospectors who scouted and tamed this splendid and diverse land.

South Island's variety of natural scenery, climate, and vegetation is matched by seasonal changes more distinct than those in North Island. Springtime fruit blossoms give way to the ripe fields of summer. Colorful foliage brightens the autumn landscape. In winter, snow blankets much of the interior.

About 28 percent of New Zealand's 3.1 million people live on South Island. With a population of about 850,000, this entire island is barely larger in population than Auckland, the country's largest city. Most settlements border the east coast.

An island overview

Separated from its sister island by narrow Cook Strait, elongated South Island stretches southwest some 800 km/500 miles. For most of its length, a diagonal geologic fault divides the island, rising abruptly from the western coast to create the magnificent mountain chain called the Southern Alps.

Thousands of years ago massive glaciers covered much of the island. Grinding down the valleys, they sculpted the mountains, sheared rocky cliffs, carved deep grooves in the southwestern coast, and gouged out long, slim lakes.

Immigrants transformed the land

Captain James Cook circumnavigated the islands and mapped the coast in 1769-70; then sealers and whalers established shore stations in the early decades of the 19th century; finally European colonists began arriving in earnest during the 1840s, establishing settlements at Akaroa in 1840, Nelson in 1841, Dunedin in 1848, and Christchurch in 1850.

The English and Scottish colonists transformed the virgin landscape, plotting neat townsites and planting thousands of trees. They erected sturdy buildings to house their churches, schools, and governmental bodies; they reserved parklands for the enjoyment of succeeding generations.

While the Maori land wars raged across North Island, Australian sheepmen opened up South Island's hilly interior. Discoveries of gold in Central Otago in 1861 were followed shortly by rich new finds on the West Coast, accelerating the exploration and settlement of these remote regions. That pioneer spirit never quite died—a strong streak of hardy individualism persists.

Sparsely settled South Island is still the home of many proud descendants of pioneer stock, hospitable hard-working farm families who share the conviviality of country gatherings, as well as the problems of flood, drought, snow, stock losses, and isolation.

Lush forest and grassy plains

Luxuriant greenery descends to the blue Tasman Sea along the wet and wild western coast. Moisture-laden clouds drop more than 200 inches of rain annually as they sweep in from the sea and strike the steep, alpine barrier.

Along the northwest coast, the towns of Westport, Greymouth, and Hokitika were born during gold rush days. Farther south is Westland National Park, where Franz Josef and Fox glaciers descend steeply toward the sea, and the virtually untouched, fiord-indented southwest coast.

Interisland ferry steams out of Picton Harbour on the 3½-hour trip to Wellington. Daily ferry service transports passengers and vehicles across Cook Strait between the two islands.

On the drier east side of the mountains, a vast network of waterways drains the alpine snowfields, hilly grasslands, broad plains, and coastal valleys. More than half of the island's population is concentrated along the Pacific coast near Christchurch (metropolitan area population 326,000) and Dunedin (population 120,000) and in the smaller towns of Timaru and Oamaru.

Other sizable towns are Invercargill, on the south coast, and Nelson and Blenheim, near the island's northern tip. South Island's leading resort is Queenstown, hub of the southern lakes district.

Scenic highways follow historic routes

Modern highways follow the coastline and cut across the mountains to link the island's eastern and western settlements. Highway 1 borders the east coast from Picton to Bluff, passing through major cities and towns. Highway 6 cuts from Nelson through the Buller Gorge to Westport and down the western coast.

Centuries ago, Maoris seeking West Coast greenstone discovered riverside routes through the mountains. Today, scenic transalpine highways follow these traditional routes. The Lewis Pass Road (Highway 7) links Waipara and Greymouth. Arthur's Pass Road (Highway 73) winds through the high country from Christchurch to Kumara Junction, north of Hokitika. Highway 6 cuts across Haast Pass from Wanaka, providing a southern route to Westland National Park.

Other main highways thrust deeply into the provinces of Canterbury and Otago and cut through the valleys of Fiordland to Milford Sound.

South Island's highlights

Beyond the cities, travelers find attractions in rich variety. Seven national parks and a maritime park preserve outstanding scenic areas for public enjoyment. On the north coast are historic Abel Tasman National Park and the delightful waterways of Marlborough Sounds Maritime Park. Nelson Lakes National Park contains a pair of slender, beech-fringed glacial lakes.

Straddling the snowy crest of the Southern Alps are four national parks—Arthur's Pass, Mount Cook, Westland, and Mount Aspiring—attracting climbers, hikers, naturalists, and others who love the alpine country. Vast and varied Fiordland offers awesome mountains, dense forests, tranquil lakes, and majestic fiords.

Many travelers enjoy Queenstown and the southern lakes, Nelson's sunny beaches, unspoiled Stewart Island, and the sleepy old mining towns of Central Otago.

Activities include fishing for trout and salmon; visiting coal mines, historic museums, or bird sanctuaries; walking on a glacier or through fern-filled rain forest; staying overnight with a farm family; dining on local scallops, crayfish, oysters, or venison; and exploring the island's remote districts on foot or horseback or by jet boat, sightseeing plane, or four-wheel-drive vehicle.

Christchurch

Nestled at the base of the hilly Banks Peninsula, New Zealand's third largest city faces inland toward a broad panorama—the flat, Canterbury Plains backed by the snowy Southern Alps. South Island's largest city (population 300,000), Christchurch is the busy yet relaxed capital of the province of Canterbury; it is also the island's transportation hub.

Though known for its peaceful ambience and unhurried pace, Christchurch is a city that gets things done. It has one of the country's busiest

Exploring Christchurch by bicycle

You'll see Christchurch in fresh perspective if you explore the city by bicycle. Level streets, a compact central area, and the vast greensward of Hagley Park offer incentives for wheeling around the city. You'll have plenty of company —many students, office workers, shoppers, and business people pedal their way to work, school, and sports activities.

You can rent leisure bikes, 10-speed touring bikes, or tandems by the hour, day, or week. Two shops rent bikes: Rent-A-Bike, N.Z. Ltd., in the Avon Carpark Building, 82 Worcester Street; and Cycle Trading Company, 226 Manchester (at Armagh). A refundable deposit is required; damage and theft insurance is optional at additional charge. Ask for city and touring maps.

Many roads have cycling lanes. A favorite of cyclists is Hagley Park. Its many paved paths wind across the green parklands and along the Avon. Enjoy the fun and freedom of pedaling slowly and silently at your own pace, savoring the fresh air and scenery. You can explore the city easily in a few hours.

If country touring is your hobby, rent a 10-speed touring bike, equipped with carrier bags, and pedal off to the Banks Peninsula, Canterbury Plains, or other destinations. Local cyclists of the Christchurch Recreational Cycling Club plan frequent Sunday jaunts covering about 30 miles (usually leaving from Victoria Square at 10 A.M.).

Cyclists keep to the left of traffic, even on bicycle paths in the park. Bikes are not permitted on sidewalks or footpaths along the Avon River in the downtown area.

Use arm signals to indicate turns and stops. For left or right turns, extend your left or right arm parallel to the ground to show a turn in that direction. To indicate an impending stop, bend your right arm at a 90° angle, hand pointing up.

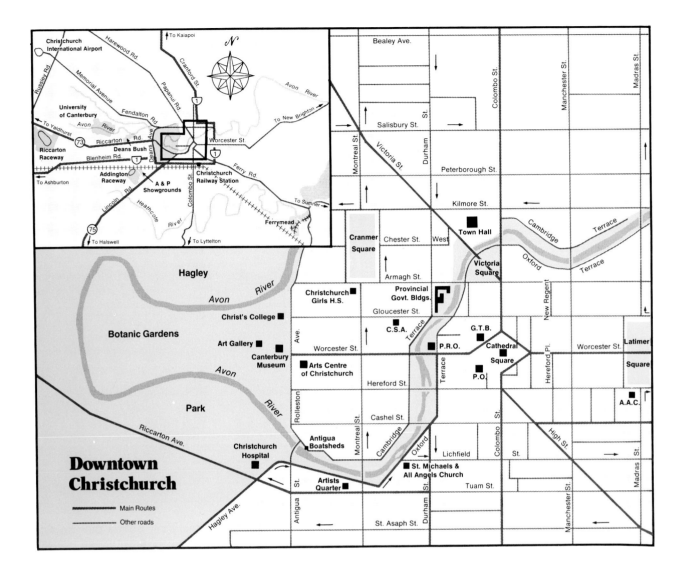

and most modern airports, a modern town hall, and an outstanding sports complex developed for the 1974 Commonwealth Games.

The Canterbury settlement was the last and most successful of the mid-19th century colonizing ventures. Four shiploads of hand-picked English colonists arrived at Lyttelton in 1850 and made a historic trek across the Port Hills to found Christchurch. Surveyors laid out the town in a grid pattern, its dignified order broken only by the serpentine course of the Avon River. Occupying a spacious square in the heart of the city is Christchurch Cathedral, a reminder of the important role the Church of England played in the settlement of Canterbury. Major arteries radiate from Cathedral Square.

Often called "New Zealand's most English city," Christchurch retains many features established by its Anglican settlers. Shaded by overhanging trees, the Avon meanders through the city, adding a gracious, old-world charm. Parks soften the city's rectangular layout, and home gardens blaze with color from spring to fall. Uniformed students wait

for bright red buses or cycle along city streets. Still in daily use are many stately Gothic buildings, constructed by early civic leaders to house the settlement's religious, educational, governmental, and cultural institutions.

Getting settled in Christchurch

You can arrive in Christchurch by air, rail, or road. Air passengers from North Island and Australian points disembark at Christchurch International Airport, only 11 km/7 miles northwest of Cathedral Square, and then fan out to various South Island destinations.

Travelers who have made the interisland ferry crossing from Wellington to Picton continue by rail to Christchurch. Trains depart from the Christchurch railway station on Moorhouse Avenue north to Blenheim and Picton, south to Dunedin and Invercargill, and west across the mountains to Greymouth.

Long distance buses of N.Z. Railways Road Services, Mount Cook Landlines, Newmans Coach

Gothic-style *cathedral, begun by Canterbury settlers in 1864, marks the heart of Christchurch. Red city buses depart from Cathedral Square.*

Lines, and Midland Coachlines provide scheduled service to all parts of the island. Cruise liners anchor at Lyttelton, south of Christchurch.

Hotels and motels. Christchurch has dozens of hotels and motels, both near the central business district and in the suburbs.

Major downtown hotels include high-rise Noah's Hotel and the older Clarendon Hotel (both overlooking the Avon a block from Cathedral Square); and the Vacation Hotel, facing Victoria Square. Smaller downtown hotels include the refurbished 1884 United Services Hotel, facing Cathedral Square, and Coker's Hotel on Manchester Street. Centrally located motor hotels include Avon Motor Lodge and Latimer Motor Lodge.

Accommodations near the airport include the Christchurch Travelodge, Commodore Motor Inn, and Hotel Russley. Among other major hotels are the Chateau Regency on Deans Avenue, Shirley Lodge Motor Hotel on Marshland Road, Canterbury Inn in Riccarton, and the DB Redwood Court Hotel on Main North Road.

Restaurants. You'll eat well in Christchurch. Restaurants range from those offering gracious continental dining and dancing to steak houses and cozy hideaways specializing in home-style cooking at moderate prices. At leading restaurants dinner reservations are advisable, especially on weekends.

In addition to hotel restaurants, here are some possibilities to consider: Allegro, 142 Lichfield Street (Italian regional specialties); Cascade Restaurant, Town Hall (overlooking Avon River, dancing); Charlie Brown Restaurant, 76 Lichfield Street (house specialties, dancing); Coachman, Gloucester Street (informal steak house, old English atmosphere upstairs).

Other favorites include the Coffee Pot Restaurant, 16–20 New Regent Street (informal, home-style cooking; Fails Cafe, 82 Cashel Street (seafood, informal atmosphere); Galleon Restaurant, 170 Tuam Street (French cuisine, entertainment); Grenadier, 24 Oxford Terrace (old English decor, French cuisine, dancing); Guardsman, 103 Armagh Street (grilled steaks and chops); Horizon Restaurant, Christchurch International Airport (magnificent alpine panorama); Swiss Chalet, 5 Hereford Place (cozy alpine decor, continental cooking).

Local transport. Taxis are available at Cathedral Square and all transportation terminals. Bright red city buses depart from Cathedral Square for city and suburban points; for route information, stop at the kiosk in front of the cathedral. Free "City Clipper" bus service shuttles downtown shoppers on weekdays and Friday evenings. A special Christchurch touch is baby strollers hooking a ride on the front of city buses, a convenience reflecting the city's relaxed pace.

Tourist information. For city maps and information on local points of interest, stop at the Public Relations Office, housed in an 1887 building at 75 Worcester Street (corner of Oxford Terrace). Travel arrangements, tour information, and accommodations reservations are handled by the Government Tourist Bureau, located in the Government Life Building facing Cathedral Square. The Automobile Association (Canterbury) office is located at 210 Hereford Street, facing Latimer Square.

Shopping and entertainment

Christchurch's main shopping district clusters around Cathedral Square. Nearby shopping arcades such as Chancery Lane and New Regent Street offer shops and a relaxed atmosphere. A new two-story shopping center links Hereford and Cashel streets near High Street.

Shops are generally open from 9 to 5:30 on weekdays and until 9 on Friday evenings. Most downtown stores are closed on Saturday and Sunday. In Riccarton, stores stay open late on Thursday nights. New Brighton shops are closed Wednesday and open on Saturday from 9 to 9.

Evening entertainment. Most ballet and theater performances, concerts, and touring shows take place at the city's handsome Town Hall. Plays are presented in the Court Theatre at the Arts Centre of Christchurch.

Major hotels and many restaurants offer live entertainment and dancing in the evening, particularly on Friday and Saturday. Dinner with a local family can be arranged through the Public Relations Office or Government Tourist Bureau.

Sports and special festivities. In the Christchurch area are numerous golf courses, river and surf fishing, and midwinter skiing at Mount Hutt.

In Christchurch you can see some of the country's top horses in action at two of the country's finest tracks. Light-harness racing (trotting) takes place at Addington Raceway; racing and steeplechase events are held at Riccarton Raceway.

Racing events featuring the best horses from North and South Islands highlight November's Carnival Week celebration. Premier classic on the racing calendar is the New Zealand Cup; the companion New Zealand Trotting Cup race takes place at Addington.

Other annual events include the New Zealand Grand National in August and the Easter Cup Carnival meetings in autumn.

On foot in Christchurch

Christchurch is a walker's city—compact, level, and varied. Begin your stroll at Cathedral Square, the city's bustling center. Along your route you'll get a close look at distinctive old and new buildings. You can linger along the Avon, sample outstanding parks and gardens, and visit some of the city's stimulating cultural centers.

Cathedral Square. Heart of the city is Cathedral Square, now a tiled pedestrian plaza softened by trees and flower-filled containers. Vendors sell fruit and flowers from pushcarts to passing office workers. Shoppers pause to rest on benches, and noontime entertainers amuse the lunch crowd.

Buildings around the perimeter of the square include not only sleek, high-rise office buildings but elegant older structures—the main post office (built 1877–79), the *Press* newspaper building, and several vintage hotels. A statue honors John Robert Godley, called "the founder of Canterbury."

Christchurch Cathedral is the finest Gothic-style church in the Dominion and the spiritual center of this essentially Anglican city. Built of stone quarried in the Port Hills, it reflects the courage, vision, and dedication of the early settlers who began construction in 1864, only a few years after they arrived. Inside, the cathedral's arched ceiling soars skyward. Memorial tablets and windows record the origins of the town and Canterbury province. If you feel energetic, you can climb the 139 steps up through the bell tower to observation balconies overlooking the city. The cathedral spire towers more than 63 meters/215 feet above the square.

Victoria Square. Two blocks north of the cathedral is Victoria Square, departure point for most sightseeing tours. The Bowker Fountain provides a graceful backdrop for a sturdy statue of Captain Cook, and a portly Queen Victoria keeps an eye on passing traffic.

Town Hall. A block beyond, bordered by the Avon River, is Christchurch's striking glass and marble Town Hall. Opened in 1972, it is the center for civic and cultural activities, performing arts events, and meetings and conventions. Events are presented in the spacious two-level main auditorium or the smaller 1,000-seat theater.

Guided tours leave the main lobby at frequent intervals on weekdays and on Saturday and Sunday afternoons. Tickets for theater and ballet performances, concerts, and other attractions are handled by the Town Hall booking office. The Cascade Restaurant overlooks the placid river, Victoria Square, and the Ferrier Fountain.

Provincial Government Buildings. Follow the Avon upstream along Oxford Terrace. Near the river at Armagh and Durham streets, you'll see the stone tower and wooden extensions of the Canterbury Provincial Government Buildings, one of the most intriguing structures in the country. Seat of Canterbury's government from 1859 to 1876, the complex is usually open weekdays from 9 A.M. to 4 P.M.; guided tours are often available on Sunday and holiday afternoons.

The Provincial Council Chamber, on the Durham Street side near the river, was built in 1865 of local stone and native timber. Almost churchlike in appearance, the neo-Gothic chamber has a magnificent gilded and painted barrel-vaulted ceiling, mosaic wall panels, and stained glass windows. Balcony seats once accommodated the public.

During Canterbury's early years, the chamber was the scene of many lively debates and historic decisions. Provincial architect Benjamin Mountfort designed the complex, as well as many of Canterbury's other early public buildings.

Walk along the river. Rimmed by grassy, tree-shaded banks and spanned by graceful stone bridges, the winding Avon provides a tranquil corridor skirting the center of the city. Couples stroll the riverside walkways, office workers eat their lunches on the lawn, and children and grandparents feed the ducks.

A statue of Captain Robert Falcon Scott facing Worcester Street recalls the city's link with the Antarctic. At Cashel Street you pass the Bridge of Remembrance, a war memorial. Continuing along Oxford Terrace, you see the distinctive wooden St. Michael's and All Angels Anglican Church, built in 1872.

Paddle a canoe on the Avon

It's pleasant to walk along the river, but the best way to enjoy the Avon's charm is by boat. You can hire a canoe or rowboat any day at Antigua Boatsheds, facing the shallow river on Cambridge Terrace near Rolleston Avenue.

You step off the sloping wooden dock and lower yourself into your craft, then slowly paddle or row upstream past the Botanic Gardens and Hagley Park. Willows droop over the water. In spring you glide beneath blossoming trees; in autumn, golden leaves cast reflections in the water. Your fellow paddlers range from pre-teens to grandparents. On sunny weekends, picnicking families relax along the grassy bank and watch the passing parade.

A city of parks and gardens

The English colonists who settled Christchurch transformed the "flat, treeless, featureless" site of the 1850s, landscaping their young town with European trees and grasslands and setting aside vast areas as public parkland. Today, pocket parks dot residential areas, and city gardeners groom their plots in competition for annual best-garden and best-street awards.

Botanic Gardens. A few minutes' walk from Cathedral Square takes you to the Botanic Gardens, a 75-acre reserve encircled by a deep bend of the Avon. Here you'll find mature trees gathered from all parts of the world (many are labeled), a rose garden, water gardens, and splendid seasonal flower displays. In late spring the woodlands are bright with daffodils, azaleas, and rhododendrons. Tropical and flowering plants are displayed under glass. From September to April you can climb aboard an electric cart—called the "Toast Rack"—for a scenic tour of the gardens.

Hagley Park. Across the Avon from the Botanic Gardens is Hagley Park, a 500-acre playground for the city's cyclists, dog walkers, golfers, joggers, horseback riders, and model yachting enthusiasts. Often there's a game of cricket, soccer, or rugby in progress, or you may see competitors engaged in croquet, lawn bowling, tennis, or other sports.

North of Harper Avenue is Millbrook Reserve, noted for its azalea and rhododendron displays.

Deans Bush (Riccarton House). Situated west of Hagley Park and north of Riccarton Road, this modest reserve contains the only remaining stand of native swamp forest originally found on these treeless plains. On the property are Riccarton House, the Deans family homestead for some 90 years (now used for receptions), and Deans Cottage, a tiny plains homestead built in 1843 and preserved as a small museum.

Canterbury Museum—a fascinating stop

For many visitors, the city's most absorbing attraction is Canterbury Museum, a treasure house of Canterbury and New Zealand lore. One of the finest museums in the Southern Hemisphere, it contains several exhibits unique in the country. The museum is on Rolleston Avenue near the Botanic Gardens entrance and is open daily (closed Sunday mornings).

A replica Christchurch street typical of colonial days (1850s to mid-1870s) shows well-stocked shops patterned after actual businesses of the era. Other colonial displays include a three-room cob house containing costumed figures and a Cobb and Co. stagecoach.

The museum's National Antarctic Centre contains a fascinating collection of articles used by Antarctic explorers—personal effects, clothing, survival equipment, and diaries from the heroic era of exploration (1900 to 1917) give insights into Antarctic hardship, exhilaration, and tragedy. Modern thermal clothing and mechanized equipment create vivid contrasts. Additional exhibits offer information on Antarctic geology, fossils, and penguins, and on life beneath the sea.

In the Pacific Hall, Captain Cook's three voyages are traced on a giant wall map, and displays include mementos collected during his travels. A 47-foot war canoe dominates Maori cultural exhibits.

Arts and crafts are flourishing

Recent developments have stimulated activity among Christchurch's artistic community, sparking new interest in the city's varied cultural life.

Arts Centre of Christchurch. When the University of Canterbury moved to a new and larger campus in Ilam in 1975, its historic town site was presented to the people of Christchurch. The handsome stone buildings at Rolleston Avenue and Worcester Street have gained a new lease on life serving as the busy home of many local artistic, cultural, educational, and recreational organizations.

Artists, musicians, and dancers maintain studios and rehearsal space in the old Gothic buildings. Cultural clubs and community service organizations meet here. A resident company presents stage plays in the 230-seat Court Theatre; the former gymnasium has become a movie theater; and a

French restaurant occupies the old Art School. Students learn new techniques in a theater workshop and an arts school, and a youth orchestra rehearses on Saturday mornings. Each Wednesday at 1 P.M. the Canterbury Orchestra presents a recital in the former University Library.

You can visit the small basement laboratory, now a museum, where famed nuclear physicist Lord Ernest Rutherford conducted his first scientific experiments in 1893-94.

Visitors are welcome to stroll through the center's quadrangles and cloisters. Tours are held on the first and third Sundays of each month, beginning at 2 P.M. (additional tours in January). On the first weekend of April, craftspeople sell their work under the trees at the annual Centrefair.

Robert McDougall Art Gallery. Located behind the Canterbury Museum facing the Botanic Gardens, this gallery houses the city's collection of early and contemporary Australasian and European paintings, sculpture, pottery, and weaving. Special exhibitions are presented during the year. The gallery is open daily (closed Sunday mornings).

Canterbury Society of Arts. You can view changing exhibitions of contemporary New Zealand art, as well as art from other countries, at the CSA Gallery at 66 Gloucester Street. Other events include musical recitals and film and photographic evening programs. The gallery is open daily (closed Sunday mornings).

Artists' Quarter. More than a dozen craftspeople create and sell their work in a cluster of wooden buildings at 40 Oxford Terrace, near Montreal Street. You'll see them at work in their studios here, and in the upper level sales gallery, you can view their handcrafted articles—including pottery, weaving, leatherwork, metalcraft, woodwork, photography, fabric printing, and stained glass work.

Other places to visit

If time permits, you may want to visit a transport museum, some of the province's educational institutions, or Christchurch's seaside suburbs.

Ferrymead Historic Park and Transport Museum. Still in the development stages is this community effort to recapture the pioneering atmosphere of Canterbury's early decades. Located on Bridle Path Road south of the Avon-Heathcote estuary, Ferrymead is open daily.

Enthusiastic volunteers have restored many early vehicles to working order. On Sunday afternoons you can ride a steam train, trams, and a London double-decker bus. Many of the vintage vehicles and machines are displayed in the Hall of Wheels, first part of a new Museum of Science and Industry rising on an adjoining area bordering Truscotts Road. Railway and tram lines link the two areas.

Plans call for additional science and industry exhibits, a six-story replica of Christchurch's first windmill, and a working pioneer township with replicas of colonial shops and houses, staffed by shopkeepers in period costume.

Educational institutions. Reminiscent of an English public school, the gray stone buildings of Christ's College are grouped around a grassy quadrangle north of Canterbury Museum bordering Rolleston Avenue. Founded during the settlement's first decade, the boys' secondary school retains a formal uniform that includes black blazer and black and white striped tie.

You'll often see uniformed schoolboys cycling along city streets or competing in outdoor sports in nearby Hagley Park.

In 1975 the University of Canterbury, noted for its School of Engineering, moved from its town site to a spacious new campus in the western suburb of Ilam. Visitors are welcome to stroll the landscaped grounds.

Lincoln College (Canterbury Agricultural College) lies 21 km/13 miles southwest of the city near the village of Lincoln. Surrounded by acres of model farmland, it trains young farmers and supervises research in agriculture and animal husbandry. Founded in 1873, the college was one of the world's first schools of agriculture. It has been an important factor in Canterbury's agricultural growth and prosperity.

Seaside suburbs. Christchurch has its own coastal suburbs. New Brighton, known for its Saturday shopping, has a long beach bordering the Pacific. The Queen Elizabeth II Park complex was the site of the 1974 Commonwealth Games.

South of the Avon-Heathcote Estuary is Sumner. Its esplanade curves past Cave Rock and along

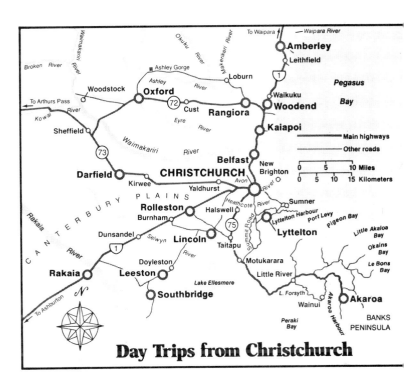

Day Trips from Christchurch

Sumner Bay. You can take the steep road over the bluff and descend to Taylor's Mistake, a pleasant sheltered beach, or climb to Evans Pass and the Summit Road.

Orana Wildlife Park. New Zealand's first drive-through wild animal park is open daily northwest of the airport on Harewood Road West. Lions are the big attraction, but the park also has tigers, camels, water buffalo, and Barbary sheep.

The Antarctic connection

No city has stronger and more enduring ties with the icy southern continent than Christchurch. During the early days of Antarctic exploration, Lyttelton was port of departure for expeditions. The riverside statue of Captain Robert Falcon Scott, the English Antarctic explorer who lost his life returning from the South Pole in 1912, is a daily reminder of these hazardous explorations.

An outstanding collection of Antarctic relics, records, and equipment has been assembled in Canterbury Museum's National Antarctic Centre (see page 80).

Today a dozen countries are engaged in scientific research on the southern continent, and tourists have flown over its vast icy mass. Christchurch International Airport is the supply base and communications center for Operation Deep Freeze, the nonmilitary U.S. scientific study at McMurdo Sound.

Seeing the area by guided tour

If you prefer to see Christchurch and its surrounding area on a guided excursion, you'll find several companies ready to show you the sights. Some tours operate the year around; others are scheduled only on certain days or during the main October-to-April tourist period. For detailed information on available excursions, check at the Government Tourist Bureau or other travel agencies.

Canterbury excursions

From Christchurch, travelers radiate in all directions to explore Canterbury and other South Island destinations.

You can head southeast across the Port Hills to Lyttelton or make a loop around the Banks Peninsula. To the north you'll find the scenic Kaikoura Coast and Hanmer Springs, a spa in the forest. Routes take motorists west across the Southern Alps or south over the Canterbury Plains.

Superb views from the Summit Road

Curling high above the city along the crest of the Port Hills, the Summit Road offers superb views—westward over Christchurch and checkered plains to the snow-capped Southern Alps, eastward over Lyttelton and its harbor encased in the crater of an extinct volcano.

From the seaside community of Sumner, you climb to Evans Pass to meet the Summit Road as it snakes for 26 km/16 miles along the northern hills overlooking Lyttelton Harbour some 300 meters/1,000 feet below. A southern section continues from Dyers Pass Road (at the Sign of the Kiwi tea house) along the western side of the harbor to Gebbies Pass.

Lyttelton. South Island's leading port, Lyttelton is connected with Christchurch by road and rail tunnels. Wooden houses cling to the steep streets above the harbor. Along the waterfront, cargo handlers service docked freighters, and weekend yachtsmen ready their boats for sailing the sheltered bays. Launch cruises leave Lyttelton every afternoon.

A quartet of 19th century churches adds historic flavor. On Sunday afternoons you can see displays on the historic port and her ships at Lyttelton's Historical Museum, located in the Community Centre at 2 Hawkhurst Road, near the road tunnel's southern entrance.

Roadhouses. Along the route are three old stone roadhouses offering shelter to travelers. Best known is the Sign of the Takahe, overlooking the city from the Cashmere hills. Modeled after a medieval baronial manor, this showplace has richly ornamented ceilings, wood carvings, intricate stonework, and colorful murals. You can stop for tea and views there and at the Sign of the Kiwi, located on Coronation Hill at the junction of Summit Road and Dyers Pass Road. The third roadhouse —the Sign of the Bellbird—has no refreshment facilities.

Scenic walks. The Canterbury Pilgrims who came ashore at Lyttelton in 1850 followed a zigzag bridle path across the Port Hills to found their colony on the plains. Today, walkers still enjoy the old Bridle Path trail. Hundreds make a nostalgic anniversary trek annually on the Sunday nearest December 16.

Walking tracks wind through the Port Hills, offering hikers spectacular views of the city, harbor, plains, and mountains.

Akaroa and the Banks Peninsula

Set apart both geographically and geologically from the rest of Canterbury, the Banks Peninsula offers a relaxing retreat about 1½ hours southeast of Christchurch. Contrasting dramatically with the placid Canterbury Plains, the peninsula is formed by two extinct volcanoes whose collapsed craters hold the splendid natural harbors of Lyttelton and Akaroa.

The road to Akaroa. From Christchurch, Highway 75 heads south through farming country to the peninsula. Lake Ellesmere, a shallow coastal lagoon, supports great flocks of waterfowl. The narrow, winding road snakes through the peninsula's

Paddling a canoe *on Christchurch's Avon River is a pleasant way to spend an hour or two. Shaded by overhanging trees, the river flows languidly past the Botanic Gardens and Hagley Park.*

green and golden hills, past farmhouses and cottages tucked into folded valleys.

Cutting deeply into the eroded old volcanic cones are narrow bays, some of them used in the 1830s by whaling parties. From the main route, short, steep side roads lead down to these unpeopled coastal inlets—Port Levy's protected harbor, Pigeon Bay and its campground, Little Akaloa with its unusual church embellished with Maori-style carvings. Other roads lead to Okains Bay, known for its bathing beach and worthwhile museum; Le Bons Bay and its sports ground; Peraki's historic whaling site.

Village with a French flavor. New Zealand's first French settlers landed at Akaroa in 1840—nearly a decade before the colonial settlements at Dunedin and Christchurch—and the village keeps alive its Gallic heritage. Located 82 km/50 miles from Christchurch, New Zealand's most English city, Akaroa is a favorite place for midsummer or weekend holidays. If you can, visit on a weekday or out of season to enjoy the village's unique charm.

Along the waterfront you'll see whalers' pots and the early customs house, but Akaroa's real character lies along the side streets above the harbor. Spreading trees shade wooden Victorian cottages, and decorative fences enclose flourishing gardens of subtropical flowers. Attractive small churches serve worshippers. One of the settlement's earliest buildings is the Langlois-Eteveneaux House and Museum; the two-room cottage is furnished in 1840s style.

Walk up wooded glades to the surrounding hills for a view over town and harbor. Le Voyageur Motel and several other small hostelries offer accommodation; L'Auberge Suzette is a highly regarded restaurant.

Two scenic river gorges

An all-day loop from Christchurch takes you through North Canterbury farmlands to the dramatic gorges of the Ashley and Waimakariri rivers. You'll find pleasant picnic and swimming areas at both river sites. In season there's good salmon and trout fishing.

Raft trips and jet boat excursions depart up the Waimakariri River from Woodstock (make prior arrangements in Christchurch).

North to Kaikoura

From Christchurch, Highway 1 curves to the north across North Canterbury's rolling hills and lush river valleys. At Waipara, Highway 7 branches inland for Hanmer Springs, Lewis Pass, and the West Coast. Anglers find good fishing in the Hurunui and Waiau rivers.

South of Cheviot you can visit and picnic at Cheviot Hills domain, now a scenic reserve. You'll see the homestead and some buildings of the vast Cheviot Hills run, one of the earliest Canterbury sheep stations. At Hundalee you cross the Conway River, marking the Canterbury-Marlborough boundary, then descend through the hills to meet the sea at Oaro.

For nearly 100 km/60 miles, Highway 1 hugs the rock-strewn Pacific shore. Ever-changing seascapes, impressive views of rugged inland mountains, and the small resort of Kaikoura are coastal highlights. Seaside camping areas and picnic sites are busy in summer.

Take time to drive to the northern tip of Kaikoura Peninsula for a memorable panorama of village and sea backed by the snow-draped Seaward Kaikoura range. A fishing fleet operates out of Kaikoura, where local crayfish are packed for export. The coastal town draws many surf fishermen and skin divers.

Forest walks at Hanmer Springs

South Island's principal thermal resort, Hanmer blossomed as a spa in the late 19th century. Today visitors come not only for the hot springs but also to enjoy invigorating mountain air and forest walks. Anglers find good fishing in nearby rivers, boaters enjoy Tennyson and Horseshoe lakes, and skiers head for nearby Amuri Ski Field.

An easy 1½ to 2-hour drive north of Christchurch, Hanmer sits on a high plateau ringed by mountain spurs of the Southern Alps. Forestry workers here tend one of the country's largest and most varied tree plantations.

The thermal pools of Queen Mary Hospital are open daily; bring your bathing suit and towel.

From the center of town, take Jollie's Pass Road to the forest. Walks lead into the woods, which are bright with color in autumn. A trail zigzags from Conical Hill Road to the summit for broad views over the forest and Waiau Plain.

From Hanmer you can arrange horseback treks through the countryside, jet boat trips on the Waiau River, and trips by four-wheel-drive into the rugged hill country.

Two routes across the mountains

Two highways follow old Maori greenstone routes across the mountains to the West Coast. Highway 7 (the Lewis Pass Road) begins at Waipara, north of Christchurch and angles south of Hanmer Springs to Reefton and Greymouth. Highway 73 (the Arthur's Pass Road) heads west from Christchurch, climbs into the alpine country of Arthur's Pass National Park, and descends to meet the West Coast Highway near Kumara.

Lewis Pass Road. Constructed during the depression days of the 1930s, Highway 7 follows a series of river valleys across 864-meter/2,840-foot Lewis Pass. Sedate Canterbury farmlands give way to

rolling golden foothills and beech forests; then you descend through the rugged greenery of the West Coast. At Maruia Springs you can swim in hot pools in an alpine setting. Just east of Reefton, the Blacks Point Museum—housed in a wooden former church—contains exhibits recalling local mining activity.

Across Arthur's Pass. Shortest, steepest, and most spectacular of the routes across the Southern Alps, the Arthur's Pass Road (Highway 73) is the main link between Canterbury and Westland. From the Canterbury Plains, it climbs into the mountains and crosses 922-meter/3,029-foot Arthur's Pass, then descends the steep and winding Otira Gorge to the railway settlement of Otira and follows the Taramakau Valley to the coast. No caravans are permitted on the Arthur's Pass-Otira section of the highway.

National park headquarters is located in the alpine village of Arthur's Pass, about 154 km/95 miles northwest of Christchurch. Displays show the region's natural features and depict the difficult construction of the road and railway. Short walks lead hikers through the bush past waterfalls and tarns; all-day climbs lead up nearby peaks.

Nature hikes and evening programs are presented in summer. In winter there's skiing at Temple Basin above Arthur's Pass township.

South to Dunedin

From Christchurch, Highway 1 cuts across the checkerboard farmlands and sheep pastures of the Canterbury Plains and turns south along the coast toward Dunedin, some 365 km/225 miles away on Otago Harbour.

Largest towns along the east coast route are Timaru, South Canterbury's coastal resort facing Caroline Bay, and Oamaru, North Otago's commercial center. Sandy swimming beaches, river and surf fishing, and other coastal activities draw visitors to many small beach communities along the seacoast.

The Canterbury Plains

From Christchurch, the flat Canterbury Plains stretch inland to the foothills of the Southern Alps. Highway 1 cuts southwest through city suburbs and farmlands to cross the Rakaia River on the country's longest bridge. Massive spreading trees shade the brick buildings of Ashburton, the district's farming center. Anglers fish the Rakaia, Ashburton, and Rangitata rivers for salmon and sea-run trout.

Highway 73 heads west to Windwhistle, gateway to the Rakaia Gorge and Canterbury lakes. Gouged out by long-departed glaciers, these mountain lakes attract local outdoorsmen. Lake Coleridge is popular for fishing and boating. In winter, tiny Lake Ida freezes to become a natural outdoor ice

Farm families open their homes to visitors

One of the most pleasant ways to meet New Zealanders is to stay a night or two with a hospitable farm family. Throughout the country, congenial families open their homes to visitors who want to sample the friendly ways of farm life or just relax for a few days in a rural setting.

A farm visit offers a relaxing change from the usual hotel room and fast-paced touring itinerary. It also gives you a first-hand look at the backbone of the country's economy (sheep outnumber people in New Zealand by approximately 20 to 1). Some stations have been farmed for more than 100 years.

After a hearty welcome from your host or hostess, you'll be invited to watch or join in the chores. If you prefer, you can use the farm as a base for touring or just relax on the verandah.

Usually you stay in a cozy guest room in the family homestead (frequently, though not always, with private bath) and eat hearty, country-style meals with the family. Evening entertainment is informal; you share conversation with your host family. Most families take only a few guests at a time to keep the experience on a personal level.

If you like, you can join in farm chores and watch sheep dogs go through their paces. Perhaps you'll want to lend a hand with the mustering, join the haying crew, learn to operate a spinning wheel, observe shearers at work, or ride along with your host to the local fat stock sale.

Other activities vary by station—often you can ride horseback around the farm, fish for trout in a nearby stream, go swimming, hunt for deer in the hills, or picnic in a rural setting.

Accommodations range from farms just a few miles from main roads and country towns to high country stations off the beaten track. If you're traveling by public transport, you can usually arrange to be met at the nearest sizable town. Some farms have separate cottages where visiting families bring their own linen and prepare their own meals.

You can obtain details on individual farms and arrange for accommodations at offices of the Government Tourist Bureau in major New Zealand cities or at Farm Holidays Ltd., P.O. Box 1436. Wellington (reservation centers also in Auckland and Christchurch). Other than in the main holiday seasons, arrangements can frequently be made on short notice.

rink. There's skiing at Mount Hutt and in the Craigieburn Mountains.

Viewed from above, the plains form a vast rural patchwork of green and gold farmlands, crisscrossed by country roads and cut by broad rivers. The plains are New Zealand's granary, a rich agricultural region renowned for its wheat, wool, and livestock. Sheep and cattle farms abound. More than a century ago, Australian sheepmen began grazing their flocks on the open plains, and today Canterbury lamb has a worldwide reputation. On the big, isolated sheep stations in the high country, sheep are raised for wool, rather than for meat.

Timaru, a holiday town

One of South Island's most popular coastal resorts, Timaru is built on gently sloping hills facing Caroline Bay. An easy, 160-km/100-mile drive across sheep-covered plains southwest of Christchurch, it is a base for exploring the spectacular highlands of the Waitaki-Mackenzie basin.

Timaru, about 30,000 population, attracts visitors the year around with its mild climate, fine tourist and conference facilities, and protected sandy beach. Center of a large farming region, it is also home port of a fishing fleet.

A long breakwater shelters Timaru's artificial harbor, the only port between the Banks Peninsula and Oamaru. North of the breakwater, fine sand has accumulated at the old whaling cove of Caroline Bay to form a sweeping beach. Thousands flock here for Timaru's annual New Year's beach carnival.

Laid out by rival surveyors, Timaru has an irregular street grid; winding Stafford Street follows an old bullock track near the waterfront. Local bluestone was used in the construction of many buildings. Timaru's 50-acre Botanical Gardens border Queen Street south of the city. Fine paintings and touring exhibitions are housed in the Aigantighe Art Gallery. Pioneer Hall Museum on Perth Street is the place to learn about local history and port development and obtain information on the district's ancient Maori rock drawings.

In the countryside, more than 200 wild animals roam rolling hills at Hadlow Game Farm. Temuka, north of Timaru, is known for its earthenware pottery and good fishing streams.

Highway 8 heads up the Tengawai River toward Fairlie. Along the way, stop at Pleasant Point to see a restored steam locomotive and railway museum. In the village of Cave, the old stone Church of St. David is a hand-built memorial to Mackenzie Country pioneers.

Waimate, on the slopes of the Hunters Hills, is the center of a varied agricultural district.

Oamaru, the white stone city

As you cross the Waitaki River, you leave Canterbury and enter Otago, a region reflecting the sturdy values of its English and Scottish settlers. Highway 83 veers westward up the Waitaki Valley into the farmlands and sheep country of North Otago.

The region's thriving commercial center is Oamaru, noted for its wide, tree-lined streets and many handsome stone buildings. Built of the local creamy white limestone (quarried at Weston), they give the town its special appearance and unity.

From the war monument in the center of town, walk south along Thames Street to admire the classic stone buildings—among them the Brydone Hotel (1880), Waitaki County Council Chambers (1880), the Borough Council Offices (1880), courthouse (1883), the post office (1884), National Bank (1871), and Bank of New South Wales (1884). The two banks were designed by R. A. Lawson, architect of Dunedin's First Church. Earlier buildings, from the 1860s and 1870s, line waterfront streets.

Public gardens off Severn Street provide a pleasant retreat, and on the city outskirts, country lanes cut through large market gardens.

For a view of Oamaru and the surrounding country, take Tyne Street south to Tamar and turn uphill to the lookout reserve.

The Otago coast

From Oamaru, Highway 1 parallels the coast south to Dunedin. Notice the use of Oamaru stone in buildings, bridges, walls, and chimneys.

A landmark of the Otago coast, the Moeraki boulders are a geological curiosity. Strewn on the sand north of Moeraki and along Katiki Beach, the spherical, gray rocks weigh several tons each and extend up to 4 meters/12 feet in diameter. Geologists say they were formed on the sea floor millions of years ago when lime salts accumulated around a center core.

At Hillgrove a side road leads east to the small fishing village of Moeraki, in the lee of Moeraki Point. Further south, picnickers can head inland to Trotters Gorge, a delightful wooded site flanked by tall limestone bluffs.

South of Katiki, Highway 1 borders the beach to Shag Point, where sea birds congregate on the rocks. At Palmerston, "the Pigroot" (Highway 85) heads inland to Central Otago.

Otago's oldest European settlement (1840) and an early port, Waikouaiti today attracts those who enjoy its sandy beach and coastal bird sanctuary. The settlement has several old churches, and local historic items are displayed in a roadside museum.

A coastal road loops along the shore of Waikouaiti Bay, offering marvelous vistas and ocean beaches. The pleasant seaside village of Karitane is a holiday retreat for Dunedin families, who come

Snowy peaks of the Southern Alps rise behind Lake Tekapo. Small Church of the Good Shepherd, built of stones gathered near the lake shore, honors the pioneers of the Mackenzie Country.

here to swim in the river and ocean, fish, go boating, and play on the sandy beach. Near the flagstaff is the homestead of Sir Truby King, a medical reformer who founded the Plunket Society, an organization dedicated to educating mothers in the care of infants.

The coastal loop continues south through Seacliff to Warrington, then rejoins Highway 1 north of Waitati.

Exploring South Canterbury

Bordered by the Rangitata and Waitaki rivers and the imposing Southern Alps, South Canterbury is a land of contrasts. Inland from the coastal beaches you'll find open farmlands, tussock-covered hills, and high mountain lakes. Trees planted by English settlers a century ago border roads and shade stately homesteads.

The coastal resort of Timaru is a touring base for exploring South Canterbury. Inland lie the rolling hills of the Mackenzie Country and the glacier-gouged lakes of Tekapo, Pukaki, and Ohau. On the southern boundary, the Waitaki River is marked by a series of massive hydroelectric dams and reservoirs.

Timaru has numerous hotels and motels. Elsewhere in the region, accommodations are limited and frequently modest. You'll find overnight facilities in Geraldine, Fairlie, Lake Tekapo, Twizel, and Lake Ohau.

Anglers come to South Canterbury for plentiful rainbow and trout fishing in lakes and streams, for hefty (to 30 lbs.) quinnat salmon migrating up the Rangitata and Opihi rivers in late summer, and for sea fishing north and south of Caroline Bay. From July through September, skiers head for Fox Peak, Round Hill, and Lake Ohau. Outdoor ice rinks attract skaters at Albury and Lake Tekapo.

Geraldine, city of trees

For sheer scenic variety, it's hard to surpass the drive from Christchurch through the Rakaia Gorge to Geraldine and on into the lonely hills of the Mackenzie Country.

Located inland at the edge of rolling downs, Geraldine once supplied isolated sheep stations. Today it serves a flourishing agricultural district. English settlers planted trees in profusion here—not the pines of the plains, but elm, larch, oak, poplar, ash, and willow. In autumn the golden foliage is a feast for the eyes. You can picnic beside the Waihi River, which flows through town.

From Geraldine Downs behind town, the panorama extends over mountains, tree-broken plains, and the coast from the Port Hills south to Waimate.

River gorges. North of Geraldine, roads follow the Orari, Waihi, and Hae Hae Te Moana rivers to historic buildings and riverside picnic areas.

At Orari Gorge Station, the New Zealand Historic Trust is restoring the original homestead buildings. Both Waihi Gorge and Te Moana Gorge have fine recreation sites, and you can swim in the Waihi River. In Pleasant Valley you pass rustic St. Anne's Anglican Church, built in 1862 of pit-sawn native timber. Horses may be rented for saddle trips up the Waihi Gorge. In Woodbury, the slate-roofed, Norman-style St. Thomas' Anglican Church contains carved oak furniture and memorial tablets.

Up the Rangitata. Peel Forest Park, 23 km/15 miles north of Geraldine, is a pocket reserve of native bush favored for its easy walks, waterfalls, and abundant birdlife. Families picnic and camp here, and anglers fish the Rangitata River.

A short distance beyond stand the historic buildings of Mount Peel station. An unsealed road continues another 46 km/29 miles beyond, fording tributary streams, to the isolated station of Mesopotamia. This remote sheep run inspired pioneer runholder Samuel Butler to write the classic 19th century satirical novel *Erewhon*, in which he describes the utter loneliness of the rolling tussock country and the dwarfing vastness of mountains and plain.

The lonely Mackenzie Country

This great upland plain first came to general notice in 1855 with the capture of James McKenzie, a Scottish rustler who discovered it while spiriting away sheep stolen from the lowlands. Though sparsely populated, the remote back country supports vast pastoral runs with thousands of hardy sheep.

Set in rolling, tree-dotted downs, Fairlie is gateway to the Mackenzie Country. About 5 km/3 miles

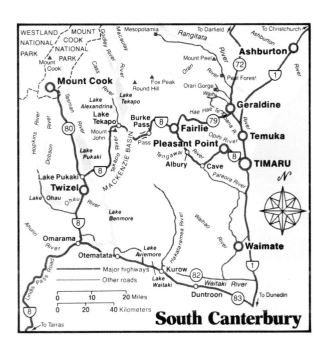

South Canterbury

northeast is Strathaven Clydesdale Stud, where working teams pull horsedrawn farm implements, and you see how farming was done in pioneer days. Fairlie's historical and transport museums offer an interesting look at days past. The Mackenzie Country Carnival is a big event during the Christmas-New Year holidays.

From Fairlie you follow the Opihi River upstream, climbing through the pleasant wooded valley to Burke Pass.

As you enter the Mackenzie Country, the transformation is abrupt and total. Spread before you is a vast, shimmering sea of tussock grasslands merging into a distant purple wall of snowy peaks. Sunlight glints off the light blue waters of glacier-fed lakes. Take a deep breath and enjoy the pure air.

The Mackenzie basin provides access to the high mountains, and its lakes feed the upper Waitaki hydroelectric power project.

The Waitaki lakes

Fed by melting glaciers and snow, the milky turquoise Waitaki lakes occupy the lower ends of glaciated valleys in the shadow of the Southern Alps. Walled in by moraines, these austerely beautiful lakes feed the great Waitaki River.

Lake Tekapo. On still days, Tekapo is a vast mirror reflecting the majestic mountain panorama. Acres of wild lupines in brilliant shades of bluish purple, pink, and yellow brighten the lake shore in summer. During bad weather, savage alpine winds churn the lake into a maelstrom and slice across the exposed hills.

Silhouetted against the mountains, the solitary little Church of the Good Shepherd conveys the isolated and enduring qualities of the Mackenzie Country pioneers in whose memory it was erected. Inside, a large window above the altar frames a splendid view of lake and mountains.

Further along the shore, a bronze collie monument honors the devoted and hardworking sheep dogs. Atop Mount John are a mountaintop observatory and a U.S. satellite tracking station.

West of Tekapo, two smaller lakes, Alexandrina and McGregor, offer good trout fishing, swimming, and camping.

Lake Pukaki. Fed by the Tasman River, Pukaki's icy finger points north toward Mount Cook. The scene is a paradox of wild beauty and forbidding solitude—pale blue lake and golden tussock contrasting with the snow-capped Alps, purpling in the western shadow. The road to Mount Cook National Park follows the western shore of the lake. Twizel is the construction center for the hydro project.

Lake Ohau. Fishermen, campers, trampers, boaters, and skiers enjoy this beautiful back country region. Unsealed roads closely follow Lake Ohau's shore, and trails lead into the beech forest.

The Waitaki Valley

Marking the boundary between Canterbury and Otago, the broad Waitaki River drains the high snowfields of the Southern Alps. Rivers flowing from the Waitaki lakes unite in the Mackenzie uplands above Benmore Dam. A series of dams and canals store and redirect lake waters to the project's power generating stations. As the Waitaki River flows eastward, it broadens into three lakes—Benmore, Aviemore, and Waitaki—and then meets the ocean north of Oamaru.

Hydroelectric dams. You can visit the power stations at Benmore and Aviemore dams, and there's an observation area overlooking Lake Benmore, New Zealand's largest manmade lake. A scenic 19-km/12-mile road loops north from Otematata around Lake Aviemore. Extensive tree planting and landscaping are softening the harsh effects of construction.

The giant 110-meter/360-foot-high Benmore Dam created a vast lake and some 110 km/70 miles of shoreline. Power boats and water-skiers cut white swaths, and sailboats glide across the water. Fishing is good in all the lakes, and in summer, visitors can take sightseeing boat trips. Below the dam, a sheltered recreation area attracts picnickers and swimmers.

Other attractions. Omarama, Otematata, and Kurow are centers for sportsmen who come to fish the lakes and some of South Island's best trout streams. In Kurow you can arrange jet boat transport to remote fishing sites. Migrating quinnat salmon are caught below Waitaki Dam in autumn.

Omarama also attracts glider pilots, who gather here in summer to take advantage of the area's favorable air currents. From Omarama the Lindis Pass Road (Highway 8) follows an old Maori trail south, linking the Waitaki Valley with Central Otago. Vast back country sheep stations—some in operation for more than a century—stretch over the lonely hills.

On the rock walls of the gorge, early itinerant hunters and fishermen drew pictures; many are now submerged beneath the lakes, but some Maori rock drawings are visible beneath a large limestone bluff just west of Duntroon (signposted over a stile).

Mount Cook

You approach Mount Cook by air—over the green and golden patchwork farms of the Canterbury Plains—or by road across the tussock-covered hills of the Mackenzie Country or Lindis Pass. On the western horizon, the snow-draped peaks of the Southern Alps rise majestically.

The heart of this spectacular alpine country—extending some 65 km/40 miles along the eastern slope—has been protected in Mount Cook National

Park. Renowned for its craggy beauty, it is a magnet for mountaineers who pit their climbing and skiing skills against its challenging peaks and glaciers. Less energetic visitors come here to enjoy the park's alpine scenery and explore its trails and tarns. Visitor facilities and accommodations are located in Mount Cook village.

Arriving at Mount Cook

Plane, motorcoach, or automobile will take you to New Zealand's premier alpine resort, Mount Cook. Mount Cook Airlines has daily nonstop service from Christchurch and Queenstown, and flights link Mount Cook with most of New Zealand's major cities. If bad weather closes the airport, planes land (conditions permitting) at the Twizel airfield, and passengers are bused the 65 km/40 miles past Lake Pukaki to Mount Cook.

Travelers with only one day to spare can take a scheduled, early-morning, 50-minute flight from Christchurch to Mount Cook, climb aboard a ski-plane sightseeing flight, have lunch, stop at the park visitor center, enjoy a short bush walk, and return to Christchurch in late afternoon.

Mount Cook Landlines provides daily coach service between the national park and Christchurch, Timaru, Wanaka, and Queenstown.

The Tourist Hotel Corporation operates accommodations at this remote site; advance reservations are essential. Most visitors stay at the THC Hermitage, recognized as one of New Zealand's finest hotels, or Glencoe Lodge. Less expensive motel flats, chalet units, and a youth hostel are also available. Information on camping and the use of mountain huts (for climbers) may be obtained at the park visitor center.

Park terrain and wildlife

Smallest of South Island's four major alpine preserves, Mount Cook National Park encompasses the highest peaks of the Southern Alps. More than 140 mountains rise above 2,100 meters/7,000 feet. Of these, 22 peaks top 3,050 meters/10,000 feet. Looming above them all is the range's mighty monarch, the highest peak in Australasia. The Maoris called it *Aorangi* (the cloud piercer). Later explorers named the 3,764-meter/12,349-foot peak in honor of Captain James Cook, first European to set foot on New Zealand soil.

Largest of the park's glaciers is the Tasman, 29 km/18 miles long and up to 3 km/2 miles wide. Other main glaciers include the Mueller and Hooker, both within relatively easy walking distance of park headquarters, and the more distant Murchison and Godley glaciers.

Botanists have identified more than 300 species of native plants in the park; labels identify many trees and shrubs along park tracks. Small alpine plants flower in high rock crevices. Wildflowers bloom from October to January; best known is the mountain buttercup (often mistakenly called the Mount Cook lily). Though not officially encouraged,

lupines stretch in a colorful midsummer carpet on the slopes below the Hermitage.

Native birds, including the inquisitive and raucous kea (mountain parrot), inhabit the forests, river beds, and rocky crags. Introduced animals—thar, chamois, and deer—browse in alpine and subalpine scrublands, destroying the vegetation. Hunting is encouraged, but shooters must first obtain a permit at park headquarters.

Enjoying your visit to Mount Cook

This splendid alpine park attracts people who love the mountains—both vacationers who come primarily to enjoy the scenery and mountaineers who expend their energies striving for the heights.

Allow time to pause and let the mountains enfold you in their beauty and calm. Listen to the bird songs, let the sun's heat warm your body, watch Mount Cook's sharp peak turn to glowing pink and purple in the sun's waning rays. On an after-dinner walk, enjoy the moonlight on the snow or gaze at a multitude of stars.

Obviously all that snow and ice doesn't arrive in the sunshine. When rain clouds settle over the mountains, far too many visitors succumb to the cozy lure of the fireplace. Even on threatening days, though, you can enjoy the displays in the visitor center and some of the shorter walks.

Blending in with its alpine background, the steeply roofed visitor center is the park's administrative headquarters and major source of information. Photographs, relief maps, and other displays add to your knowledge of the park's history, terrain, plants, and wildlife. You can ask about park trails and guide services or check road conditions or the weather forecast. During holiday periods, park rangers conduct nature walks and evening programs.

At the Hermitage or Glencoe Lodge, you can arrange for sightseeing flights or guided excursions.

Sightseeing flights. One of the "don't miss" experiences in New Zealand is a flight by ski-plane over the icy peaks and glaciers of the Southern Alps. Weather conditions permitting, ski-equipped aircraft operate from Mount Cook airport.

Two flights are available: a 40-minute excursion to the Tasman Glacier, and the 1-hour Grand Circle flight over the main divide.

Within a few minutes after takeoff, your small plane is flying above the gleaming white slopes, saw-edged ridges, and jumbled icefalls to the head of the Tasman Glacier. Your pilot lowers the retractable skis, and the craft skims to a gentle stop on the granular ice. You step out onto a high snowfield once accessible only to veteran mountaineers.

Tasman Glacier trip. Each morning and afternoon a bus departs from the Hermitage for the 2-hour trip up the rocky, single-lane road to a viewpoint of Tasman Glacier and surrounding peaks. On a still day, you can often hear the ice creak and crack, and occasionally you'll hear the rumble of a distant avalanche.

Hiking park trails

Even if clouds move in to obscure the mountains, you can get out and walk some of the tracks fanning out from park headquarters. As long as you dress for it and watch for worsening conditions, a brisk hike can be invigorating—even in wet weather.

At park headquarters you'll find printed trail information and booklets on Governor's Bush and the Kea Point nature walk. You can rent boots, heavy socks, and any other necessary equipment at the Hermitage.

Bush tracks. The Governor's Bush trail loops through a remnant of silver beech forest behind the post office; beginning below Glencoe Bridge, it takes about an hour to complete.

Even shorter is Bowen Track, a 15-minute hike on the knoll opposite the youth hostel. The track ends with a view up the Hooker Valley to Mount Cook.

Alpine meadows. The Kea Point nature walk begins in front of the Hermitage, traverses open slopes and jungly scrub, then comes out in the open overlooking Mueller Glacier. Wildflowers bloom on subalpine slopes from October to January. Allow at least 3 hours.

In summer you can take the 2½-hour Sealy Tarns hike through wildflower country to these small mountain lakes, where you can swim and enjoy stunning views.

Behind Glencoe Lodge the track to Red Tarns zigzags up the slope. Outstanding views of Mount Cook and other high peaks await hikers at the end of the 1½ to 2-hour trek. Energetic climbers continue up 1,468-meter/4,819-foot Mount Sebastopol.

Up the Hooker Valley. Forking off the Kea Point path, the Hooker Valley Track crosses the Hooker River on a pair of swing bridges on the way to the terminal face of the Hooker Glacier. Experienced mountaineers and guided parties continue up to Hooker Hut and Copland Pass.

Beginning at the Ball Hut road bridge, the Wakefield Track follows the trail along the Hooker River used by parties traveling to the Tasman Glacier in the early 1900s.

Mountaineering and skiing excursions

Though climbers began arriving at Mount Cook in the 1880s, the peak was not conquered until Christmas Day, 1894. Mount Cook National Park encompasses one of the world's best mountaineering areas; many of New Zealand's famous alpinists started their training here. Ski-equipped planes give skiers access to previously inaccessible regions on the upper snowfields.

Alpine climbs. Ardent mountaineers find a wealth of challenges, as the park includes many of the finest and most demanding climbs in the Southern Alps. At least one experienced mountaineer should go with each party, and climbers should always notify a park ranger of climbing plans before starting out. You can arrange for climbing instruction and guide service at the Hermitage; equipment is available for hire or purchase. The mountaineering school operates from November through March.

Full day guided trips can be arranged to Hochstetter Icefall, Hooker Hut, Mueller Hut, and other destinations. On longer trips, mountaineers arrange to stay overnight at alpine huts.

Skiing the high snowfields. Ski-equipped planes provide an easy and timesaving way for experienced alpine skiers to enjoy the high snowfields on the Tasman, Mueller, and Murchison glaciers. Excellent skiing is generally available from June to September.

In recent years ski-touring and ski-mountaineering have become popular; groups bunk overnight at high-country huts. At the Hermitage visitors can rent equipment, arrange for ski mountaineering instruction, or hire an experienced alpine guide.

Dunedin

Spread over the hills at the head of one of the country's loveliest harbors, Dunedin was envisioned by its Scottish founders as the "Edinburgh of the South." The first settlers landed at Port Chalmers in 1848 to colonize the Presbyterian settlement.

After gold was discovered in Central Otago in the 1860s, the tiny frontier colony thrived. Prosperity ushered in a golden era in architecture, culture, and industry. Dunedin soon became the wealthiest and most influential town in New Zealand—the model for the rest of the country.

Today Dunedin is New Zealand's fourth largest city (population 120,000) and capital of Otago, the largest province. It is a commercial and manufacturing center, a busy port and transportation hub, and the gateway to Central Otago and the Southern Lakes.

A gracious and dignified city, Dunedin has its own special charm. Reminders of its Scottish heritage are evident in its street names and in the sturdy appeal of its handsome stone buildings. You'll find the country's only kiltmaker and whisky distillery here, and a statue of Scottish poet Robert Burns overlooks downtown activity from the Octagon, a small park in the center of town.

You can reach the city by air, rail, and road. Highway 1 and the main South Island railway line parallel the waterfront a few blocks east of the town center. Air New Zealand and Mount Cook planes land at Dunedin's attractively landscaped airport 29 km/18 miles southwest of the city near Mosgiel.

Getting settled in Dunedin

Dunedin is a planned city, its streets and suburbs fanning out from the Octagon, the grassy park around which one-way traffic circulates.

Gothic clock tower *rises above the slate-roofed bluestone buildings of the University of Otago. You're welcome to stroll among the century-old buildings of the country's first university.*

Bisecting the Octagon is Dunedin's main thoroughfare. It is named George Street north of the park, Princes Street to the south. Most of the main downtown stores, banks, hotels, and restaurants are concentrated along or near this street. Stuart Street branches at right angles from the Octagon.

Downtown hotels, all within easy walking distance of the Octagon, include the Townhouse, City Hotel, Southern Cross, and DB Wain's Hotel. Cherry Court Lodge enjoys a garden setting a few blocks north of the park, and Leisure Lodge Inn borders the Leith near the Botanic Gardens. Melrose Motor Lodge overlooks the Town Belt and harbor. In south Dunedin is the Shoreline Motor Hotel.

For dinner, try the Savoy Restaurant on Princes Street at Moray Place (old English atmosphere); Restaurant Lucerna, 218 George Street (continental dishes); the City Hotel restaurant; or Chequers, 43 Moray Place (cozy ambience, smorgasbord lunches). A suburban favorite is La Scala on Alton Avenue, southeast of the city in Musselburgh.

Most evening entertainment revolves around the hotels. Concerts are presented at Town Hall, and traveling artists perform at the Regent Theatre.

For tourist information on Dunedin and Otago province, stop during weekday office hours at the Otago Council (Inc.) office, 119 Princes Street (P.O. Box 901). Brochures outline points of interest on Dunedin walks and motoring tours. You can pick up travel reservations and tour information at the Government Tourist Bureau in Cargill House, 123 Princes Street, just a few doors away.

A bus tour of the city and Otago Peninsula leaves daily at 2 P.M. in front of the G.T.B. office.

A walk around town

If you enjoy exploring a city on foot, you'll like Dunedin's compact central district. In an hour or two, you can stroll some of the downtown streets, enjoy a few of the city's parks and architectural gems, and absorb a bit of Dunedin's history.

Many fine Victorian buildings give the city its distinctive character, recalling the era when Dunedin was the most important settlement in the country. In older parts of the city, houses reflect Scottish touches added by the early settlers.

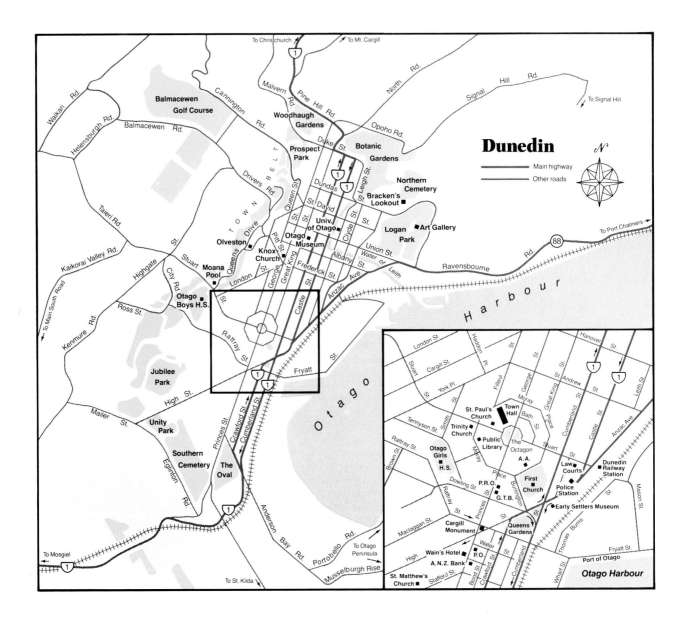

The Octagon.

The Octagon. Heart of the city is the grassy Octagon, where you stand beneath aging trees and survey the passing scene alongside the statue of Scotland's bard. Shoppers pause here to chat, and office workers eat lunch on the grass on pleasant days.

Facing the park are impressive St. Paul's Cathedral, the Municipal Chambers with its adjacent Town Hall, and the Regent and Fortune theaters. Nightly between 9 and 9:15, the Star Fountain puts on a colorful display utilizing water jets, music, and special lighting effects.

First Church. Walk east down Stuart Street, detouring a block south on Moray Place for a look at the First Church of Otago. One of the country's finest churches, it was designed by R. A. Lawson—architect of many of Dunedin's most distinctive buildings—and dedicated in 1873. Interior features

include a lovely rose window and imaginative plant and animal motifs carved in Oamaru stone.

Railway station. Returning to Stuart Street, continue east past the Law Courts to Dunedin's elegant old railway station. Its facade features granite pillars supporting an arched colonnade. A delightful touch is the New Zealand Railways' motif (NZR) used with abandon—etched in glass, patterned in mosaic floor tile, even created in stained glass (in the second-floor windows depicting a smoke-belching steam train).

Early Settlers Museum. Turn south and follow Anzac Avenue to the Early Settlers Museum, repository of a collection of vintage vehicles (steam locomotives, a cable car, a Cobb & Co. stagecoach, and Dunedin's first fire engine), old paintings and photographs, and relics of whaling and mining days. The museum is open weekdays from 9 to

4:30; from late October to Easter it is also open 10 to 4 Saturdays, 2 to 4 Sundays.

Angle a block south on Cumberland Street past Queens Gardens, a tranquil island in a sea of traffic. Then walk west on Rattray Street to the ornate Gothic Cargill Monument at Princes Street.

Classic buildings. Some of the city's well-designed 19th century buildings are still in use in the stock exchange area. Many are constructed of Port Chalmers or Oamaru stone and include interior furnishings of native and imported woods.

Among buildings of special note are these on Princes Street: the 1874 Lawson-designed A.N.Z. Bank, built in classical Greek style; Wain's Hotel, built in 1878 with carvings above its street-level bay windows; and the 1883 Bank of New Zealand, noted for its fine ceiling in the banking hall. Another century-old church is St. Matthews on Stafford Street; it contains a rebuilt 1880 organ.

To return to the Octagon, walk north up Princes Street.

Dunedin's hilly green belt

To fully appreciate Dunedin's harbor setting, head for the hills. Framed between rugged peninsulas, narrow Otago Harbour cuts inland. At its head, Dunedin's buildings rim the water and climb the encircling hills.

Dunedin's planners reserved a band of greenery —called the Town Belt—on the higher slopes of the hills facing the harbor. Queens Drive, a 7-km/ 4-mile scenic road, winds through this wooded retreat, offering motorists and walkers a succession of magnificent vistas.

Favorite close-in view points include Unity Park, Bracken's Lookout (Northern Cemetery), and Southern Cemetery. For sweeping panoramas, head north of the city to Signal Hill or Mount Cargill.

One of the city walks (map brochure available) takes you through part of the reserve. It starts near Queen and Regent streets and follows Queens Drive north through Prospect Park and the Woodhaugh Gardens.

Other Dunedin highlights

Dunedin's handsome architecture delights the eye. It also provides tangible evidence of the prosperity and talent that enriched the burgeoning town during the late 19th century. Wealthy residents began assembling some of the country's outstanding collections of art and historical items.

A drive around Dunedin and its suburbs leads you to these and other attractions:

Otago Museum. One of the finest museums in the country, the Otago is noted for its Pacific collections of Oceanian art, Polynesian and Melanesian cultural displays, marine life and maritime exhibits, and fine arts collections. In Maori Hall, you'll see a reconstructed meeting house and storehouse, examples of carving, tools and artifacts, greenstone, and wearing apparel. The adjacent Hocken Library is a repository of historic New Zealand books, manuscripts, maps, photographs, and art.

Located on Great King Street, the museum is open on weekdays and Saturday and Sunday afternoons.

Botanic Gardens. Established in 1868, this north Dunedin showplace is lovely in any season but at its best in spring with massed rhododendron and azalea displays and daffodils popping out of the lawn. Colorful autumn foliage brightens the upper area during April. The main entrance to the gardens is at Pine Hill Road and Great King Street.

Art Gallery. Located in Logan Park, the gallery is noted for the Smythe collection of watercolors, paintings by Frances Hodgkins, and frequent special exhibitions. The museum is open weekdays and Saturday and Sunday afternoons.

University of Otago. New Zealand's first university was founded in 1869; it moved to its present site 9 years later. Walk through the stone archway and the quadrangle, enjoying the old stone buildings, mature trees, and a placid stream called the Water of Leith.

A & P shows—a warm and festive look at rural life

Take an enjoyable look at New Zealand's rural life style by attending one of the Agricultural & Pastoral Society shows held in farming communities throughout the country. Most take place on Saturdays from October through March. Tourist information offices, local newspapers, and word-of-mouth alert you to upcoming shows.

The smaller A & P shows are the most fun. From outlying farms and ranches, families bring their prize livestock, produce, and homecrafts to the showgrounds. Activities are informal, and the whole family participates.

Early in the day, most men congregate near the livestock exhibits. They stand in small groups discussing the merits of different breeds of sheep and cattle. Youngsters nervously groom their animals before the livestock judging and riding events. In the exhibit building, women arrange their preserved and baked goods, sewing and knitting projects, garden produce, and cut flowers. Children's art work is displayed on the walls.

Sheep dog trials and horse jumping events are afternoon highlights. Burly wood choppers and skillful sheep shearers have their own competitions. Food vendors, amusement rides, and displays of new farm equipment vie for attention. Children scamper about trying to see everything at once.

Later, thirsty spectators may gather at a local pub to rehash the day's events.

Olveston. Built for a wealthy and well-traveled Dunedin businessman and bequeathed to the city by his daughter, this 35-room mansion depicts a bygone era of gracious living. The Jacobean-style house, completed in 1906, stands on a landscaped acre sheltered by tall trees. It is a showplace of Edwardian grandeur, containing antique furniture and elegant household articles shipped here from all parts of the world.

Located at 42 Royal Terrace (at the corner of Cobden Street off Queens Drive), the building is open daily for guided tours.

The beach scene. The surf-and-sand set heads for St. Clair and St. Kilda, two beachside communities south of Dunedin. You can watch surfers ride the waves, play a round of golf, swim in a heated salt water pool, or follow the horses at Forbury Park Raceway.

From St. Kilda, a short, scenic drive cuts across the sand dunes to a lookout at Lawyers Head.

Day trips from Dunedin

Short excursions from Dunedin offer visitors a look at the hilly Otago Peninsula with its numerous attractions, the deep-water harbor at Port Chalmers, and the historic Taieri Plain.

The Otago Peninsula loop

Southeast of Dunedin, the hilly Otago Peninsula offers a delightful rural excursion. Small settlements and weekend cottages dot the harbor's sheltered slopes, contrasting with the wild and lonely beauty of the Pacific side. Dry stone walls, tinted with moss and lichen, lace the peninsula. Sea birds abound, not only the famous royal albatross but also shags, yellow-eyed penguins, godwits, and oystercatchers.

Part of the fun *of country driving is meeting an occasional flock of sheep being herded along the road. Sheep dog (far right) responds to his master's whistle and keeps strays with the rest of the group. Keep alert; stray animals occasionally wander onto the road.*

Take the Portobello Road along the harbor, then return along the high road that follows the crest of the peninsula hills, offering views of the rugged coastline and secluded bays.

Glenfalloch. Nestled in a fold in the hills above the harbor, this 30-acre woodland garden reflects a century of loving care. The original 1871 homestead still stands. Now owned by the Otago Peninsula Trust, the garden peaks in spring when primroses bloom under English oaks and azaleas and rhododendrons create dramatic displays. Bush walks lead up the glen; a small stream trickles down the hill to the harbor.

Larnach Castle. Crowning a 1,000-foot wooded hill in the center of the peninsula, this sumptuous residence was built in the 1870s by Dunedin banker W. J. M. Larnach for his first wife, a French heiress.

Building the hilltop mansion far from town was an audacious project. Designed in Scotland, the 43-room Neo-Gothic castle took 3 years to build, another 12 to complete the handsome interior. Materials and master craftsmen were brought here from around the world—marble from Italy, glass from Venice, tiles from England, woods from many countries. The 40,000-square-foot house required 46 household servants to maintain. Larnach added the 3,000-square-foot ballroom as a 21st birthday present for his favorite daughter.

Now being privately restored, the house is open daily to visitors. After completing your self-guided tour of the interior, take the spiral stone stairs up to the battlements for a commanding panorama from Dunedin across the harbor to the heads and open coast. Before leaving, stroll through the gardens and visit the dungeons (used by Larnach for storing firewood) and brick-paved stables.

Harborside attractions. The Portobello Marine Biological Station occupies a site facing Otago Harbour. Part of the University of Otago, it maintains a variety of marine life in tanks and pools.

Otakou (corrupted by early whalers to "Otago") was the site of an ancient Maori settlement from which the province took its name. A plaque near the water marks the site of the 1830s whaling station. Behind the Otakou Maori Church, built in 1940 to replace an earlier structure, are a small museum and a cemetery. Three important South Island Maori chiefs are buried here.

Albatross colony. The world's largest sea bird— the royal albatross—breeds in a mainland colony at Taiaroa Head at the northern tip of the Otago Peninsula. Adult birds have a wing span up to 3½ meters/11 feet. During high winds, you sometimes see the giant birds circling above their nesting grounds.

The birds arrive at Taiaroa late in September. In early November they build their nests, and each female lays a single white egg about 5 inches in diameter. Chicks hatch in January.

By prior arrangement, small parties may visit the colony from late November to mid-January and from mid-February through September. In-

quiries and reservations are handled by the Government Tourist Bureau in Dunedin.

Port Chalmers, Otago's seafaring town

Otago's first settlers arrived by sea, landing at Port Chalmers in 1848. The port town faces a sheltered, deep-water bay on Otago Harbour's northern shore about 14 km/9 miles northeast of Dunedin.

Thousands of fortune hunters landed here in the 1860s on their way to the gold fields. New Zealand's first export cargo of frozen meat was shipped from Port Chalmers in 1882. Antarctic explorers Scott, Shackleton, and Byrd called here on their expeditions to the southern continent.

Today Port Chalmers' prosperity rests on its modern wharf and container shipping facilities.

Overlooking the town is St. Iona's Presbyterian Church, its spire-topped stone clock tower commanding the skyline. On the headland dominating the harbor stand a restored flagstaff—erected in 1862 to regulate harbor traffic—and a lookout.

Numerous 19th century buildings dot the old seafaring town, many of them constructed of Port Chalmers stone. At 55 Harrington Street is Stonehenge, best preserved of four remaining stone houses built in the 1880s. Holy Trinity Church, constructed in the mid-1870s, has a hammer-beamed ceiling, stone walls, and an unusual organ. St. Mary's Star of the Sea Church opened in 1878; its interior emphasizes the community's link with the sea.

The local fishing fleet anchors at Careys Bay, just north of Port Chalmers. At low tide you can see the rotting hulks of several old sailing ships off the shore of Deborah Bay. The coastal road continues to Aramoana, where holiday homes face an ocean beach; flocks of sea birds feed here.

Mosgiel and the Taieri Plain

Colonists who settled on the fertile Taieri Plain prospered during the gold rush by supplying provisions for the miners. They built large homesteads and developed farms where they improved stock breeds and pioneered new farming methods. Many colonial buildings of the 1860s and 1870s are still in use in Taieri farms and communities.

The country's first woolen factory, in operation since 1871 in Mosgiel, was the first major industry on the Taieri Plain. You can arrange to visit the modern plant on weekdays and see raw wool converted into finished fabric.

Many buildings are closely linked with early Taieri settlers. Of special interest is the East Taieri Church, one of architect R. A. Lawson's many splendid works. Built in 1870, the brick and stone church is elaborate by Presbyterian standards. The 1877 manse and cemetery are nearby.

Gold seekers forded the Taieri River at Outram. Taieri Historic Park features historic buildings, moved here from other sites, and a riverside recreation area. Outram contains a number of restored 19th century buildings.

West of Outram, traffic to the gold fields took the hilly old Dunstan Road to Styx (Paerau), Dunstan (Clyde), and other diggings. Highway 87 follows the prospectors' route some 35 km/22 miles northwest to Clarks Junction, then continues north along the Rock and Pillar Range to Middlemarch and Hyde. In Macraes Flat, 19 km/12 miles southeast of Hyde, sturdy old Stanley's Hotel still serves thirsty travelers as it has since gold mining days.

Central Otago

Sun-baked in summer and numbingly cold in winter, "Central" is a grand and desolate region of craggy ranges, stark ravines, fruit orchards, and tawny tracts of wind-rippled tussock stretching toward the distant horizon. Sleepy old mining towns and abandoned stone cottages drowse in the golden sun beneath cobalt blue skies.

Sheep-run holders who opened up this parched hinterland in the late 1850s earned their wealth by lonely isolation and hardship. A few years later, prospectors established the first settlements; colorful names bestowed during mining days still identify many towns, hills, and gullies.

Settlers transformed the once-barren landscape with greenery, planting trees along river banks and roadways and in windbreaks. More recently, dams and irrigation channels have made farming feasible and added to the country's hydroelectric power.

You can make a 2-day loop from Dunedin into Central Otago or sample the country on your way to Queenstown or the West Coast. In Alexandra, the region's main town, you can stay in the DB Golden Central Hotel or any of several small motels. Cromwell, center of the Clutha Valley hydroelectric project, has a variety of accommodations. Simple overnight facilities are available in Clyde, Roxburgh, Naseby, and Ranfurly.

Up the Clutha River

About 60-km/37-miles southwest of Dunedin near Milton, Highway 8 branches off the east coast road and cuts northwest into the bare, brown, and beautiful hills of Central Otago—gold country.

Lawrence. Poplars and birch trees line the highway as you approach Lawrence, a once-raw mining town that has grown old gracefully. Its Victorian buildings reflect its history — prosperity followed by gradual decline. Lawrence lies at the convergence of two gold-bearing streams: Gabriels Gully, where Gabriel Read made the discovery in May, 1861, triggering the Otago gold rush; and Wetherstons, also the scene of feverish activity.

Roxburgh. Fruit orchards and a massive hydroelectric power dam dominate Roxburgh's site. Peaches, apricots, apples, and strawberries are raised commercially; most are airlifted to northern markets. Seasonal pickers converge on the town at harvest time, and "pick-your-own" orchards attract Otago families on weekends. Coal mining (at Coal Creek) and sheep farming are also important.

North of town, giant Roxburgh Dam holds back the waters of the Clutha River. Completed in 1962, the dam flooded river banks that had seen nearly a century of gold mining activity. Behind the dam, a long narrow lake extends some 32-km/20-miles upriver; it's a boaters' favorite.

Alexandra, hub of Central Otago

Prospectors rushed here after gold was discovered in 1862, but for many years Alexandra was outshone by its twin town of Dunstan (Clyde). Gold dredging gave the town a new lease on life in the 1890s.

Today Alexandra is the hub of a prosperous fruit growing district. Apricots, peaches, nectarines, plums, cherries, apples, and pears are shipped all over the country. Alexandra's spring blossom festival is a big event. In late March and April, deciduous trees turn bright with autumn foliage.

The small Bodkin Museum, southeast of Pioneer Park on Thomson Street, is open weekday afternoons. Here you'll see interesting gold mining exhibits, including articles used by Chinese miners. A giant hillside clock, lighted at night, overlooks the town.

For an overview of Alexandra, the Clutha and Manuherikia rivers, and the surrounding hills, drive on Highway 85 to the northeast edge of town, turn right across the combined rail/road bridge, and take Little Valley Road to the observation point atop Tucker Hill. On your return, detour up Graveyard Gully to Shaky Bridge, a restored suspension span across the Manuherikia River.

Near Alexandra, side roads lead up many old gold mining gullies, some now planted in fruit trees. Anglers and water-sports enthusiasts head for trout-stocked reservoirs. In winter, local families enjoy ice skating and curling on frozen lakes behind Idaburn and Lower Manorburn dams.

The Cromwell Gorge

Upriver from Alexandra, the Clutha and its tributaries drain the great glacial valleys of Wanaka, Hawea, and Wakatipu. Joined by the Kawarau River at Cromwell, the Clutha funnels into the rocky Cromwell Gorge.

For nearly 20 km/12 miles the deep river flows steadily onward between steep barren slopes, relieved by only an occasional apricot orchard.

Major changes are in the air that will alter the region's character. Extensive power development is planned in the Upper Clutha basin. Cromwell's population (now 1,200) is expected to increase 600 percent over the next decade as construction workers arrive to build five dams. A dam at Clyde will flood the Cromwell Gorge; two more Clutha dams are planned between Cromwell and Luggate, and two dams will be constructed on the Kawarau River between Cromwell and Queenstown.

Clyde. The once-boisterous mining settlement of Dunstan has a sleepy charm these days. On a walk around town, you'll come across many stone buildings, constructed with rock quarried during road building through the Cromwell Gorge. You can see mining memorabilia in the Goldfields Museum in the 1864 stone courthouse on Blyth Street.

Cromwell. Perched above the junction of the swift-flowing Clutha and Kawarau rivers, Cromwell keeps the gold era alive. From December to May, you can learn about mining methods—from simple gold pan to massive quartz stamper and dredging equipment—at The Goldminer on Main Street. A pleasant walk along the Kawarau River begins in the garden by the bridge.

From Cromwell you can visit several deserted gold towns, marked by abandoned stone buildings, piles of waste rock, and scattered trees. Highway 8 leads north along the Clutha to Lowburn and Bendigo. South of Cromwell, unpaved roads lead to Bannockburn and old mining sites in the Carrick Range.

Golden ghosts of the Maniototo

From Alexandra you head north up the Manuherikia Valley. Settlements are small and scattered. Side roads lead to sheep stations—some stocked since the 1860s—and old mining settlements in the

Central Otago

— Main highways
— Other roads

0   10   20   30 Miles
0   20   40 Kilometers

foothills of the Dunstan Mountains and Raggedy Range.

Off the main road are St. Bathans and Naseby, both former gold mining centers worth a detour. About halfway between Alexandra and the coast is

Enjoy a bird's-eye view of glaciers and fiords

One of the most thrilling treats for visitors in this air-minded nation is flightseeing—sightseeing by small airplane.

These maneuverable, low-flying aircraft have helped to open up remote and rugged parts of New Zealand, both for agriculture (top-dressing and seeding steep farmlands) and the recreation. Fishermen and hunters can fly in to remote bases and have the plane return for them later.

In most of the main tourist centers you can climb aboard a single or twin-engine plane or helicopter for a bird's-eye view of the region's lakes, mountains, fiords, or coastline. Photographers will find the most expansive views from the seats beside or immediately behind the pilot. Pastures, river valleys, bush, and urban activity quickly slip away as your small craft climbs. New Zealand's varied scenery takes on a dramatic new perspective.

Perhaps the most spectacular trip is the flight through the rugged white wonderland of the

Southern Alps. Ski-equipped planes leave from Mount Cook, Franz Josef, and Fox Glacier. You thread through snowy peaks, fly over gaping crevasses, and then land briefly on one of the high snowfields.

In Rotorua, Taupo, and the southern lakes district, you soar above bush-rimmed lakes. You can gaze into gaping volcanic craters and look down on steaming geothermal valleys. Flights from Queenstown and Te Anau take you over Fiordland's dense bush and above hikers' huts along the Milford Track.

If you crave an aerial view of bush-covered headlands bordering azure sea, consider flights over the Marlborough Sounds waterways (from Picton) or the Bay of Islands (from Paihia). Above Auckland you look down on Waitemata Harbour and the islands of the Hauraki Gulf. From Kaitaia, fly along Ninety Mile Beach to Cape Reinga—and see Northland's kauri gum fields and mangrove swamps, as well.

Meeting *the mail boat,*
this Marlborough
Sounds resident picks
up mail, freight,
and a visitor,
then heads back to shore.

Ranfurly, farming center and largest town (population 1,000) on the Maniototo Plains. Highway 85 continues east across the Pigroot, a well-worn route to the gold fields.

St. Bathans. A string of tired Victorian buildings, anchored by the Vulcan Hotel, descends St. Bathans' sloping street. After the miners left, the excavated valley flooded to form Blue Lake. Years of hydraulic mining created the high, fluted cliffs surrounding the deep pool. Nearby Vinegar Hill and Cambrians also saw extensive mining activity.

Naseby. One of the most attractive of the mining towns, Naseby has a peaceful, unhurried charm. Trees shade most of its streets. Some buildings, including the 1863 Ancient Briton hotel, are built of sundried brick. The Maniototo Early Settlers' Museum has memorabilia of mining days and early curling contests, as well as an outdoor display of vintage vehicles.

In summer, Naseby is popular with campers; in winter, visitors come here to ice skate and to enjoy the Scottish sport of curling.

Northeast of Naseby, the narrow and unpaved Dansey Pass road cuts a twisting route across the Kakanui Mountains to the Waitaki Valley. Heaped tailings and ragged cliffs identify the Kyeburn Diggings. The present Dansey Pass Hotel, built in the 1880s, provides refreshment and accommodation for travelers in this lonely region.

Ranfurly. No ghost town, Ranfurly is Maniototo's administrative and supply center. It lies in the heart of a vast inland plain broken only by occasional clumps of pines and poplars. South of Ranfurly are isolated stations and scattered farming settlements, some—such as Hamiltons and Patearoa—dating from mining days. The paved road ends at Patearoa, but a graveled route continues to Paerau (Styx), where you'll still see buildings from the early 1860s. Styx was an overnight coach stop on the Old Dunstan Road at the Taieri River crossing.

Over the Pigroot. East of Ranfurly, Highway 85 is known as the Pigroot, another old coach road that linked Palmerston with the Otago gold fields. Rough roads lead off to abandoned diggings and empty old roadside coaching inns, and vast lonely expanses of golden tussock stretch toward the far-off mountains.

Marlborough Sounds

Narrow, watery fingers deeply indent the lush green Marlborough coastline on South Island's northeast tip. These drowned coastal river valleys, called the Sounds, create more than 600 miles of shoreline, a maze of sheltered waterways, inviting bays and coves, and wooded peninsulas sloping steeply to the sea. Pleasure craft now sail the waters first explored by Captain James Cook.

You can reach the Sounds by train or bus from Christchurch, or you can take a 30-minute flight from Wellington to Blenheim. But the most satisfying approach is by ship.

Many travelers first glimpse South Island from aboard one of the interisland auto/rail ferries linking Wellington and Picton. On a 3½-hour ferry trip, you cross Cook Strait and cruise up Tory Channel into Queen Charlotte Sound, savoring the region's remoteness and leisurely pace.

Picton, at the head of Queen Charlotte Sound, is the main port and chief holiday center of the area. Blenheim, 29 km/18 miles inland, is the province's main farming center.

The prime holiday season in this sunny region extends from late spring to late autumn (November through April). If you plan to be there during the peak season (December through February), make your reservations well in advance. In winter you'll often enjoy clear days and cool nights.

Newmans Coaches link the province's main towns with Nelson and Christchurch; rail service connects Picton with Christchurch and intermediate towns. Visitor information is available in Blenheim.

Settling in ... accommodations

Most vacationers headquarter near the water, where accommodations run the gamut.

In Picton, the Picton Motor Inn, Harbour View Motel, and Whalers Inn overlook marina activity, and the DB Terminus Hotel is located about 50 yards from the waterfront. Most motels are located near the central district and along Waikawa Road, east of the harbor.

Blenheim's leading downtown hotels are the Autolodge Motor Inn and the DB Criterion; the town also has a number of good motels.

If you enjoy rustic accommodations, the licensed Portage Hotel on Kenepuru Sound may be to your liking. You reach it by road from Picton or by water taxi. Numerous unlicensed guest houses and simple motel-style accommodations are scattered on secluded bays throughout the Sounds.

Picton, busy deep-water port

Most Sounds activity centers on Picton, the small bustling ferry port (population 3,100) at the head of Queen Charlotte Sound. Here, pleasure boats and sightseeing launches cluster along the waterfront, and interisland ferries steam in and out of port.

Holiday activity centers on London Quay, bordering Picton's foreshore, where you can arrange for sightseeing trips, look over local crafts, and watch waterfront activity. A museum on the foreshore features whaling equipment and artifacts.

Vacationing families come here to play in the sun—swim, fish, water-ski, hike—or to explore the endless waterways by boat. For a pleasant stroll, cross the humpbacked bridge arching above the marina and follow the path along the harbor shore to Bob's Bay, a sheltered cove where you can swim and picnic.

Sightseeing excursions. On London Quay several operators offer half-day and full-day launch sightseeing cruises on Queen Charlotte Sound. Water taxi service, mail boat and fishing trips, and summer evening cruises also begin here.

A favorite launch trip goes up Grove Arm, across Onahau Bay, and back to Picton via Lochmara and Double Cove, where tame fish swim to the surface when food is thrown to them.

On a longer trip you can picnic at Kumutoto Bay or Ship Cove, near the mouth of the sound, where Captain Cook's ships anchored in the 1770s. Queen Charlotte Sound was one of his favorite Pacific anchorages—he paused here on five separate occasions during his explorations.

You can also arrange for scenic flights over the Sounds and half-day or full-day sightseeing trips by minicoach to Nelson and Port Underwood and along Queen Charlotte Drive.

Scenic drives. From Picton, scenic roads branch west along Queen Charlotte Sound and east to Waikawa and Port Underwood.

Queen Charlotte Drive closely follows the shore of Grove Arm, climbing to headland viewpoints, then dipping to waterside to meet bays and coves. Side roads lead to the Cobham Outward Bound School at Anakiwa and to settlements bordering scenic Kenepuru Sound. Allow about an hour for the leisurely drive to Havelock.

Waikawa Road passes Picton's marina, then continues northeast toward Waikawa. Take the marked side road to Victoria Domain for a fine view. Anchored boats bob on the sheltered waters of Waikawa Bay. A winding road continues across the saddle between Queen Charlotte Sound and Port Underwood. Its fame dates from the late 1820s, when Port Underwood became the center of feverish whaling activity. Whaling ships from many countries operated in these waters.

Fishing Marlborough's rivers and sounds

Anglers enjoy excellent fishing, both in the Sounds and in Marlborough's well-stocked trout streams.

The sheltered waters of the Sounds attract many fishermen, boaters, and skin divers every year. Cod, terakihi, snapper, garfish, groper, and butterfish are plentiful. Surfcasters concentrate along the east coast from Kaikoura north to Cape Koamaru. Charter excursions and public fishing trips depart from Picton; small boats with outboard motors can also be hired.

Fly fishermen head for the Rai and Pelorus rivers. Brown trout are also abundant in the Wairau and Opawa rivers and in Spring Creek. In the summer, salmon migrate up the lower reaches of the Wairau River.

Marlborough Sounds Maritime Park

Picton and Havelock, at the head of Pelorus Sound, are departure points for launch trips to scenic shore and island reserves in the Sounds. Roads lead to some reserves, though the most enjoyable way to explore the park is by boat.

More than 100 separate reserves make up the maritime park. Some offer good picnicking and camping sites, as well as trails for bush walking. Others—particularly offshore islands in the Sounds and Cook Strait—are breeding grounds for native birds and animals. Historic reserves reflect the region's rich history—preMaori occupation, Maori culture, early European explorers, the 19th century whalers.

Largest of the reserves is Tennyson Inlet, accessible from Highway 6 by road from Rai Valley. The inlet is noted for its dense forests and varied birdlife.

Permits are required for camping, shooting, or visiting protected wildlife reserves. For information, contact the park ranger in Picton.

Blenheim, the district's farming center

A tidy town of parks and gardens, Blenheim lies 29 km/20 miles inland, surrounded by vineyards and farm lands. It is Marlborough's largest town and administrative center, having a population of 17,000.

Blenheim is New Zealand's newest wine-producing area; Montana Vineyards opened its Riverlands Winery here in 1977. West of town you'll see acres of vineyards.

Focal point of the business district is triangular Market Place, featuring a filigreed band rotunda. Stop in at the Marlborough Public Relations Office here for information on what to see and do in the province.

Parks and gardens. From Market Place, walk a block west on High Street to Seymour Square, colorful with seasonal flower displays. In the park you'll see the town's memorial fountain and stone clock tower. Marlborough historical exhibits are located in the public library across the street. On Fridays an indoor craft market is held in the former St. Andrew's Presbyterian Church facing the square.

Other pleasant places to stroll include Riverside Park, with its footbridges spanning a stream, and Pollard Park, a favorite for its rose gardens, sports grounds, and flower-bordered walkways along a creek.

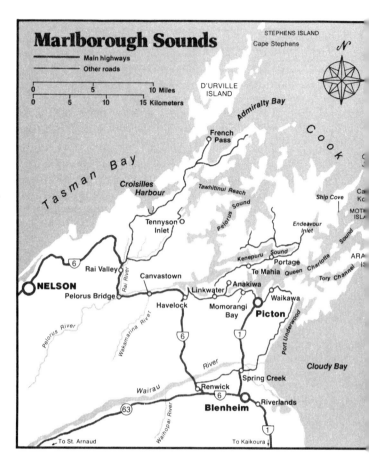

Brayshaw Museum Park, southwest of town on New Renwick Road, contains a miniature railway, vintage machinery and vehicles, and historical displays.

Excursions from Blenheim. About 5 km/3 miles southeast on Highway 1 is Riverlands cob cottage, a restored, mud-walled pioneer house built about 1860. A cobblestone path leads to the small cottage-museum, now refurbished with period household articles and costumed figures in colonial dress.

At the Renwick Motel in Renwick, visitors can arrange rides into the countryside in a horsedrawn gig, a variation of the Irish jaunting cart.

Over the mountains to Nelson

From Havelock, Highway 6 winds through the dairy country of the Pelorus and Rai valleys, across forested mountains, and down the Whangamoa valley into Nelson province.

Along the highway at Havelock, an old bush logging engine outside a former church marks the local museum. A small commercial fishing fleet moors here at the head of Pelorus Sound.

At Canvastown you pass a roadside display of 1860s mining equipment from the goldfields up the Wakamarina River. The mining activity was concentrated upstream at Deep Creek.

Allow time to stroll through a pocket of virgin bush at Pelorus Bridge Scenic Reserve. A short, self-guided nature trail called the Totara Walk offers a look at native ferns and trees—rimu, miro, tawa, kamahi, a giant totara—and leads down to a swimming hole in the Pelorus River.

You can pick up picnic supplies in Rai Valley, noted for its excellent local cheese and breads. The bakery, next to the post office, is known for baking loaves in unusual shapes and sizes.

Nelson and the Sunshine Coast

One of the earliest settlements of the colonizing New Zealand Company, Nelson has its roots deep in the soil. Apples, hops, and tobacco dominate the broad agricultural patchwork of the Waimea Plains and Motueka Valley.

Both Nelson province and its largest city—also named Nelson—honor Britain's great naval hero, and you'll see additional reminders of the region's links with sailors of various periods and nations. Other sizable towns include Motueka, Takaka, and —on the West Coast—Westport.

Nelson's sunny weather and sheltered coastline act as a magnet attracting many visitors, and lodging is hard to find whenever the weather is warm. Many Kiwis book a year ahead for the school holidays in late December and January.

Two national parks—Abel Tasman and Nelson Lakes—preserve dramatic areas of rugged seacoast and glacial lakes.

Newmans Coach Lines operates regular service linking the city of Nelson to the West Coast, north to Takaka, and east and south to Picton, Blenheim, and Christchurch. You can fly to Nelson from Wellington and Christchurch (via Hokitika and Westport).

Sunny, relaxing Nelson

Facing a sheltered harbor, and encircled by wooded mountains at the head of Tasman Bay, Nelson is one of the country's oldest cities. It was settled by colonists in 1841.

Dominating the city is Church Hill, topped by an Anglican cathedral built of local Takaka marble. Good viewpoints for enjoying the panorama of city and bay are Cleveland Terrace and Princes Drive, both features of the city scenic tour.

Main downtown hotels are the DB Rutherford and the DB Nelson. Motels near Tahunanui Beach cater to vacationing families.

For information on attractions in Nelson and the province, stop at the Public Relations Office at the corner of Trafalgar and Halifax streets. Leaflets suggest local walks, a city scenic drive, and day trips from Nelson.

A downtown stroll. For a look at Nelson's central district, begin your walk at the city's traditional meeting place, the church steps leading down to Trafalgar Street. The city's main downtown artery, Trafalgar bisects the business district and crosses the tree-bordered Maitai River.

Queens Gardens offers a sylvan oasis about a 10-minute walk east of Trafalgar Street (on either

Ride the mail boat through the Marlborough Sounds

You're sure to enjoy exploring the wooded coastline and countless bays of the Sounds aboard a mailboat run. From Havelock, launches leave on daylong trips (weekdays except Wednesday) to deliver mail and supplies to outlying settlements on Pelorus and Kenepuru sounds. Telephone the day before— Havelock 34—to confirm schedule and space. Trips also depart from Picton.

Plan to arrive early—about 8 A.M.—at the Havelock wharf, and bring your lunch. Dress warmly; you may want to carry rain gear if the weather is changeable.

You'll climb aboard a launch piled high with mailbags, newspapers, boxes and bags of foodstuffs, hardware, and farm equipment—rolls of fencing wire, perhaps, or a shiny shovel tagged for its new owner. If rain threatens, a tarpaulin is tied over the cargo.

Your fellow passengers may be residents returning to their homes, campers stopping for a few days at one of the scenic reserves, fishermen who will be dropped off at a remote site and picked up on the return journey, or student travelers stopping at the Havelock youth hostel.

The launch cruises mile after mile of unspoiled waterways, past coves and bays where lush greenery slopes down to the waterline. Occasionally the boat may nose up to the bank to deposit or reclaim a party of campers or fishermen. You'll pass scenic and wildlife reserves. If you have binoculars, bring them along to watch native birds.

Since many families living on outlying homesteads get "out" infrequently, the mailboat is their major link with the outside world. As you approach each destination, you'll see at least one person—frequently an entire family and a dog or two—awaiting your arrival. If no dock is available or the tide is low, a couple of youngsters or their father will row out to meet the boat and get groceries and mail.

Hardy or Bridge Street). Nearby, in an 1898 building on Bridge Street, the Suter Art Gallery contains one of the country's best small collections (open daily from noon to 4; extended summer hours).

The Cawthron Institute, a private soil and agricultural science research institute and museum, is headquartered at 170 Milton. Exhibits illustrate the value of science to agriculture, mining, and forestry.

Spreading trees shade the close-in sports grounds of the Botanical Reserve at the east end of Hardy Street. One of the city's favorite walks is the 30-minute trek up 483-foot Botanical Hill, where you have a panoramic view of the city, port, and Maitai Valley.

Along the water. Industrial and recreational waterfront activity centers on Port Nelson, north of the business center near the entrance to Nelson Haven. Farther south is the magnificent white sweep of Tahunanui Beach.

A touch of the past. Nelson's early residents left a rich legacy of opulent houses and horticultural treasures. Many European trees they brought and planted have now grown to impressive maturity.

Just a few minutes south of Church Hill, the city-owned Melrose mansion reflects the Victorian architecture of the 1880s. Located in spacious grounds at Brougham and Trafalgar streets, it is used for a wide range of community activities.

Isel Park, about 2 miles south of town, is the setting for Isel House and the Nelson Provincial Museum. Thomas Marsden, one of the original settlers of the New Zealand Company, surrounded his two-story homestead with a 12-acre garden planted with trees from around the world. The house, located off Main Road in Stoke, is open from 2 to 4 weekends (also Tuesday and Thursday in January).

Behind Isel House, the Nelson Provincial Museum contains exhibits depicting local maritime history and the early days of the colony. Museum hours are 10 to 4 Tuesday through Friday (also Mondays in January), 2 to 4 weekends.

Not far away—on Nayland Road in Stoke—is Broadgreen, a restored 1855 cob house flanked by tree-shaded lawns and a large rose garden. Modeled after a Devonshire farmhouse, the two-story house has thick walls made of packed earth originally dug from the cellar. Refurnished with period furniture, Broadgreen is open to visitors on weekends from 2:30 to 4:30 or by appointment.

Visit a craftsperson. Nelson's climate, scenery, and clay have attracted a number of artists, potters, weavers, and other craftspeople. You can meet some of them in their studios and galleries. A folder available at the Nelson Public Relations Office lists local craftspeople who welcome visitors.

North along Tasman Bay

Below Richmond, Highway 6 branches northwest along the shore of Tasman Bay.

Coastal settlements. Blossoming apple and pear orchards brighten this countryside in October. The coastal road (via Mapua and Ruby Bay) cuts through the heart of the apple district. In season you'll pass roadside stalls piled high with fresh produce. Collectors find interesting sea shells along the shore of Ruby Bay.

Near Motueka, wire-hung hopfields and bright green fields of tobacco mark the center of New Zealand's hop and tobacco-growing industries. Large numbers of seasonal workers flock here each summer to help with the harvest. The Motueka Valley offers a sleepy river route through farming country to meet Highway 6 at Kohatu.

Fishing boats operating from Port Motueka land scallops and oysters from August to early November.

North of Riwaka, a short side road branches off to Kaiteriteri, a sheltered bay bordered by a curve of beach.

The Moutere Valley. Highway 60 follows an inland route near the Moutere River. Upper Moutere, settled by German immigrants in the 1840s, retains a faint Bavarian aura.

Lower Moutere is the site of the Riverside Community, a family-operated commune founded by pacifists during World War II.

Takaka Hill. At the base of the hill, a side road leads inland from the highway to a wooded picnic site near the source of the Riwaka River. Often you'll see fishermen dipping their lines.

As Highway 60 curves and climbs Takaka Hill, pull off the road and gaze back across the panorama of the Motueka Valley and Tasman Bay.

Marble quarried on Takaka Hill (also called Marble Mountain) has been used in the construction of some of New Zealand's most imposing buildings, including Nelson's cathedral and Wellington's Parliament Buildings. Near the summit you'll see strange marble outcroppings and unusual funnel-shaped rock basins. In summer you can view the delicate formations inside Ngarua Caves, near the top of Takaka Hill.

Beaches and a national park

Continuing north, the highway twists down the mountain's steep northern slope to the dairy country of the Takaka River valley. Until this road was completed, Golden Bay was relatively isolated from the rest of the province.

The town of Takaka contains several motels and motor camps, convenient for visitors making a day trip into Abel Tasman National Park. You'll find the park information office in Takaka and a visitor center at Totaranui Beach.

The 33-km/20-mile route from Takaka to Totaranui offers the only access road into the park. Along the way, look for good beaches at Pohara, Ligar Bay, and Tata. Pohara Beach has an adjacent campground and recreational facilities.

Abel Tasman National Park. New Zealand's

Vacationing families *swim in the sea, go sailing, or just relax on the sand at Nelson's Tahunanui Beach. Sunny days and sheltered, golden sand beaches attract visitors to Tasman Bay. A national park honors Dutch navigator Abel Tasman, who discovered New Zealand in 1642.*

smallest national park honors the country's first *pakeha* visitor, Dutch explorer Abel Tasman, who sailed these waters in 1642. A memorial overlook above Ligar Bay commemorates the site where he anchored.

The first 11 km/7 miles of the road from Takaka to the park are sealed (paved), but the surfacing ends at Tata Beach. The winding, graded road (not recommended for caravans) soon begins to climb into the forested hills. Spreading tree ferns rise above you to shade the road; streams cascade down gullies toward the bay. Trails wind through the park's primeval rain forest and along the shore.

At Totaranui, bush-covered headlands frame the golden sand beach and deep blue bay. Here you'll find a small campground and the visitor center containing displays on the park's vegetation, sea and land birds, and other natural features.

Other area attractions. Tame eels in the Anatoki River are fed daily (10 to 11 A.M. and 3 to 5 P.M.), weather permitting, from the end of August to early May. To reach Anatoki, turn west off Highway 60 just south of Takaka.

Northwest of Takaka is Waikoropupu (Pupu) Springs, where an estimated 200 million gallons of pure cold water flow from fresh-water springs each day. The road to the springs leaves Highway 60 north of Takaka.

Tramping through luxuriant bush

Many backpackers have discovered the Heaphy (Hee-fee) Track, a one-time prospectors' trail cutting across the grassy downs and subtropical valleys of northwest Nelson province.

Beginning southwest of Collingwood (via Bainham), the 72-km/45-mile route climbs through rimu and beech forest and then descends through the red tussock country of the Gouland Downs to the fern-filled valley of the Heaphy River. Here you'll find not only luxuriant stands of nikau palms but also giant sandflies—insect repellent is a "must" for travelers.

The magnificent final section of the track follows the bush-bordered seacoast south to end at the Kohaihai River north of Karamea. Trampers can arrange taxi service at both ends of the trail.

Tramping groups generally take 4 to 6 days to make the trek, staying overnight in trail huts along the route. Most hikers prefer the months of February and March, after the summer rains. But be prepared for all kinds of weather in this region that receives up to 200 inches of rain annually.

Experienced trampers who prefer a more challenging and less popular route seek out the Wangapeka Track, another miners' trail south of the Heaphy. It goes westward from Wangapeka through mountains and river valleys to end south of Karamea near Te Namu.

Trampers should check with New Zealand Forest Service rangers in Nelson or Takaka for current information on track conditions before setting out on either trek.

Collingwood and the northern tip

From Collingwood you can arrange four-wheel-drive trips to Farewell Spit and other off-road destinations near South Island's northern tip. Collingwood Motors organizes daily safari trips from mid-December to February (trips leave on Wednesdays only for the rest of the year; groups of

people can make special arrangements for other times).

Heading for the beach? You'll find safe swimming and easy boat launching at Paton's Rock, and alluring shells and colored pebbles at Parapara, both south of Collingwood. Surfcasting, swimming, a campground, and a store are to be found further north at Pakawau. On the north coast near Cape Farewell, Wharariki Beach offers wave-cut rock formations, a seal colony, and sea birds.

For an inland summer destination, drive southwest through the rich dairyland of the Aorere River valley to see limestone formations and glowworms in Te Anaroa Caves (open during the summer holidays). Take along picnic supplies (including some Collingwood cheddar cheese) for lunch beside the river.

Inland Nelson

Two main highways lead southwest to Nelson Lakes National Park and the Buller River.

From Blenheim and Renwick, Highway 63 follows the Wairau River upstream to meet Highway 6 at Kawatiri, north of the park. From Nelson, Highway 6 winds over the Spooner Range and through pine forest plantations to meet the Buller River, paralleling the water to Westport.

Nelson Lakes National Park. Beech-covered mountains rise steeply from the water to enclose a pair of slender glacial lakes—jewel-like Rotoiti and Rotoroa—now preserved in a national park.

Swimming, boating, water-skiing, and picnicking attract many visitors to Lake Rotoiti. More isolated Lake Rotoroa draws anglers, hunters, and trampers. In winter, skiers come to enjoy the fine runs on Mount Robert.

Tourist accommodations and park headquarters are located in St. Arnaud, on the northern shore of Lake Rotoiti. Here on weekdays visitors can obtain information on park trails and activities.

Along the Buller River. Lake Rotoiti's outflow becomes the Buller River, principal stream on the West Coast. For most of its scenic route, it churns through a steep, wooded gorge, providing one of the most scenic river drives in New Zealand.

Murchison, near the junction of highways 6 and 65, serves both surrounding farmers and the traveling public. Originally a gold mining settlement, Murchison has been rebuilt since 1929, when it stood near the epicenter of a devastating earthquake. Exhibits from the local gold rush and earthquake fill the town museum. Maruia Falls, about 22 km/14 miles south on Highway 65, was created when the earthquake changed the course of the Maruia River.

About 14 km/9 miles west of Murchison, Highway 6 crosses the line of the Murchison earthquake fault. You'll be able to see land displacement across the river.

At Inangahua Junction, Highway 69 branches south to Reefton; Highway 6 continues through

Take a walk through the verdant bush

Numerous trails thread through New Zealand's burgeoning forests. If you allow time for strolls along some of these paths, you'll discover one of the country's greatest delights.

Depending on the weather and time of day, you can experience the forest in a variety of moods. On fine days, dappled sunlight turns towering trees and lush undergrowth into a palette of greens. Climbing vines and tree orchids cling to mossy trunks. Above your path, evergreens (podocarps) and tree ferns form a verdant canopy.

If you're an early riser, you can enjoy in solitude the crystal tones of a bellbird and the beads of dew outlining a spider's web. In the moist West Coast rain forest, umbrella mosses and brightly colored fungi add a fairylike touch. So do the toadstools that cup rainwater after a nighttime shower.

Many trails are suitable for walkers wearing street shoes; other paths require sturdy walking shoes or boots. Sandy sections of some trails may be soggy after a heavy rain.

Some of the best bush walks wind through scenic reserves and national parks. Visitor centers have displays on local trees and plants and provide information on park trails and points of interest. Elsewhere, inquire at Forest Service offices and local tourist centers for information on scenic reserves and bush walks.

the scenic Lower Buller Gorge to Westport. Evergreens, beech forest, and ferns cover the slopes.

The West Coast

When New Zealanders refer to "The Coast," they're talking about the wild, wet West Coast of South Island, a slim strip of land hemmed in between the jagged peaks of the Southern Alps and the rough waters of the Tasman Sea.

Though Maoris traveled here over difficult mountain routes in search of greenstone, early European visitors found few attractions. Only the lure of gold in the mid-1860s could stimulate migration to this long-isolated region.

A century ago prospectors swarmed to the Coast, boom towns appeared overnight, and fortunes were won and lost by hard-working, hard-drinking miners. Renowned for their friendliness and hospitality, today's "Coasters" reflect the lively spirit and camaraderie of that nostalgic golden era. No group represents this fun-loving region better than the colorfully dressed Kokatahi Miners Band, a musical aggregation whose travels and outrageous exploits are well documented in coastal folklore.

Averaging only about 50 km/30 miles in width, the narrow coastal strip offers variety in geography, climate, and terrain. Lofty peaks, snow-covered the year around, tower along the spine of the Southern Alps. Icy glacial fingers inch slowly down the alpine valleys, terminating less than 1,000 feet above and only a few miles inland from the sea. A luxuriant native rain forest covers the lower slopes.

The West Coast's main towns—Westport, Greymouth, and Hokitika—originated during the gold rush when supply ships anchored near the mouths of the larger coastal rivers to trade with miners. Franz Josef and Fox glaciers have drawn scenery-loving travelers since the late 19th century.

You can reach the West Coast by automobile, N.Z. Railways Road Services coach, train (from Christchurch to Hokitika and Greymouth), or plane (Air New Zealand to Hokitika and Westport). Local sightseeing information is available in the main towns and at Westland National Park tourist centers. Because coastal weather tends to be unpredictable, you should be prepared for rain.

A room for the night

Most travelers stay in Westport, Greymouth, and the Glaciers area, but you'll find modest accommodations and camping areas in some of the smaller towns, as well.

Westport has a number of hotels (including the DB Westport and DB Buller) and motels. In Greymouth, Revington's is a comfortable older hotel in the center of town. Other accommodations include the DB Greymouth Hotel and King's Motor Hotel. Many fishermen enjoy the Mitchells Hotel at Mitchells, 47 km/29 miles southeast of Greymouth on the shore of Lake Brunner. Hokitika offers both hotel and motel rooms.

Activity in the Glaciers area centers around the excellent THC Franz Josef Hotel and the Fox Glacier and Vacation hotels at Fox Glacier; motel accommodations are also available in both communities. The DB Haast Hotel is located at the western end of the scenic mountain route near Haast.

Westport, coal shipping center

Although gold brought prosperity to Westport, coal—"black gold"—has sustained it. Bituminous coal mining began in the Paparoa Range in the 1870s. Westport—at the mouth of the Buller River—continues as the country's major coal shipping port. Large freighters anchor at riverside wharves to load coal, timber, and cement.

You can obtain information on Buller attractions and excursions at the town's information center in the Buller Motorways showroom on Palmerston Street. Along the main street, intricately detailed ironwork decorates the pillars and facades of vintage buildings. City parks include Victoria Square, a grassy gathering spot near the center of town, and Westport Domain, a section of subtropical bush at the upper end of Palmerston Street.

Westport's leading attraction is Coaltown, a new community museum featuring the area's coal mining industry. Housed in a converted brewery at the upper end of Queen Street, it includes a simulated coal mine, displays of old-time mining equipment and artifacts, and a model of the famed Denniston Incline coal conveyor. Other exhibits depict the area's pioneering and transportation history and the early New Zealand brewing industry.

From the Buller bridge, a road leads west from Highway 6 to the airport, Carters Beach (a popular swimming and sunning spot) and Cape Foulwind. Topped by a lighthouse, the headland is New Zealand's closest land point to Australia.

Farther south at dune-backed Tauranga Bay, low tide uncovers fascinating tidepools. Walk up the headland at the north end of the beach for a look at the seal colony just offshore.

Visit a coal mine

If you want to learn more about the West Coast's coal mining industry, arrange to visit an operating coal mine independently or on a tour. If you go on your own, stop first at the Mines Department office in Westport for a permit.

One of the most renowned of the coal towns was Denniston, 25 km/16 miles northeast of Westport. From Waimangaroa a twisting road climbs high into the Paparoa hills.

Now a virtual ghost town, Denniston once had a population of 2,000. From here the famed Denniston Incline conveyed millions of tons of coal from the mine bins some 600 meters/2,000 feet to the railway below. Acclaimed as an engineering feat when it was established in 1880, the Incline operated until the late 1960s. Now coal from several underground mines is trucked to Waimangaroa and then transported by rail.

Farther north at Granity, also a Buller coal center, another mining road climbs past Millerton's burning mine to the hilly site of Stockton. Here an 8-km/5-mile-long aerial cableway carries coal from Stockton's open cast mine down to Ngakawau.

Karamea and the "winterless north"

From Westport, Highway 67 heads north along the coast toward the isolated community of Karamea. Along this route to the "winterless north" you can hunt for gemstones, go surfcasting along the beach, or enjoy short walks through the bush.

North of Ngakawau the road threads between steep hills and the sea and then veers inland across the Mokihinui River to wind slowly through thick forests atop Karamea Bluff. Stop at the top for a memorable view. Short trails lead to a giant matai tree and to tiny Lake Hanlan.

Remote Karamea, cradled between mountains and the sea, is an isolated dairy center about 98 km/60 miles north of Westport. Subtropical fruits flourish in the district's mild climate.

North on Highway 67 about 9 km/6 miles, a logging road branches east to the Oparara River, where a limestone arch bridges the water.

If time permits, continue about 15 km/9 miles north of Karamea to the road's end at the Kohaihai River, cross the footbridge, and walk part of the spectacular coastal section of the Heaphy Track.

Gold rush memories and scenic grandeur

South of Westport, Highway 6 curves southwest across Addisons Flat. Little remains of the gold diggings that once drew thousands of miners here. Experimental farms are now under cultivation on the coastal plain, whose *pakihi* soils were once considered swampy wasteland.

In its heyday, Charleston was a boisterous boom town containing some 80 hotels. Today it has only one—the European Hotel—that keeps the gold rush era alive with its collection of photographs and mining relics. Charleston's tiny roadside post office serves a wide coastal area.

Dense greenery *borders the bush trail to Lake Matheson in Westland National Park. Bird life abounds in New Zealand forests.*

After climbing into the hills south of Charleston, the coastal highway hugs the shore as it cuts through some of the wildest coastal scenery in New Zealand.

Subtropical greenery covers the slopes of the craggy coastline to the very edge of the Tasman Sea. Large nikau palms, tree ferns, flax, and hebe species border the exposed coast; farther back from the sea rise rimu, miro, beech, and rata trees. Bush birds include the bellbird, tomtit, and weka.

One of the coast's best-known features, the stratified Punakaiki Pancake Rocks jut into the sea about midway between Westport and Greymouth. Centuries of surf action at this spot has tunneled out rocky grottoes, surge pools, and blowholes beneath the thinly layered limestone headland. On a clear day you can see the Southern Alps.

Greymouth, gateway to Shantytown

Largest town on the West Coast, Greymouth is hub of a coal and timber-producing district. Like most other coastal communities, it flourished during the time of the 1860s gold rush. Today, visitors flock to nearby Shantytown, a replica mining town. For local tourist information, stop at the West Coast Public Relations Office, 66 Mawhera Quay.

The Grey River carves a broad valley—known as The Gap—through coastal limestone to the sea. On clear days you can gaze eastward to a snowy panorama of Mount Cook and other high peaks of the Southern Alps. The best view is from the south breakwater. Another memorable vista is from King Domain; the steep track starts from Mount Street (leave your car in Smith Street if you're driving) and climbs to several lookouts.

During the spring whitebait season, you may see local fishermen netting for the tiny transparent fish in the Grey River and other West Coast streams. Tuna fishermen call at Greymouth from January to May.

Wild game may be seen daily at Hunting and Safari (N.Z.) Ltd.'s wildlife park at Paroa.

Highway 73, the Arthur's Pass Road across the mountains, reaches the coast south of Greymouth.

Coal miners' train. You can board the Rewanui coal miners' train weekdays at 1:50 at Greymouth's Riverside Station for a ride into the Paparoa hills to an operating underground coal mine.

The train goes northeast to Runanga and Dunollie and then climbs steep Seven Mile Canyon to Rewanui. A 25-minute stopover gives you time to look around the buildings, bins, and conveyor belts of the Liverpool Mine. The train arrives back in Greymouth at 3:38 P.M.

Shantytown. Popular Shantytown offers a glimpse of life in a West Coast gold mining town of the 1880s. Set amid native bush southeast of Greymouth, it is open daily from 8:30 to 5.

A century-old church, general store, hotel-saloon, and typical shops line the main street. A few buildings have been moved here from other sites; others are reproductions of earlier structures. Among the

sights you'll see are an 1837 printing press, an excellent gemstone display, vintage vehicles and equipment, and a replica Chinese den containing articles used by these early miners.

You can climb aboard a stagecoach for a tour of the grounds or ride through the bush on the Kaitangata steam railway. A short trail leads to the gold sluicing area, where you can pan for gold.

West Coast gold country

Discoveries of gold along West Coast streams triggered a massive rush as prospectors of all nationalities flocked to the Coast. Full-fledged towns —complete with hotels, banks, bars, and shops— sprang up almost overnight. In late 1864 only 800 people had settled here, but a year later the population had boomed to 16,000. By the end of 1866, some 50,000 miners had arrived in search of riches.

Miners struck gold in such places as Blackball and Moonlight. In the Ngahere region, Nelson Creek, Red Jacks, and Notown were all thriving gold sites. Yet the boom collapsed almost as suddenly as it had begun. After the rush to Addisons Flat in May 1867, most prospectors moved on to the new Coromandel gold fields, though mining continued in Westland on a sizable scale until the mid-1880s. And all activity is still not over—the Kaniere electric-powered dredge continues to recover gold from the Taramakau River.

For information on side trips from Greymouth to former mining centers, ask for brochures on Westland walks at the Public Relations Office in Greymouth. Forest Service rangers in Hokitika and Totara Flat (on Highway 7 southwest of Ikamatua) can also help.

Up the Grey Valley. From Greymouth, follow the north bank road upriver through Blackball to the timber and rail center of Ikamatua and then return to the coast on Highway 7.

Coal miners still live in Blackball, where you'll see the old mine's dilapidated outbuildings. Several roads and trails—including the Croesus and Moonlight tracks—head into the Paparoa hills.

Near Ngahere on Highway 7, roads and trails lead up creeks where miners panned a century ago. Waiuta, in the hills southeast of Hukarere, was productive as recently as 1950.

Highway 7 continues northeast to Reefton, a major junction on the Lewis Pass Road. In Blacks Point, just east of Reefton, a former church houses a collection of mining memorabilia.

Lake Brunner and Greenstone Valley. Fishermen, hunters, and yachtsmen head inland to Lake Brunner. Mitchells, on the southern shore, is the fishing and boating center and starting point for bush walks.

The road from Kumara to Mitchells follows part of the old 1865 miners' route through the Greenstone Valley. In Kumara you can examine historic items in the Holy Trinity Anglican Church. Built by gold miners, the church has been in use since 1878.

Hokitika for greenstone

Boisterous "capital of the gold fields" in the lively 1860s, today Hokitika is Westland's administrative center and headquarters of the greenstone processing industry. Tourist information is available at 29 Weld Street.

Mining displays and early photographs at the West Coast Historical Museum on lower Tancred Street recall gold rush days. Exhibits include a working model of a gold dredge and a mining shaft cross-section. Museum hours are 9:30 to 4:30 weekdays, 2 to 4:30 weekends.

Northeast of town on the airport road, a plane table identifies more than 50 peaks visible in a panorama of the Southern Alps. Scenic flights are available.

Craftsmen. From the nearby Arahura Valley, early Maoris obtained highly prized jade called greenstone to make their weapons, cutting tools, and personal ornaments. Modern West Coast craftsmen fashion the hard stone into jewelry, *hei-tiki* pendants, and other decorative objects on weekdays at two Hokitika factories—Westland Greenstone Company on Tancred Street, and Hokitika Jade Company Ltd., 110 Revell Street.

Glassblowers demonstrate free-form glassblowing on weekdays at Hokitika Free Form Glass Co. Ltd., 130 Revell Street.

Excursions. You can visit a working gold sluicing claim, pan for gold, and even enter some of the mine shafts and tunnels at the Blue Spur Gold Mine, about 5 km/3 miles east of Hokitika. The mine is open to visitors daily.

Lake Kaniere—one of Westland's loveliest—often mirrors a view of forested hills backed by the snow-topped Southern Alps. Located 18 km/12 miles southeast of Hokitika, the lake is popular for boating, swimming, and water-skiing. Yachting and speed boat regattas ruffle the waters on summer weekends.

Back country explorers and trampers can follow the Hokitika River upstream via Kokatahi and Kowhitirangi. For trail information, check with the Forest Service ranger in Hokitika.

South to the Glaciers

From Hokitika, Highway 6 crosses the Hokitika River on a long combined road/rail bridge and curves inland up the valley. Franz Josef Glacier lies 147 km/91 miles southwest, Fox Glacier another 25 km/15 miles beyond.

Lake Mahinapua, west of the highway a few kilometers south of Hokitika, attracts picnickers and yachtsmen. You can walk in (30 minutes) from the highway or follow a loop road and approach the lake from the west through a green tunnel of bush.

Another former gold town, Ross is noted for the cherry trees that flower along its main street each spring. In a local factory, opossum furs are manufactured into purses, hats, and other objects.

From the Waitaha River south to Lake Ianthe, you pass through a forest corridor of tall rimu, lush ferns, and other dense bush. West of Lake Wahapo, a signposted road forks 13 km/8 miles to the coastal settlement of Okarito. Here a marked track leads uphill to the Okarito trig and one of the Coast's outstanding alpine panoramas. From September to February, a white heron colony nests at Okarito Lagoon.

Westland National Park

On the western slope of the Southern Alps some of New Zealand's most spectacular alpine country has been set aside in Westland National Park. Most visitors focus on Franz Josef and Fox glaciers, a pair of broad, icy tongues that push steeply down from permanent snow fields to within a few kilometers of the sea. You'll also enjoy the park's rain forests, lakes, and coursing rivers, all backed by the range of snow-clad peaks.

Getting your bearings. Accommodations and tourist facilities are concentrated in the communities of Franz Josef and Fox Glacier. N.Z. Railways Road Services provides regular bus service from Christchurch, Hokitika, Wanaka, and Queenstown.

Look for park headquarters in Franz Josef. A visitor center serves tourists at Fox Glacier. Each offers exhibits on park geology, botany, and wildlife; printed trail information; and other park publications.

During your park visit you can sign up for a glacier sightseeing flight or a glacier walk. Although you can drive a car near the base of the glacier, you should not hike on the ice without proper equipment. On your own, explore some of the bush tracks and nearby lakes; don't let a rain shower keep you indoors.

Check at the park office to see if any nature walks or evening programs are scheduled during your visit.

Walk on a glacier. Hikers in good physical condition can join one of the guided glacier walks leaving daily from the Franz Josef Hotel and from Fox Glacier (inquire at the hotel or park visitor center). The half-day excursions involve fairly strenuous hiking over terminal moraine and ice. Hikers are issued well-oiled boots, heavy socks, and—in rainy weather—knee-length slickers.

On sunny days, protect your eyes and skin against glare from the snow. For comfort on the walk, plan to have both hands free.

You'll follow a guide over glacially polished rocks and the pulverized rubble of the glacier's terminal moraine and then head upstream along the river of glacial melt, murky gray with finely ground rock flour. Once on the glacier, the guide chops steps with his ice axe when necessary. That occasional grinding and cracking of ice you'll hear is a sign of the glacier inching forward under tremendous pressure from the vast ice field above.

Fly through the snowy Alps. Perhaps the most exciting way to view the Alps is from the air.

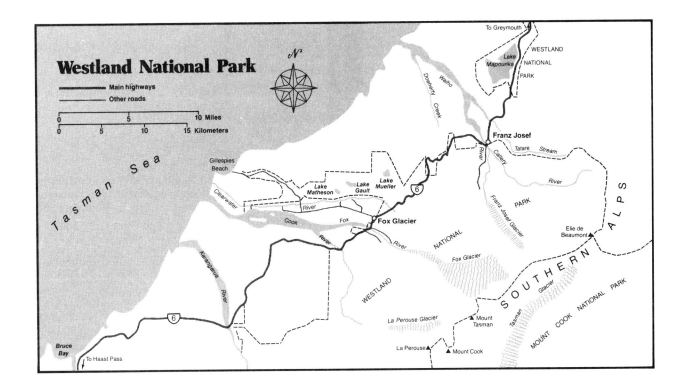

Westland National Park

Main highways
Other roads

Ski-equipped planes of Mount Cook Line depart frequently during good weather. But demand is great; sign up as soon as you arrive so you won't be disappointed. Planes depart from airports at Franz Josef and Fox Glacier on 40-minute and 1-hour flights. On the longer trip, you fly over the divide and down the Tasman Glacier on the eastern slope. On most flights, the pilot lands the small plane on a glacial snow field so passengers can walk on the ice and take photographs.

Mount Cook Line also operates helicopter flights over the Franz Josef Glacier region. Flights in the 4-passenger helicopter operate on demand only.

A pause at Franz Josef

Named by explorer Julius von Haast in 1865 for the emperor of his native Austria-Hungary, Franz Josef is the shorter and steeper of the two glaciers, descending the western slope of the Southern Alps some 11 km/7 miles to terminate about 300 meters/900 feet above sea level.

After you've stopped at the park visitor center to arrange for glacier excursions, visit St. James' Church to see the alpine view framed in the chancel window.

Bush walks. If you have time for only one walk, take the Terrace Track through the rain forest to historic Callery Gorge, stop at the warm springs, and return along the Waiho River. The *Callery Gorge-Warm Springs Walk* booklet describes natural features and points out traces remaining from gold mining days on the Waiho.

From Glacier Road, a 5-minute walk leads to

Peters Pool, a "kettle" lake with a glacier reflection. You can continue on the Douglas Track past the swing bridge over the Waiho, and return through bush and moraine areas to the road.

Viewpoints. If you arrive in Franz Josef from the north, your first view of the glacier comes across Lake Mapourika. Another vista comes as you cross Tatare Bridge north of town.

Closer views can be seen from the Franz Josef Hotel grounds and from Glacier Road, which branches off Highway 6 just south of the Waiho River.

Fox Glacier's walks and views

The curvy, 24-km/15-mile route from Franz Josef to Fox Glacier winds over spur ranges before descending into the broad valley known as the Cook River flats. The cozy settlement of Fox Glacier is headquarters for excursions into the southern part of the park. The glacier was named for Sir William Fox, one-time premier of New Zealand.

Stop at the visitor center to see its exhibits of park plants, birds, and geology, and for printed information on trails and other park features.

Bush walks. The walk to Lake Matheson is a delight at any time of day, but the classic panorama——Mount Cook and Mount Tasman reflected in the lake's dark waters—is most striking at sunrise, when the first rays streak the clouds and strike the snowy peaks.

It's an easy 30-minute walk to the raft viewpoint, about another 30 minutes on a rock trail to the "view of views" at the far end of the lake. Take along the *Lake Matheson Forest Walk* booklet to help you identify trailside plants. The Lake Gault track branches north from the Matheson trail.

Just south of the township, the Minnehaha Track is a 20-minute loop from the highway through the bush to the edge of the quiet Minnehaha stream.

Several promising tracks begin along the South Approach Road (Glacier View Road) south of the river.

If Westland mists part, some of the most inspiring glacier views come along the steep switchback track up Cone Rock. In less than an hour, you'll climb some 300 meters/900 feet above the Fox River for a grandstand view of the large glacier. After a rain, though, handholds are slick, and you'll dodge one waterfall after another.

A shorter and less strenuous track leads to the Fox Chalet Lookout, also offering splendid views.

The effects of the glacier's advance and retreat are particularly noticeable on the Moraine Walk through the Fox Valley. Along the way you see forests of varying ages, terminal moraines marking the glacier's advance in earlier centuries, and erratic boulders pushed along the valley by the ice.

Other diversions. You'll discover breathtaking vistas of Fox Glacier and the high peaks from several viewpoints. One of the best is from the Clearwater River bridge on the road to Gillespies Beach. From the South Approach Road, you see the glacier framed by trees, and there's a good view of Mount Tasman from the Fox River bridge.

After dark, you can walk to the glowworm grotto signposted just south of town. Here, glowing iridescent green lights attract night-flying insects. (For more on glowworms, see page 49.)

Gillespies Beach, west of Fox Glacier, was once an isolated gold mining settlement. Gorse now covers the old tailings behind the dunes. Captivating coastal scenery and alpine views await visitors.

If you plan to hike north to the seal colony (1 to 1½ hours round trip), check first at the park visitor center, since part of the beach route is passable only at low tide. An alternate path takes you inland over parts of the old miners' road.

Down the South Westland coast

From Fox Glacier, Highway 6 continues 118 km/73 miles south to Haast junction. Forest lines much of the route; in summer, white plumes of toe toe, scarlet-blooming rata, and yellow gorse add color accents.

You can picnic beside the sea at Bruce Bay, where the road briefly skirts the coast before turning inland, or farther south at Lake Paringa and Lake Moeraki, both good fishing lakes. Just north of the Moeraki River bridge, a short side road leads to the start of the Munro Track, a 40-minute walk to the beach through a forest thick with large tree ferns and native fuchsia.

The highway meets the coast again at Knights Point, where a windy viewpoint high above the sea offers vistas of bush-covered headlands, golden sand beaches, and jagged offshore rocks.

About 5 km/3 miles south of Knights Point, you can walk to the beach along Ship Creek, where shipwreck remains are sometimes visible below the bridge at low tide.

Lonely road to Jackson Bay

After crossing the Haast River bridge, longest of New Zealand's single lane bridges, most motorists turn inland to follow Highway 6 across Haast Pass, 64 km/41 miles distant. A hardy few continue along the coast toward Haast township, Arawata, and Jackson Bay. Experienced trampers head up the Okuru River into Mount Aspiring National Park.

Just south of the Arawata River bridge, a signposted, unpaved side road leads 4 km/2 miles to the start of the Ellery Track. The 45-minute forest walk beside the outlet stream brings you to secluded Lake Ellery, surrounded by tree-clad hills.

Jackson Bay, 48 km/28 miles below Haast Junction, was a sheltered anchorage for early whalers and sealers. The bay was also the site of one of Westland's most isolated early settlements.

The Wanaka country

Ancient glaciers scooped out the deep troughs that hold lakes Wanaka and Hawea. Today these water-filled valleys attract water sports enthusiasts and fishermen.

The town of Wanaka contains resort amenities and is the departure point for hikers heading into Mount Aspiring National Park. Winter visitors head for the ski fields at Treble Cone.

Lake Hawea is a favorite of fishermen for its rainbow trout and landlocked salmon. Many boat owners come here in summer to escape Wanaka's crowds. Small holiday houses hug the cliffs above the shoreline.

Accommodations at Wanaka include the fine THC Wanaka Hotel overlooking the lake, as well as numerous motels. Hawea also has several small motels. A pleasant campground borders Lake Wanaka at Glendhu Bay. Regular bus service connects Wanaka with major West Coast, Canterbury, and Otago destinations.

Wanaka's lake resort

Clustering at the southeastern end of Lake Wanaka, the township of Wanaka faces glacier-molded hills. The lakeside resort draws water sports buffs, who boat, swim, water-ski, and fish on the long, narrow lake. For an overview, walk from the business district to the lookout above town, in front of the white war memorial.

In season you can arrange for lake sightseeing and fishing trips, scenic flights, and rental boats and fishing equipment. At the Gin and Raspberry Stables in Cardrona you can rent horses for

Ski-equipped *airplanes offer an exhilarating ride over rugged peaks of the Southern Alps to land passengers on the high glaciers.*

escorted or independent trail riding in the Cardrona Valley.

Day excursions. Short drives lead to sheltered Albert Bay, pleasant for a picnic and afternoon swim; and to Glendhu Bay and West Wanaka, center of water sports activities. Willows and poplars along the lakeshore form an attractive golden border in autumn. Hiking trails lead up Mount Iron and Mount Roy.

The Crown Range Road. A scenic alternative to Highway 6 from Wanaka to Queenstown is the Crown Range Road, an unpaved 70-km/44-mile route (closed in winter). Not recommended for nervous drivers, Highway 89 wends south from Wanaka through the Cardrona Valley, passing Cardrona's sagging old hotel and continuing to the summit of the Crown Range. From the crest you survey the entire Wakatipu Valley.

The road then plunges in zigzag curves to the valley, where it crosses the Arrow River and meets Highway 6 northeast of Queenstown.

Mount Aspiring National Park

Southernmost of South Island's alpine preserves, Mount Aspiring National Park encompasses the high slopes on both sides of the divide between the Haast and Te Anau-Milford highways. Its name comes from its highest and most magnificent peak, 3,035-meter/9,957-foot Mount Aspiring.

A mountaineer's park, Mount Aspiring draws hikers and climbers who probe its remote river valleys and ascend through beech forest to rugged, glaciated peaks. The alpine region is one of New Zealand's finest climbing areas. Numerous alpine huts offer shelter from variable mountain weather.

In Wanaka you'll find park headquarters and a visitor center where you can obtain trail and weather information and view displays on the park's flora, fauna, and history. Ranger stations are located at Makarora (on the Haast Pass road) and at Glenorchy (near the head of Lake Wakatipu).

Highway 6 cuts across the northern end of the park, offering hikers access to the Wilkin Valley and other tributaries of the Haast and Makarora rivers. From Wanaka, motorists can follow a lonely road (unpaved beyond Glendhu Bay) up the scenic Matukituki Valley to the park boundary for views of Rob Roy Glacier, Mount Avalanche, and Mount Aspiring's pyramid peak. To reach the Dart, Rees, and Routeburn valleys, follow the Glenorchy road from Queenstown.

Queenstown

Backed by steep mountains, Queenstown lies in a curve of Lake Wakatipu at the head of its own small, horseshoe-shaped bay. It is South Island's principal resort, drawing visitors the year around with its lake and mountain scenery, exhilarating climate, changing seasons, and varied excursion possibilities.

Water sports and back country trips attract summer vacationers. At Coronet Peak, skiing is the main winter lure. The town's permanent population of 2,600 balloons during the summer holidays and winter ski season.

Born as a canvas town during the Otago gold rush, Queenstown prospered as miners uncovered rich finds in the Arrow, Shotover, and Kawarau rivers. When the easily won gold was gone, most of the bushy-bearded prospectors moved on to the new West Coast goldfields, and sheepmen staked out the grassy slopes for vast high country stations.

Queenstown offers a bewildering array of activities; your main problem may be deciding what to do first.

Getting settled in Queenstown

Queenstown attracts visitors the year around, and travelers are wise to reserve accommodations ahead at any time of year—particularly during the school holidays, on long weekends, and during ski season. You can make travel and accommodation reservations at the Government Tourist Bureau office on Shotover Street. Information on tours and excursions is available at booking offices facing the mall at the foot of Ballarat Street.

Hotels. Major Queenstown tourist hotels are the Travelodge, near the steamer wharf; the Lakeland Resort Hotel, a 10-minute walk from town on the Lake Esplanade; the Country Lodge on Fernhill Road; and two Vacation hotels on Frankton Road.

Queenstown's smaller hotels include Vacation (O'Connells), Wakatipu, and Mountaineer Establishment, all centrally located; and the Hotel Esplanade, terraced above the water facing Frankton Arm. Among many fine motels are the A-Line Motor Lodge and the Ambassador, Lakeside, and Modern motels. Motorists with a yen for gold rush atmosphere enjoy Arthur's Point Hotel, located 5 km/3 miles north of town. The renovated 6-room stone-walled inn was built in the 1860s as a wayside oasis for miners traveling on the route to the Shotover gold fields.

Restaurants and nightlife. Most of Queenstown's evening activity centers around its numerous hotels; many feature music, dancing, or cabaret entertainment during peak seasons. In winter, after-ski activity is lively in local hotels and pubs.

The area's best and most elegant restaurant is Packers' Arms, a stone-walled inn that first served

Haast Pass opens up the southwest coast

Originally an old Maori route to the West Coast, the Haast Pass was first crossed in 1863 by prospector Charles Cameron and geologist-explorer Julius von Haast, who named the pass after himself. In the late 19th and early 20th centuries, packhorses transported supplies to isolated West Coast settlers. Cattle had to be driven up the coast or over the Haast Pass track, goods came and went by ship, and radio and aircraft provided primary means of communication.

Not until 1960 did completion of the Wanaka-Haast route end a century of isolation for the people of Haast. A few years later the coastal highway finally linked up with the Haast route, opening the West Coast to tourism and enabling travelers to enjoy the region as part of a circular trip.

Lowest cut-through in the Main Divide at 568 meters/1,847 feet, Haast Pass forms the boundary between Otago and Westland. Snow seldom closes the highway, but rainfall is abundant—up to 250 inches a year. All too often, clouds obscure the scenery.

Silver beech trees fill the wetter forests west of the Main Divide; mountain beech predominate on the drier eastern side of the pass. Waterfalls drop from hanging valleys into the glacial-cut gorges of the Haast and Makarora rivers.

Camping areas, picnic tables, and rest rooms are located at several roadside points, but you may have to share facilities with aggressive sandflies.

Southeast of the Pleasant Flat picnic area, a short track leads through a silver beech forest to 90-foot Thunder Creek Falls. At the Gates of Haast, the clear, pale blue waters of the Haast River foam over immense boulders in the narrow gorge. The old bridle trail, used by prospectors, cattle drovers, and other early travelers, parallels the highway near the pass.

East of the divide, you descend on unpaved highway along the Makarora River through the northern part of Mount Aspiring National Park. Side roads lead to high country sheep stations.

Highway 6 cuts through brown tussock lands to skirt the northeastern shore of Lake Wanaka. It angles across The Neck—where the ancient Hawea and Wanaka glaciers met to gouge out the lake beds—and then continues south along Lake Hawea to Wanaka.

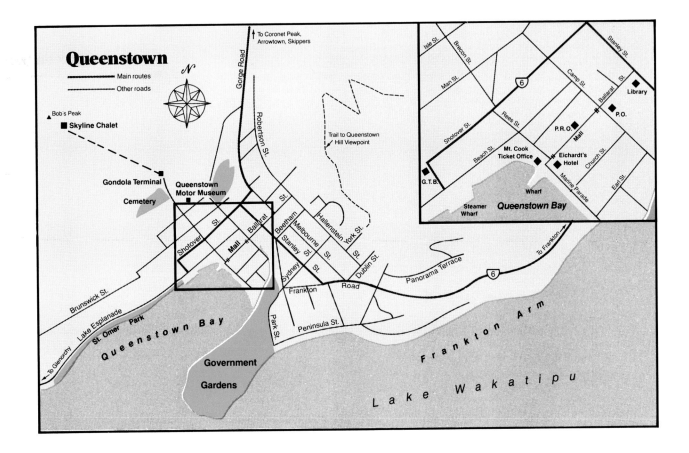

miners during the 1860s gold rush. The restaurant is located a short distance north of Arthur's Point.

Take the gondola to Skyline Chalet on Bob's Peak and enjoy sunset views over the lake and mountains. Cabaret entertainment is featured some evenings.

Other local restaurants include the Continental Restaurant on the Mall (grills and dishes with a continental flavor); The Beefeater in Shotover Arcade (steaks and salads); Country Lodge, Fernhill Road (a la carte dining); and The Cow on Cow Lane (Italian food, generous portions).

Transportation. N.Z. Railways Road Services provides regular bus service to Wanaka and the West Coast, Dunedin, Invercargill, Te Anau, and Milford. Mount Cook Landlines coaches link Queenstown with Mount Cook and Christchurch. Mount Cook Airlines serves Queenstown with regular flights to main South Island destinations and connecting service to North Island.

A stroll around town

Small and compact, Queenstown is geared for pedestrians. Tourist activity centers around the Mall at the foot of Ballarat Street, a busy and colorful block where you'll find information and tour-booking agencies, major shops, and several of the town's historic buildings. One of these has been

converted into the Wakatipu Trading Post, a two-story arcade of shops and boutiques. Eichardt's Hotel, at the foot of the street facing the lake, began serving thirsty travelers in 1871.

Perpendicular to the mall, Marine Parade borders the waterfront. You board the hydrofoil or Kawarau jet boats at the small pier, where children toss bread to tame trout and greedy ducks swimming below. Along the gravelly shore, benches shaded by weeping willows invite you to pause and enjoy the scenery and lake activity.

Lake Wakatipu. Shaped like an elongated S, Lake Wakatipu fills a deep and narrow 83-km/52-mile-long glacial trough. Rugged mountains rise abruptly around its shore. Third largest of New Zealand's lakes, it is noted for its seiche action— a rhythmic oscillation in water level that rises and recedes as much as 5 inches within 4 or 5 minutes. Scientists say the oscillation is due to changes in atmospheric pressure or mountain-funneled winds. Maori legend claims the motion is caused by the heartbeat of a giant at the bottom of the lake.

Lakeside parks. You'll enjoy a stroll through Government Gardens, a wooded peninsula park jutting into the lake and separating Queenstown Bay from Frankton Arm. A small stone bridge arches across the park's lawn-bordered pond. You can watch lawn bowlers in summer. St. Omer Park offers a grassy lakeside promenade along the bay beyond the steamer wharf.

Colorful gondolas *lift Queenstown visitors up Bob's Peak to the Skyline Chalet for expansive views southeast over the lake. The Remarkables range lifts abruptly along Wakatipu's eastern shore.*

Gold rush show. Upstairs in the Shotover Arcade on Beach Street, Colonial Sounds depicts the sights and sounds of Queenstown during the gold rush days in a 30-minute audio-visual show.

Motor museum. Vintage touring and racing cars, motorcycles, and pioneer aircraft—all in working order—may be seen daily at the Queenstown Motor Museum on Brecon Street, just below the gondola terminal.

Panoramic viewpoints

The steep slopes rising from the lake offer sparkling views of Queenstown, Lake Wakatipu, and the sawtooth peaks of the Remarkables along the eastern shore.

Take a gondola ride up Bob's Peak in a four-seat bubble car to Skyline Chalet, a glass-walled mountainside restaurant and tearoom perched high above Queenstown. Reserve ahead for dinner and arrive in time to enjoy the sunset.

One of the best views is from Deer Park Heights, a game reserve near Frankton. The chairlift ride to the summit of Coronet Peak provides a splendid view over the river basin, Crown Range, and high peaks.

If you want some exercise as well, take the trail up Queenstown Hill behind town (starting at the end of York Street) or the longer trek up 1,752-meter/5,730-foot Ben Lomond.

Excursions from Queenstown

Using Queenstown as your touring base, you can explore this historic district and its attractions by boat, plane, motor coach, four-wheel-drive vehicle, gondola, ski lift—even by horseback.

Popular excursions fill rapidly; book early. Some tours are seasonal; others require a minimum number of participants. You can obtain current tour information and make reservations at the Mount Cook Travel Office, corner of Rees and Ballarat streets, or at the Public Relations Office.

A broad selection of boat trips

You can cruise Lake Wakatipu on a sturdy old steamship, speed across the water on a hydrofoil, skim through scenic river gorges in a jet boat, float leisurely with the current aboard a raft, or charter a boat for a few hours of fishing.

Lake steamer. The grand old lady of the lake is the T.S.S. *Earnslaw*, a white-painted, coal-burning steamship that made her debut on Lake Wakatipu in 1912. Last of the steamship fleet that once plied the lake, she makes morning and afternoon cruises to Walter Peak station and a lunch cruise up Frankton Arm from late October through April.

Jet boat trips. Hamilton jet boats were developed in New Zealand for navigating the country's shallow rivers. Fast, versatile, and highly maneuverable, they provide a thrilling trip for sightseers and handy transportation for outdoorsmen.

In Queenstown you can arrange to shoot the rapids of the Shotover River or jet the Kawarau, both historic gold-bearing rivers. Drivers explain how the water jet propels the craft and demonstrate the boat's maneuverability.

A courtesy minibus transports passengers from Queenstown to the Shotover dock, just upstream from Arthur's Point bridge. Your boat cuts through the narrow rocky canyon, and passengers gasp as the driver skims close to cliff walls and spins around the river's curves.

You board the Kawarau jet boat at the Queenstown wharf for an hour-long trip up the Kawarau River. You'll head up the Frankton Arm, shoot over the spillway at Kawarau Dam, and continue past the mouth of the Shotover River and Kawarau Falls into the Kawarau Gorge.

You can also explore the Kawarau valley on a heli-jet excursion, combining helicopter sight-seeing with a jet boat trip on the Kawarau River.

Hydrofoil. Departing from the wharf at the foot of the mall, the 17-passenger hydrofoil *Meteor III* takes passengers on a 1½-hour, 37-mile cruise on Wakatipu, speeding along smoothly on its foils with its hull above the water. You'll pass lakeside sheep stations and see mountain scenery in the upper reaches of the lake. During school holiday periods, shorter trips depart at frequent intervals.

River rafting. From September through May, you can float down the Shotover River on an inflatable raft. Without noise or fuel fumes, you float downstream past pine-studded cliffs and grazing livestock, enjoying views of the valley and distant mountains. Overnight rafting trips explore the Upper Shotover, Dart, Hunter, and Matukituki river valleys.

Fishing boat. If fishing is your passion, you can charter a boat and guide for a few hours or a day of trolling on Lake Wakatipu or fly fishing on one of the local rivers. Tackle is provided.

Sightseeing by bus and plane

After you've explored compact Queenstown on foot and surveyed its water trips, it's time to venture farther afield.

Half-day bus excursions depart Queenstown for Coronet Peak, Skippers Canyon, Arrowtown and Waterfall Park, and Deer Park and Golden Terrace Mining Town A full-day trip follows the lake road from Queenstown to Glenorchy and on to the Routeburn Valley.

For another full day, you can depart Queenstown on the early N.Z. Railways Road Services bus, travel through farming country to Te Anau, continue on the Milford Road to Milford, have lunch and take a launch trip on Milford Sound, and return to Te Anau by dinner time (or continue back to Queenstown, if you prefer).

Scenic flights depart from Queenstown airport over Lake Wakatipu and the rugged mountainous country to the west. You can take a 1¼-hour round-trip flight to Milford Sound, passing over the Milford Track with eye-level views of Sutherland Falls and snowy peaks.

Exploring the rugged back country

Four-wheel-drive vehicles provide access to some of the district's scenic and unspoiled valleys. You can raft down several remote rivers and go trail riding to old mining areas.

Skippers Canyon. Best known of the back country excursions is the trip up historic Skippers Canyon. The narrow, single-lane road snakes high above the Shotover River, where a century ago miners panned for gold. Rocky monoliths jut above the craggy terrain. Intense sun scorches the parched valley in summer; biting winds and snow ravage the gullies in winter.

You'll see stretches of the packhorse trail to the Upper Shotover gold fields and part of the old road built by Chinese workers, who were lowered over the cliff to hammer out the route. Occasionally you pass the dilapidated remains of a long-abandoned building.

Other trips. From Queenstown you also can arrange day excursions by four-wheel-drive vehicle to Moke Lake, the ghost towns of Macetown and Sefferton, and up the Rees and Dart valleys. Most trips stop for billy tea (brewed in a can over an open fire); all-day trips include lunch.

Danes Back Country Experiences operates several trips that combine travel by four-wheel-drive vehicle with river rafting: 1-day and 3-day trips up Skippers Canyon and rafting down the Shotover River, and a 3-day trip up the Hunter and Matukituki valleys. "Fly-in, raft-out" trips operate on the Dart River. All equipment except personal gear is provided on overnight trips.

Trail riding. Escorted horseback riding trips depart from Moonlight Stables at Arthur's Point. Following trails used by miners more than 100 years ago, you ride up the Shotover Gorge and on to the old gold mining areas of Moonlight Valley and Moke Creek.

See a cattle show

Visitors learn about New Zealand's beef and dairy industry at the Cattledrome; shows are held daily at 9:30 A.M. and 4:15 P.M. at the exhibition center on Skippers Road. Inside the building you'll see a film on New Zealand farming and learn about pedigreed cattle as trained animals walk to their places on stage. Cows are milked with glass milking machines. If you like, you can try your own hand at milking.

Coronet Peak—for skiing and scenery

In winter, Queenstown turns into an alpine skiers' resort. The challenging terrain of Coronet Peak, an easy 19 km/12 miles north of Queenstown, offers excellent skiing from mid-June until October.

Facilities at Coronet Peak are among the best in Australasia. A twin-seat chairlift transports skiers from the cafeteria-restaurant at 1,140 meters/3,800 feet to the 1,350-meter/5,400-foot summit. A triple chairlift provides access to experts' slopes, and three Poma lifts take novice skiers to learners' areas. On fine days, many skiers soak up the sun from the restaurant deck.

Coronet Peak has a ski shop and a ski school; you can rent skis, boots, and poles in town or at

the ski area. Skiers find ample accommodations and plenty of after-ski activity in Queenstown. Various ski packages cover transportation, accommodations, and lift fees.

In summer, sightseers take the chairlift ride to the summit station, then climb to a glassed-in viewpoint for a breathtaking panorama over the Lake Wakatipu region and the Southern Alps. On chilly days, you bundle into army greatcoats to ward off the biting wind during your ride.

Mining memories linger in Arrowtown

The 20-km/12-mile trip to Arrowtown is a diverting one. Memories of gold rush days come to mind as you cross the Shotover River and pass rebuilt 1860s inns still serving travelers. Side roads lead to Skippers Canyon and Coronet Peak. As you motor through the peaceful Wharehuanui Valley, you may meet a herd of cattle ambling along the road.

Mellow old Arrowtown has a lively past. After gold was discovered in the Arrow River, a midwinter 1863 flood wiped out the riverside canvas town. Permanent stone and wooden buildings were built on higher ground; many have been converted into shops and restaurants. A former bank, thick-walled and bar-windowed, houses the mining memorabilia and pioneer possessions of the Lakes District Centennial Museum.

Century-old sycamores form a shady canopy over upper Buckingham Street and its wooden cottages. You'll find the empty Arrowtown jail off Cardigan Street. If you stroll the upper streets, you discover old stone buildings mortared with river sand, dry rock fences, attractive village churches, and clapboard houses with pillared porches and ornamental ironwork.

Gravestones in the cemetery record poignant tales of early death—miners who drowned in floods, children "too gentle for this bustling world." You can picnic under the willows by Bush Creek or along the river.

Return to Queenstown past Lake Hayes, its glassy surface mirroring the pastoral countryside and mountain backdrop.

Along Frankton Arm

East of Queenstown, Highway 6 skirts Frankton Arm, outlet of the Kawarau River into Lake Wakatipu. A small zoological garden borders the river near its outlet. The Kelvin peninsula marks the arm's southern shore.

Located 3 km/2 miles east of town on the Frankton road, Golden Terrace Mining Town seeks to re-create life in a mid-19th century mining village. Typical gold rush buildings are furnished in period style. Outside displays feature mining equipment and old vehicles.

One of the best views of the lake district comes from a private game reserve atop Deer Park Heights on the peninsula. Plan ahead—to enter the

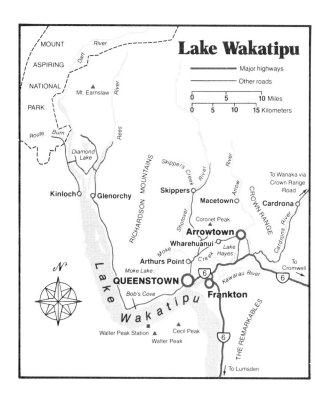

reserve you'll need a $2 token, available at the Queenstown Public Relations Office or at small grocery stores in Frankton.

From Frankton, the road to Deer Park Heights climbs to a viewpoint high above Frankton Arm. On the drive you'll see several kinds of deer roaming the grassy park, as well as thar, chamois, mountain goats, and wapiti (elk). From the summit you look down on Queenstown, nestling in its own bay, and mountains rising steeply around the rim of Wakatipu's waters. Coronet Peak looms high over pastoral valleys and several small lakes.

Visit a sheep station

You can combine a cruise on Lake Wakatipu with a visit to a high country sheep and cattle station. In Queenstown you board either the T.S.S. *Earnslaw* or one of the station launches for a half-day or full-day excursion to Walter Peak station across the lake.

Homesteaded during the 1880s, the station now attracts day visitors from Queenstown. Homestead buildings have been restored or rebuilt to their original state and furnished with articles of historical interest. Most of the station's vast acreage is still operated as a high country pastoral farm, carrying up to 6,000 Merino sheep and 3,500 Hereford cattle.

Visitors learn about the station's history and present-day farming activities, enjoy morning or afternoon tea (also barbecue lunch on the full-day tour), tour some of the early buildings, walk through the garden, and watch demonstrations of wool spinning and sheep dogs at work.

From October through April you can visit the station in the morning, have tea, and go on to Te Anau on a 2½-hour back country trip. The Walter Peak bus follows a graded but unpaved road, splashing through occasional stream fords, as you wend through the station's remote summer pasture lands. A return trip leaves Te Anau at 12:30 P.M., arriving in Queenstown about 5.

Hiking the Routeburn Track

Queenstown is departure point for hikers following the Routeburn Track, a 40-km/25-mile alpine trail winding through the inspiring country of Mount Aspiring and Fiordland national parks. The trail cuts along river valleys and through untouched beech forest, past cascading waterfalls and saucerlike alpine tarns, and across a challenging, 1,280-meter/4,200-foot mountain pass. Portions of the trail are exposed and can be dangerous in bad weather. Huts along the trail provide overnight shelter for hikers.

The track is usually open from mid-November through April, though there may still be some snow early in the season.

You can hike the trail independently or with a guided group from either end—beginning at road's end north of Kinloch or from the Divide on the Milford Road near the Hollyford junction. You can arrange to connect with hiking trips on the Milford or Hollyford tracks.

For those who prefer not to carry a heavy pack, Routeburn Walk Ltd. (P.O. Box 271, Queenstown) conducts 4-day guided excursions over the trail. Hikers carry only their personal gear; all food, utensils, and sleeping equipment are provided. Parties are small—usually 12 hikers and two guides. Huts at Routeburn Falls and Lake Mackenzie are complete with down sleeping bags, mattresses, and hot showers.

Fiordland

New Zealand's largest and most remote national park, Fiordland encompasses the entire southwest corner of South Island. Incredibly beautiful and wild, it is an intriguing region of rugged mountain ranges, dense rain forest, solitary alpine lakes, sparkling rivers, and splashing waterfalls. Majestic fiords indent its western coast. Much of Fiordland is virtually unexplored wilderness, still inhabited by such rare birds as the takahe and kakapo.

Less than 15,000 years ago this region was locked in thick ice. Glaciers sculpted the land on a larger-than-life scale, gouging out long narrow lakes, carving out coastal fiords, shearing high mountain valleys. Captain James Cook sailed along the coast in 1770 and returned in 1773, putting in at several fiords and anchoring at Dusky Sound for rest and ship repair.

Spectacular scenery and outdoor activities attract visitors; you'll find few commercial diversions here. The region's most accessible destinations are the lakes of Te Anau and Manapouri and majestic Milford Sound. But the best of Fiordland lies off the roads, to be experienced in solitude, on foot or by boat.

Sports enthusiasts come here for water sports, to fish for trout and salmon, and to hunt deer and wapiti. You can arrange for guides and float planes into remote lakes. Many visitors enjoy scenic flights and launch trips, others join hiking groups on the Milford and Routeburn tracks.

You can obtain information on park activities and trails daily at Fiordland National Park headquarters in Te Anau or at the Clifden ranger station. Rangers conduct field trips and evening programs during the summer holidays.

Getting settled in Fiordland

Te Anau, headquarters for most Fiordland excursions, has a variety of accommodations led by the THC Te Anau Hotel and Campbell Autolodge (both facing the lake), Fiordland Motor Lodge, and Luxmore Inn. At Manapouri, most motorists stay at the Manapouri Motor Inn.

On the Milford Road, modest accommodations are available at Te Anau Downs Motor Lodge at Te

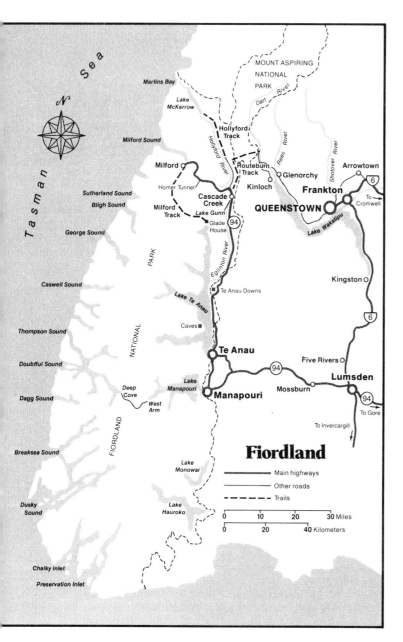

Fiordland

Main highways
Other roads
— — — Trails

0   10   20   30 Miles
0   20   40 Kilometers

Te Anau, gateway to Fiordland

Largest of the southern lakes is Lake Te Anau, which marks Fiordland's eastern boundary for some 60 km/40 miles. Its three long fingers probe deeply into the park's thickly wooded mountains. At the lake's southern tip is the town of Te Anau (population 2,000), gateway to this wilderness country and base for excursions south to Lake Manapouri and Doubtful Sound and north to Milford.

From Te Anau, visitors cruise on the lake, explore the glowworm cave, and go flightseeing. If you prefer, you can arrange to rent a bicycle, stroll along the lake, follow a nature trail, or arrange for a day of fishing or golf. You can also plan guided back country hunting and fishing trips.

Information on excursions may be obtained from Fiordland Travel Ltd. or Mount Cook Travel Bureau. Inquire at Fiordland National Park headquarters for park information and suggestions on local walks.

Lake trips. Launches make regular trips the year around from Te Anau to the Te Ana-au Caves.

From November through March you can make a day excursion to the head of Lake Te Anau, traveling by coach to Te Anau Downs and continuing by launch to Glade House, start of the Milford Track. You return in the afternoon by the same route.

Other seasonal launch trips cruise to Gorge Falls on the lake's South Fiord and across the lake to Brod Bay (for swimming, picnicking, a nature walk, and a tramp up Mount Luxmore). Special evening cruises operate in midsummer.

Te Ana-au Caves. Maoris probably discovered and named this "Cave of Rushing Water," but it was not rediscovered until 1948. Located about 16 km/10 miles north of Te Anau on the lake's western shore, the site can be reached only by boat.

Geologically young, it is known as a "living cave," since it is still in the process of formation. A powerful underground stream cascades from Lake Orbell, hollowing out the limestone cliffs of the Murchison Mountains. A short boat ride takes you into the cavern, where electrically lighted walkways guide you past frothing waterfalls and limestone formations. A punt transports visitors along the cave's underground river into the glowworm grotto.

Flightseeing excursions. Short, scenic flights by floatplane or land-based aircraft take passengers over Te Anau and Manapouri lakes, up through uninhabited valleys, and over thick forests and hidden lakes to western fiord country. A 1¼-hour flight goes over the Milford Track past Sutherland Falls to Milford Sound and returns to Te Anau via the Eglinton Valley. In summer you can arrange a day excursion to Milford, flying one way and traveling by bus the other.

Float planes depart from the Te Anau lakefront; other flightseeing trips leave from the Te Anau/Manapouri airport.

Anau Downs, 29 km/18 miles from Te Anau. Cascade Lodge at Cascade Creek is being renovated following fire damage. Campsites with fireplaces and toilets are located along the Milford Road; for information, check at park headquarters in Te Anau.

Facilities at Milford are limited to the 40-room THC Hotel Milford, facing the sound, and the Milford hostel, used mainly by Milford Track hikers.

N.Z. Railways Road Services coaches make daily return excursions from Te Anau to Milford Sound and provide regular service to Queenstown, Dunedin, and Invercargill. Mount Cook Lines fly daily from Te Anau/Manapouri to Queenstown, Mount Cook, Christchurch, and North Island points.

By coach to Milford. N.Z. Railways Road Services buses leave Te Anau in the morning for Milford with a stopover of several hours—long enough for lunch and a cruise on Milford Sound—before the return trip to Te Anau.

Fishing and hunting trips. Experienced guides are available for day excursions or longer fishing and hunting trips in Fiordland. Permits, available at park headquarters, are necessary to hunt in Fiordland National Park. You can charter float planes for travel to remote lakes and sounds.

Island-studded Lake Manapouri

Many travelers consider Manapouri the most beautiful lake in New Zealand. Thick forests border its meandering shoreline, and some 30 bush-clad islets stud the blue water. Flanking the lake on three sides are high mountains, their snow-tipped peaks mirrored in lake waters. Boat trips depart from Pearl Harbour on the Waiau River.

Up West Arm. Most popular excursion for overseas visitors is the full-day trip (bring your lunch) up the lake's West Arm by launch to visit the underground power station. You continue by coach to Doubtful Sound, where you board a launch for a cruise on this unspoiled fiord. The trip operates daily from October through May, four times a week in winter.

On arrival at West Arm, you board a coach and descend through a steep spiraling tunnel to the powerhouse, 213 meters/700 feet below ground. Hewn from solid rock, it houses seven turbines, each driving a powerful generator. Water from the lake enters vertical penstocks and falls through the turbines, then passes through a 10-km/6-mile-long tailrace tunnel for release into the sea at Doubtful Sound, on the other side of the mountains. The station furnishes power for the aluminum smelter at Bluff.

On to Doubtful Sound. Construction of the power station opened up some of New Zealand's most spectacular scenery, allowing visitors to see virtually untouched country at close hand. Coaches use the upgraded construction road to transport visitors over 671-meter/2,250-foot Wilmot Pass to Doubtful Sound.

At Deep Cove you board a launch for a 2-hour cruise on Doubtful Sound, one of the region's most majestic fiords. Noted by Captain James Cook (as Doubtful Harbour) in 1770, it is 10 times larger than Milford Sound.

Vertical cliffs thrust high into the sky or mist as you cruise into Hall Arm. Great waterfalls stream over sheer rock faces. In fine weather, mountains and greenery are reflected in the protected waters of the fiord.

Other boat trips. At Pearl Harbour you can arrange to rent a rowboat or take a jet boat trip on the Waiau River. In summer you can take a launch to Stockyard Cove, one of the lake's loveliest bays, enjoy a beach picnic and a walk through conifer forest, then have the launch return for you later in the day.

By air to Milford

You can reach Milford in three ways: by air over the rugged Fiordland wilderness, through mountain valleys along the Milford Road, or on foot along the Milford Track. Each offers an unforgettable experience.

The flight over Fiordland to Milford Sound offers a thrilling perspective of this rugged and remote region. It's a good idea to book space ahead, especially in summer.

In Queenstown or Te Anau you board a small plane for an aerial look at Fiordland's mountains, forests, and waterways. You fly over the route of the Milford Track, gazing down on hikers' huts along the trail, past 580-meter/1,904-foot Sutherland Falls plunging in a spectacular triple cataract from Lake Quill's glacier-carved basin, then down the Arthur Valley to land at Milford's small airstrip.

After a brief stop, you again take to the air, soaring high for a bird's-eye view of world-famous Milford Sound. Your plane returns by a different route, flying between crinkled icy peaks and down alpine gorges that broaden into river plains.

The memorable Milford Road

If you travel to Milford by car or bus, you'll follow the 119-km/74-mile Milford Road (Highway 94), an alpine route cutting through some of New Zealand's most untouched country. The highway is paved for the first 38 km/24 miles, then turns to graded gravel until the final short section before Milford Sound.

N.Z. Railways Road Services coaches provide daily service between Te Anau and Milford. If you're motoring, plan to leave early so you can make a leisurely trip. By late morning, fast-moving buses raise great clouds of dust on the unpaved part of the road. Caravans and trailers should not be driven beyond Cascade Creek.

The Eglinton Valley. From Te Anau you follow the shore of Lake Te Anau north to Te Anau Downs, then veer up the broad wooded valley of the Eglinton River, well known to fly fishermen. Beech-covered mountains frame a view of distant peaks, and colorful lupines brighten the valley floor in summer.

You pass the tiny Mirror Lakes before arriving at Cascade Creek, the only travelers' oasis (rustic accommodations, meals, gasoline) between Lake Te Anau and Milford. If you want to stretch your legs, take the 40-minute self-guided nature walk that begins across the creek from the lodge.

Continuing past lakes Gunn, Fergus, and Lochie, you reach the Divide, the lowest pass (541 meters/1,742 feet) in the Southern Alps. From here trampers depart for Lake Howden and the Routeburn and Greenstone tracks to Lake Wakatipu.

Down the Hollyford Valley. A side road leads down the Hollyford River, a sparkling stream that empties into the Tasman Sea at Martin's Bay. From October to June hikers and fishermen can arrange trips down the Hollyford Track, past Hidden Falls and along Lake McKerrow. Some excursions include water and air transport and lodge accommodations at Martin's Bay.

About 8 km/5 miles from the highway at Gunn's Camp, a small museum contains a fascinating collection of mementos, old photographs, and yellowed clippings on various aspects of Fiordland lore—ill-fated settlements, legendary local characters, shipwrecks and plane crashes, early Milford Track hikers, the construction of the Homer Tunnel.

Through the Homer Tunnel. Mountains crowd closer as you continue climbing to the Homer Tunnel, a single-lane, rough-hewn bore piercing the Darran Range.

One-way traffic moves through the short tunnel —westbound to Milford from the hour to 25 minutes past, eastbound to Te Anau from the half-hour to 55 minutes past. If you have a short wait, take a stroll or just pause and enjoy the scenery.

West of the tunnel, the switchback road descends the steep upper Cleddau Valley. About 7 km/4 miles below the tunnel, a signposted trail leads to the Chasm. Take the 5-minute walk through beech forest to a railed platform overlooking the turbulent Cleddau River as it thunders through a narrow rocky gorge and drops in frenzied cascades on its route to the sea.

"The finest walk in the world"

Hikers find the Milford Track more than just a scenic adventure—it's a total experience. Thousands have traversed this wilderness trail between Lake Te Anau and Milford Sound. Yet each feels a sense of achievement as he gazes down from the summit of Mackinnon Pass or catches the first awesome glimpse of Sutherland Falls.

Trampers experience many of the same challenges the pioneer Milford hikers did in the 1890s— rivers to be crossed, a mountain pass to be conquered, the caprices of rain and weather. Yet today's walkers take for granted comforts beyond the dreams of those early tourists, one of whom called this footpath through Fiordland "the finest walk in the world."

The trail leads up densely wooded valleys to open alpine grasslands, carpeted with mountain wildflowers early in the season. Every curve of the trail opens fresh views of glacier-flanked peaks, rugged canyons, serene lakes, and thick forests.

Sparkling waterfalls hurtle over cliffs. You'll balance on shaky suspension bridges to cross ravines and fast-moving streams. Birds erupt into song in the bush. A fitting climax to your trek is majestic Milford Sound.

Hiking excursions. From mid-November through March, parties of 40 persons depart each Monday, Wednesday, and Friday (daily from mid-December to mid-January) from Te Anau on the 53-km/33-mile tramp to Milford Sound. Each hiker sets his or her own pace, forging ahead or lingering to fish, swim, or take photographs. Along the route hikers stay in huts, each equipped with dormitory-style bunks, electricity, hot showers, toilet facilities, and drying rooms. Meals are provided.

You must book space months in advance (through the New Zealand Government Tourist Office) for these popular excursions. Hikers carry only clothing and personal articles needed on the trail; "city clothes" are sent by coach to Milford.

Along the Milford Track. Excursions cover 5 days on the route, beginning with an afternoon launch trip across Lake Te Anau to Glade House, start of the trail. Hikers cover the Milford Track in three main sections. From Quintin Hut, a trail leads to the base of famous Sutherland Falls, which plunges from a glacier-carved basin.

Though the trail is "good going," it is challenging even in fine weather, for you must ford numerous streams and cross a 1,067-meter/3,500-foot alpine pass. In bad weather it's a difficult and demanding route, even for experienced and physically fit hikers.

From Glade House you climb through native beech forest along the Clinton River to Pompolona Hut. The third day of the trip is the most challenging, with a steep climb through open alpine country to Mackinnon Pass, followed by a switchback descent to Quintin Hut. On the final day of hiking, you follow the Arthur River downstream, skirting Lake Ada, to Sandfly Point, where a launch transports hikers the final step across Milford Sound. The trip terminates after lunch the following day at Milford.

"Freedom walkers." A limited number of independent hikers (called "freedom walkers") can tramp the Milford Track, carrying all equipment and supplies. Trail access is controlled by Fiordland National Park headquarters in Te Anau; advance contact is necessary. Because of variable weather and track conditions, only experienced hikers with proper equipment are permitted on the trail. The track can be walked only in one direction—from Te Anau to Milford.

The grandeur of Milford Sound

Milford Sound rates a special place in the memories of many travelers. Far from any population center, it is a destination renowned solely for its beauty.

From the head of the fiord you gaze upon one of New Zealand's classic views. Steep granite peaks, wooded on their lower slopes, frame the glacier-carved inlet and cast mirrored reflections on its dark, calm waters. Dominating the scene is the triangular pinnacle of mile-high Mitre Peak.

Along the cliffs, several waterfalls tumble from high hanging valleys more than 150 meters/ 500 feet into the sheltered sound.

Only a few moored boats and a scattering of buildings at the head of the sound break the unity of mountains, forest, and water. Crayfishing boats anchor in Deepwater Basin during the summer fishing season. Sightseeing launches schedule frequent trips.

Be prepared for plenty of rain in any season. Passing clouds can bring drenching rainstorms, creating dozens of new waterfalls. Overnight visitors can enjoy Milford's quiet moods. In early morning, shafts of sunlight pierce the mist to illuminate Mitre Peak. At day's end pastel sunset tints streak the cloud-strewn sky.

Launch excursions. A primary reason for your trip to Milford is a cruise on the sound, the best way to enjoy its unspoiled beauty and grandeur. Launches depart from the Milford wharf on 1 and 2-hour cruises; if you have enough time, take the longer trip—it goes all the way to the open sea.

You'll cruise past 1,692-meter/5,560-foot Mitre Peak, Milford's landmark, and glacier-topped Mount Pembroke. Spray blows over you as the boat noses close to Stirling and Bowen falls. Often the captain spots a seal or two playing near shore.

Short walks at Milford. If you enjoy a before breakfast walk or an afternoon stroll, you'll find several short walks near the head of the sound. Trail information is available at the reception desk at Hotel Milford.

Wear a raincoat or waterproof parka on the

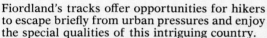

On foot in Fiordland

Fiordland's tracks offer opportunities for hikers to escape briefly from urban pressures and enjoy the special qualities of this intriguing country.

The types of country you can traverse here vary greatly, but the tramps have much in common. Routeburn concentrates on the high country (above sandfly level); Milford ranges from open alpine terrain to lush rain-forest valleys; Hollyford is a low-level river track. Their proximity and complementary nature make it possible to combine two—or all three—walks on the same hiking holiday.

A hiker's adventure. Hiking the Milford or Routeburn tracks is a tramping adventure, not a tourist excursion. The trips can be difficult for the inexperienced or out-of-condition hiker; sections of the trails are demanding and strenuous, particularly in foul weather.

On the trail you enter a remote world almost untouched by man. Dwarfed by gigantic mountains, you follow a twisting track through dense forest, across alpine grasslands, along swift-flowing rivers, and past cascading waterfalls. Naturalists delight in the varied flowers, trees, ferns, and shrubs. Tumbling streams glint in the sun like molten silver, and only the liquid trill of a forest songbird or the shrill call of a kea breaks the stillness.

You cross the larger streams on suspension bridges or large fallen trees; smaller streams are forded. Be prepared for wet weather; a passing cloud can suddenly deepen creeks and create dozens of new waterfalls.

Most of your trail companions will be New Zealanders, Australians, and Americans, but other international hikers add spice to the group. You'll carry a "cut lunch" and share "scroggin" (a high-energy mix of nuts, raisins, and ginger) and hot "billy tea" brewed from snow-fed streams. Evenings are a time for talking and the comfortable camaraderie that comes from shared experiences.

Keep your pack light. If you're joining one of the group trips on the Routeburn or Milford tracks, you'll receive a recommended packing list. Each hiker carries personal gear in a backpack; you can hire one, but your own probably will be more comfortable.

One hiker's formula: "Be prepared for bad weather, carry a minimum amount of clothing, and be very fit." You'll want a waterproof hooded jacket and comfortable footwear. High-topped basketball shoes or lightweight boots (well broken in), worn with two pairs of woolen socks, provide shock absorption and traction. A complete change of warm clothing and underwear is essential insurance against a downpour.

Miscellaneous equipment includes a small flashlight, adhesive tape, sunglasses, and insect repellent. Milford hikers can purchase evening refreshments and small items at hut shops.

Coping with sandflies. In Fiordland and many other wet lowland areas, "getting away from it all" means walking straight into the domain of the sandfly. During his May, 1773, sojourn at Dusky Bay, Captain James Cook noted in his log that sandflies were so " numerous and . . . so troublesome that they exceed everything of the kind that I have ever met with." The tiny pests are still with us.

Thriving in moist and humid regions up to 3,000 feet elevation, these silent and persistent insects harass persons when the air is calm, particularly at dawn, dusk, or before rain. The small, black sandflies are least belligerent in hot sunshine, in cold weather, and during strong winds or heavy rain.

Only the females bite. In many people these bites set up a series of reactions, resulting in an allergy to subsequent bites. Vulnerable hikers rely on a powerful insect repellent or vitamin B_1 tablets to discourage sandflies from biting. Antihistamine drugs minimize side effects from the bites.

Float plane *lands on Milford Sound, disturbing Mitre Peak's mirrored reflection. Visitors can fly over the fiord or board a sightseeing launch and cruise past waterfalls to the open sea.*

Bowen Falls trail; it begins near the wharf and follows the shore along the cliff face. The stream provides the hotel's water supply and hydroelectric power.

The 1½-hour Lookout Track starts behind the hotel, where a 5-minute climb gives you a view over the hotel's red roof to the water. Beyond this point you need agility and sturdy footwear to clamber over exposed roots and rocks and to scramble on slippery slopes.

The Deep South

In the 1840s, whalers roved the southern seas and pastoral runholders claimed most of Southland's grazing lands. But real settlement got a late start in this region.

During the Otago gold rush of the 1860s, fortune seekers converged on the boom town of Switzers (now Waikaia), but for the most part Southland residents prospered only indirectly by providing food and other supplies for the miners.

Southland's future lay in less spectacular but more enduring assets—primarily its rich grass-lands, but also coal and timber. Wool and meat are exported to world markets, and dairy products add their share to Southland's wealth.

Mills began to ship timber to Dunedin in the 1860s, and coal has been minded in the Ohai-Nightcaps district since 1880.

Though legally Southland has no provincial standing, its boundaries cover the southwestern part of South Island, encompassing the western fiord country, skimming the southern shores of Lake Wakatipu, and running east to Gore to meet the south coast near Waikawa. Off the South Island "mainland" is unspoiled Stewart Island.

Southland contains some 110,000 residents, approximately half of whom live in Invercargill. You approach New Zealand's southernmost city by car or bus along Highway 6 from Queenstown or along Highway 1 from Dunedin and Balclutha. You can also reach Invercargill by air or rail.

Most travelers stay in Invercargill, where accommodations include the centrally located Kelvin Hotel, the gracious older Grand Hotel, the Don Lodge Motor Hotel, and Ascot Park Hotel/Motel. You'll also find a number of smaller hotels and motels. Anglers can make Gore headquarters for fishing in Southland rivers. Bluff's small hotels cater to travelers taking the Stewart Island ferry.

Farming, fishing, and illicit whisky

Only scattered small farm towns break the open plains between Lake Wakatipu and the south coast. Sheep and cattle munch on the rich grasslands; they'll provide meat and wool for the export market. Well-stocked trout streams—among them Aparima, Oreti, and Mataura—draw fishermen.

Highways radiate in all directions from the junction town of Lumsden—north of Queenstown, west to Te Anau and Milford Sound, south to Invercargill, and east to Gore and Balclutha. Near Mossburn, red deer browse in the tussock and manuka at the West Dome Deer Ranch. Southland's second largest town is Gore (population 9,000), surrounded by lush rolling pastures and grain fields.

West of Gore are the Hokonui Hills, synonymous with illicit whisky. The Scottish sheepmen who settled this district brought with them knowledge of whisky distilling and a taste for the brew. Until World War II, moonshiners and Customs men engaged in a continuing battle of wits over the stills.

At the foot of the hills, Dolamore Park has a pleasant, forest-rimmed picnic area and trails winding through bush. The Mataura Plain is cattle and dairy country; Mataura, Edendale, and Wyndham are the main centers.

The foothills above Ohai and Nightcaps have been mined for coal for nearly a century. Coal from the underground and open-cast mines fuels many Southland industries. If you want to visit a mine, check the state Coal Mines Office in Ohai.

All aboard the Kingston Flyer

Each summer a shrill whistle and the hiss of escaping steam herald the approach of the Kingston Flyer, as New Zealand's vintage steam train chugs leisurely through the wooded hills and farm country near Invercargill. Children wave as the train passes scattered homes and villages, and grazing sheep scurry in alarm as the smoke-belching engine nears.

The Kingston Flyer currently operates a variety of day excursions from Invercargill. For information on the routes and schedule, check with the New Zealand Government Tourist Office.

Beginning in the 1880s, express passenger trains provided fast service between Gore, Lumsden, and Kingston, transporting tourists to scenic Lake Wakatipu and its surrounding mountains. A few years ago a pair of the old coal-fired locomotives and some of the historic old dark green carriages were brought out of retirement, carefully restored, and redecorated to 1920s elegance.

You can choose your seat in the combined first class car and guard's van, the "birdcage" or gallery carriage, refreshment car, or passenger carriages. Brasswork gleams and woodwork is varnished to high luster. Match striker plates, ornate luggage rack brackets, and gas lamps add a nostalgic touch. The traditional spittoons have been removed, though, and horsehair seats have been replaced with foam-padded vinyl in some carriages.

Light refreshments and souvenirs are sold in the refreshment car.

Passengers on the Invercargill-Bluff route can break their trip with the Foveaux Walk, a 2½-hour coastal stroll around the island's southern tip. Pack a picnic and reboard the train in Bluff.

Invercargill, Southland's market center

Thriving capital and economic center of Southland, Invercargill spreads across the open plains along the New River estuary. The city shares Dunedin's Scottish origins. Broad streets—many named for Scottish rivers—and numerous parks mark its level site.

Invercargill was a busy river port during the late 1850s and 1860s, but in later decades Bluff gradually gained dominance in coastal shipping. Today, Invercargill is New Zealand's eighth largest city and the market center for the surrounding district. Massive freezing works ring the city, preparing fat Southland lambs for world markets.

Air New Zealand planes land at Invercargill's airport, located about a 5-minute drive west of the business district. Hunters and fishermen can charter floatplanes for trips into Fiordland's remote lakes and fiords. The rail station faces Leven Street, one block west of Highway 6 (Dee Street). N. Z. Railways Road Services buses link Invercargill with Dunedin, Christchurch, Te Anau, and Queenstown.

Visitors can obtain local information at the Southland Progress League office, Crawford House, Don Street. Tour information and travel reservations are handled by the Government Tourist Bureau, 29 Esk Street.

Queens Park. The city's showplace is Queens Park, a 200-acre reserve north of the business district. Its outstanding gardens flourish in Southland's equable climate. In season you'll enjoy extensive displays of iris, rhododendrons, and roses. Tropical plants thrive under glass in the Winter Garden. Nearby, sleek bronze animal statues rim the shallow children's pool. Sunday concerts attract families in summer.

Sports fields include an 18-hole golf course, hockey and cricket grounds, bowls and croquet greens, and tennis and squash courts.

Southland Centennial Museum. Near the southern boundary of Queens Park, the Southland Centennial Museum and Art Gallery contains exhibits on the region's Maori culture, whaling and pioneer relics, and natural history displays.

Anderson Park. The City Art Gallery is housed in the former home of Sir Robert Anderson, whose family gave the city the house and its well-tended gardens and surrounding bush. It is located about 7 km/4 miles north of Invercargill.

Other points of interest. South of the main shopping area, parklands border Otepuni Creek as it flows through the city.

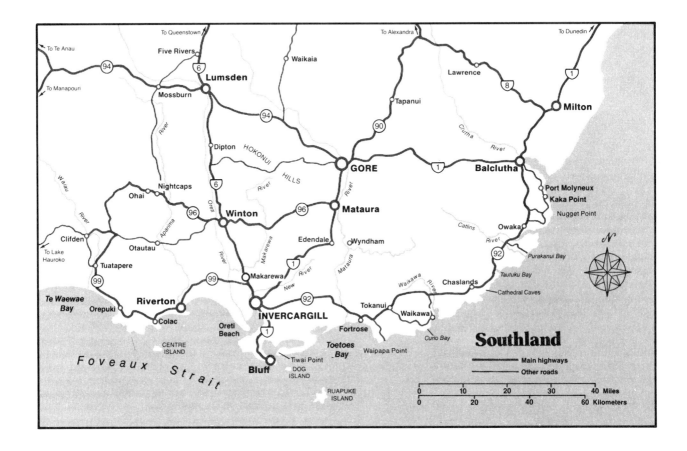

On the city's eastern boundary, Southland Racecourse features trotting and galloping meets during the year.

Bordering the upper Waihopai River near the city's northern boundary is Thomsons Bush, an 85-acre scenic reserve largely covered by native bush. In summer you can rent canoes and paddle along the quiet stream.

Along Foveaux Strait

The protected waterways and coastal beaches lining Foveaux Strait are Southland's playground. Just west of Invercargill, weekend boatsmen race, row, and water-ski on the long straight stretches of the Oreti River estuary, and fishermen cast for trout. Yachts and power boats cruise the strait and the sheltered bays.

Beaches border Foveaux Strait from the New River estuary west to Riverton. On warm weekends and during the long summer twilights, local families converge on Oreti Beach west of Invercargill. Toheroas are taken from the beach during the short winter clamming season.

Riverton exudes the mellow charm of an unpretentious seaside resort; families come here on holiday, particularly during the New Year carnival period. Fishing boats and pleasure craft moor along the estuary's south shore. Flanking the seaside road to Howells Point, you pass The Rocks, a

local landmark. Farther west on Highway 99, the village of Colac faces Colac Bay and Centre Island.

Timber country

Tuatapere, a timber town in the Waiau Valley, is the major milling center producing lumber for Otago and Southland markets. Fishermen come here for trout and Atlantic salmon. You can picnic or camp in a wooded park on the riverbank. Axmen from around the country converge here on New Year's Day to participate in woodchopping contests.

Lying near the Waiau River in limestone cave country, Clifden is the gateway to Lake Hauroko and southern Fiordland. You can obtain trail information and hunting permits at the park ranger station.

One of the park's southernmost lakes, Hauroko lies in a wild and beautiful bush setting. A camping area is located near the park boundary. Bush tracks begin near road's end, following the lake shore and leading into the park. Remains of a Maori burial cave have been discovered on Mary Island.

The southeast coast

Highway 92 follows a slow and winding coastal route from Invercargill to Balclutha. Side roads detour to unspoiled beaches and seaside points of interest, some best observed at low tide. An unsealed stretch of roadway cuts through bush reserves where trees and ferns spill down to the sea.

At the east end of Toetoes Bay, hidden reefs extend beyond the Waipapa Point lighthouse to mark the eastern entrance to Foveaux Strait.

Curio Bay fossil forest contains the petrified logs of a subtropical forest, buried by volcanic ash millions of years ago. When the land mass re-emerged from the sea, waves cut the sandstone to reveal the petrified stumps and broken logs.

Southeast of Chaslands, a steep trail leads down to Waipati Beach and the Cathedral Caves. Accessible only at low tide, the interconnected, high-ceilinged sea caves cut far back into the cliffs. Check tide times before exploring, and take a flashlight if you plan to venture into the caves.

Side roads and paths lead to unspoiled, bush-backed Tautuku Beach and cascading Purakaunui Falls. Near Owaka and the Catlins River, Jacks Bay Blowhole is impressive at high tide and in stormy weather. Just beyond is Penguin Bay, where in late afternoon penguins come ashore to nest in the bush. In Owaka the small Catlins Historical Society Museum on Waikawa Road contains displays on the region's pioneering and economic history.

South of Balclutha you can visit the lighthouse on Nugget Point, then continue north to Kaka Point, a favorite family vacation retreat. Little remains—except a magnificent coastal view—at Port Molyneux; the port town was by-passed by the railroad and its harbor blocked by debris from the flooding Clutha River.

Bluff and the southern tip

Built on a natural harbor, Bluff is Southland's seafaring town. The port is a major meat and wool exporting center. Storage tanks and coolstores rim the sheltered inlet. Ferry service links Bluff with Oban on Stewart Island.

Across the water on Tiwai Point gleam the silver buildings of the Comalco aluminum smelter. Aluminum oxide is shipped here from Queensland, Australia. During the smelting process, oxygen is extracted to yield aluminum, and the molten metal is cast and alloyed with other metals before it is exported.

The Manapouri power scheme, developed in conjunction with the smelter, provides the massive amounts of electricity needed for the project.

Bluff is also home port of Southland's commercial fishing fleet, including the sturdy boats that dredge Foveaux Strait for the succulent Bluff oysters. The country's oyster lovers wait expectantly for the opening of the March-to-August season; the shellfish are airfreighted to all parts of New Zealand.

Houses cover the low slopes of Old Man Bluff, the hill that gave the town its name. Turn uphill by the post office and follow the road to the summit, where you'll enjoy a windswept panorama over Bluff Harbour and the town, the sprawling South-

land plains, and islands in Foveaux Strait.

National Highway 1 ends at Stirling Point lookout, where a signpost gives kilometer distances to various points worldwide. A walking track begins at road's end, winding around the bush-covered bluff toward the island's southern tip.

Stewart Island

Separated from South Island by the waters of Foveaux Strait, Stewart Island is less a destination than a way of life. For residents and visitors alike, its attractions lie in its unspoiled beauty, glowing skies, and unhurried pace. Time is unimportant; only the tide governs daily activities. You'll find few cars, few roads, and little tourist development here. Most of the island is a nature reserve.

Despite its southerly latitude, the island enjoys a mild—if frequently wet—climate, seldom very warm or very cool. But on the southern tip, raw icy blasts sweep north from the Antarctic. Year-round rainfall provides most of the island's water supply. Brilliant dawns and sunsets streak these southern skies, and occasionally the aurora australis—the "southern lights"—adds special radiance.

Mountainous and heavily forested, Stewart Island is roughly triangular in shape, about 60 km/40 miles long and 30 km/20 miles wide. Steep, wooded promontories rise sharply from the clear sea. Its irregular shoreline contains many fine harbors and beach-rimmed coves. Numerous islets lie off the coast, including the Muttonbird (Titi) Islands, where Maoris traditionally collect young birds each autumn.

Visitors come in all seasons, but most enjoy the summer months best, when the whole island is alive with native birds and the scent of flowers perfumes the air. Yet even in winter, the skies retain their glow, and coastal waters lure fishermen.

You reach Stewart Island by plane from Invercargill or by a 2½-hour ferry trip (usually Tuesday and Friday) on the *Wairua* from Bluff, approximately 30 km/20 miles across Foveaux Strait. In bad weather the strait can be a turbulent stretch of water. Check transportation schedules in Invercargill; air and ferry reservations are essential.

Getting acquainted with Oban

Stewart Island's only sizable settlement is Oban, a fishermen's town facing the crescent of Half-moon Bay. Low buildings rim the bright blue water and blend into the encircling wooded hills. Sheltered from westerly winds by the island's forested ranges, the tranquil village basks in the sun. Only a tiny stretch of the northern coast has been touched by roads and habitation.

The island has about 400 permanent residents; many are descendants of European whalers who intermarried with the island's Maori inhabitants. They ride their fishing boats westward into the heavy swells in search of the crayfish and cod that provide the residents' main source of income.

Most visitors arrive by ferry and depart the same afternoon. To experience the island's special appeal, though, you need to stay several days. In summer you must book accommodations months ahead. Simple but comfortable facilities include the South Seas Hotel facing the bay, a small motel, several private guesthouses, and a few cabins and campsites at Horseshoe Bay.

On boat days, a mini-bus meets the ferry and takes day-trippers on a short tour of the northern hills and bush-rimmed bays. While the ferry is in port, you can visit the town's museum, on Ayr Street near the foreshore, to see whaling relics and exhibits of island plants and birds.

Exploring the coastline

One of the best ways to enjoy the island's bays and beaches is by boat. You can arrange to charter a launch for a day of fishing or a cruise along the coast to Port William or Paterson Inlet. Inquire at the general store on the Oban waterfront or check the notice board outside. In summer regular launch trips operate for fishing and sightseeing.

Only a strip of land divides Oban and Halfmoon Bay from Paterson Inlet, the large landlocked harbor on the northeast side of the island.

Wooded to the water's edge, Paterson Inlet is a favorite sailing ground for pleasure craft. You can cruise into Price's Inlet—perhaps stopping to see relics of a Norwegian whaling base at Surveyors Bay—or venture further up Paterson's southwest arm.

A favorite stopping point is enchanting Ulva Is-land, near the inlet entrance. Its sandy beaches are ideal for a picnic; trails wind through its unspoiled forest; and bird life abounds. Nearby Native Island was the site of a Maori settlement.

Shell hounds head for Ringaringa Beach, about a mile from Oban, or Horseshoe Bay.

Hiking island trails

Enjoy Stewart Island's blending of land, forest, and sea from numerous walking tracks that hug the coastline and cut through the bush. A light waterproof jacket and sturdy footwear may come in handy at any time of year.

From Oban you can take the 15-minute walk up to Observation Rock for a splendid view over Halfmoon Bay to the north and Paterson Inlet to the south. Another short walk heads north to Horseshoe Bay and beyond to bush tracks up Garden Mound or to Lee Bay. Day trails lead to Butterfield Beach, Golden Bay, Thule, Ringaringa Beach, and the lighthouse.

For the more ambitious, the New Zealand Forest Service has opened walking tracks into some of the more remote and wild parts of the island. Huts offer overnight shelter on the longer bush tracks; you bring your own food and equipment and replace the firewood you use. Information is available from the ranger in Oban.

The island has a unique wealth of native plants and rare birds. Rimu, rata, miro, and totara trees stretch skyward from the mossy floor. All bird life is protected; you may see tuis, parakeets, bellbirds, kakas, and perhaps a rare weka or kiwi searching for insects in the dense undergrowth. Deer roam the island.

Additional Readings

Fiat Book of Common Birds in New Zealand: Mountain, Bush, and Shore Birds by Janet Marshall, F. C. Kinsky, and C. J. R. Robertson. Wellington, New Zealand: A. H. & A. W. Reed Ltd. Color illustrations and descriptions aid in bird identification. A companion volume describes town, pasture, and fresh-water birds.

Fiat Book of New Zealand Trees by Nancy M. Adams. Wellington, New Zealand: A.H. & A. W. Reed Ltd. This pocket-size guide contains color illustrations and detailed descriptions to aid the reader in identifying native trees.

How to Get Lost and Found in New Zealand by John W. McDermott. Wellington, New Zealand: A. H. & A. W. Reed Ltd. An entertaining first-person account of one couple's travels through the country.

Microtone Colour Book Series. Christchurch, New Zealand: Bascands Limited. Color photographs illustrate a series of pocket-size books, each focusing on a particular subject— individual cities, national parks, native birds, animals, wildflowers.

Mobil Guide to North Island and **Mobil Guide to South Island** by Diana and Jeremy Pope. Wellington, New Zealand: A.H. & A.W. Reed Ltd. Revised periodically, these comprehensive books resemble Michelin guides in format. Alphabetical city and area listings are supplemented by detailed maps and information on Maori legends and regional history.

New Zealand on $20 and $25 a Day by Beth Bryant. New York: Arthur Frommer, Inc. Low-cost accommodations, food, and touring suggestions are emphasized in this guide.

The North Island of New Zealand and **The South Island of New Zealand** by Errol Brathwaite. Auckland, New Zealand: William Collins N.Z. Ltd. A New Zealand author describes his country in these two books in the Companion Guide series.

Wake Up to New Zealand by Colin Simpson. Sydney, Australia: A. H. & A. W. Reed Pty Ltd. One of Australia's best-known travel writers chronicles his New Zealand travels.

Index

Gardens *in New Zealand put on a colorful show. Trees planted in Queenstown's Government Gardens glow with autumn color.*

Photographers

Cornelia Fogle: 2, 31, 35, 38, 43, 46, 51, 62, 75, 78, 83, 91, 98, 103, 106, 114, 122, back cover. **Bruce Moss:** 59, 67, 70, 111. **National Publicity Studios:** 7, 10, 18, 23, 26, 54, 127. **Jim Rearden:** 15, 94. **Richard Rowan:** 86.

Artwork by William Dunn